FIRST CAME DR. ABRAVANEL'S BESTSELLING
BODY TYPE DIET. NOW, THIS NEW NATIONAL
BESTSELLER BRINGS YOU AN INNOVATIVE
LIFETIME PROGRAM FOR TOTAL HEALTH FOR
YOUR INDIVIDUAL BODY TYPE.

Your body type is not like everyone else's. Therefore, no one
health plan can work for everyone. Here is a total, personalized health care program for you and your body.

DISCOVER YOUR BODY TYPE

It's easy. Simply answer the questions of the Personal Metabolic Inventory (PMI) to pinpoint which of the four body
types you are. Now you are ready to apply Dr. Abravanel's
lifetime health-care program to your individual body type
and its specific needs.

BALANCING DIET, PURIFICATION DIET, AND
HEALTH AND WEIGHT MAINTENANCE
BODY TYPE NUTRITIONAL SUPPLEMENTS
THE BODY TYPE EXERCISE PROGRAM
STRESS REDUCTION FOR YOUR BODY TYPE
THE BODY TYPE LONG WEEKEND
OF REJUVENATION
BODY TYPE SELF-ACUPRESSURE MASSAGE
BODY TYPE LIFE EXTENSION

Through good nutrition, proper exercise, and deep relaxation, you, like many thousands across the country, will learn
to understand your body, nourish its strengths, offset its vulnerabilities, and reap the many lifetime rewards of Dr. Abravanel's revolutionary program of optimum health.

Bantam Books by Elliot D. Abravanel, M.D. and Elizabeth A. King

DR. ABRAVANEL'S BODY TYPE DIET AND LIFE-TIME NUTRITION PLAN

DR. ABRAVANEL'S BODY TYPE PROGRAM FOR HEALTH, FITNESS, AND NUTRITION

QUANTITY PURCHASES

Companies, professional groups, churches, clubs and other organizations may qualify for special terms when ordering 24 or more copies of this title. For information, contact the Special Sales Department, Bantam Books, 666 Fifth Avenue, New York, N.Y. 10103. Phone (800) 223-6834. N.Y. State residents call (212) 765-6500.

DR. ABRAVANEL'S BODY TYPE PROGRAM FOR HEALTH, FITNESS, AND NUTRITION

ELLIOT D. ABRAVANEL, M.D. AND ELIZABETH A. KING

ILLUSTRATIONS BY MENTOR HUEBNER

BANTAM BOOKS
TORONTO · NEW YORK · LONDON · SYDNEY · AUCKLAND

To Each Other

This or any other Diet and Fitness
program should be followed only under
a Doctor's supervision

DR. ABRAVANEL'S BODY TYPE
PROGRAM FOR HEALTH, FITNESS, AND
NUTRITION

A Bantam Book

PRINTING HISTORY

Bantam Hardcover edition / April 1985
2nd printing . . . May 1985
3rd printing . . . May 1985
Bantam paperback edition / February 1986

ISBN 0-553-25332-8

Published simultaneously in the United States and Canada

Bantam Books are published by Bantam Books, Inc. Its trade-
mark, consisting of the words "Bantam Books" and the por-
trayal of a rooster, is Registered in the United States Patent and
Trademark Office and in other countries. Marca Registrada. Bantam
Books, Inc., 666 Fifth Avenue, New York, New York 10103.

PRINTED IN THE UNITED STATES OF AMERICA

O   9 8 7 6 5 4 3 2 1

CONTENTS

PART III: BODY TYPES AND BEYOND

INTRODUCTION

We live in an age of great progress in medicine. The dramatic breakthroughs, especially, are widely publicized—genetic engineering, organ transplants, incredible feats of cardiovascular surgery. But with all this high-science and high-technology medicine, it sometimes seems that the only real advances are ones you have to be sick to use. Those of us who aren't sick but still want to be healthier are left to deal on our own with the most important practical questions—questions like what to eat, how much to exercise, and how best to deal with stress.

Yet the truth is that there is a great deal of new research now becoming available that *directly affects the most basic questions of your health*. All the biochemical and other studies that have gone into investigating more abstract questions have *vital implications for the way you eat and exercise, what vitamins you take, what preventive medicine you need*. This research is, for the most part, widely scattered over the scientific literature. It makes it possible for us to answer many of the age-old questions of personal, front-line health care from a more definite standard of scientific knowledge.

THE CURRENT
STATE OF
KNOWLEDGE

Because most of the research is read only by a few specialists, in most of these areas—nutrition, exercise, nutritional supplementation, stress reduction—there is no general agreement, either in the scientific community or in the popular press. You know yourself that you can go to ten nutritionists and come away with ten different, "perfect" diets. Exercise is also debated widely: how much should you do, how often, what kind? Or, to take the other side of this question, how much rest do you need? Is there a "best" kind of rest? No one answer seems definitive.

Vitamin supplements are another battleground. You don't need any, or you need a hundred dollars' worth a week, or anything in between—take your pick. As for life extension, today's hot topic, experts say variously that you'll live longer if you take a daily handful of antioxidants, or if you go on a university hypertension program, or if you consume no coffee, sugar, or fat. And what about consciousness, that most essential and elusive of human qualities? Is it truly a factor in health and longevity? What's it worth in years? The answers to all these questions depend entirely on which book you picked up last, or whom you caught on this morning's talk show.

THE STANDARD
OF YOURSELF

In fact, the diversity of opinions lags behind the new knowledge already discovered in most, if not all, of these areas. Yet the diversity is not likely to resolve itself quickly. There will continue to be different ideas of what's best to do, at least for the foreseeable future, which means that *deciding what's best for you to do at any given moment is ultimately up to you*. Like it or not, the responsibility for day-to-day health decisions is on your own shoulders.

And because this is so, I feel a responsibility to you. What I would like to do in this book is give you two things. First, I want to give you an insight into the new understanding of health that the latest biochemical research makes possible. You'll see that it is now possible to understand why different people eat, exercise, work, and rest the way they do, and what changes they need to make to be healthier and feel better.

Second, I want to give you a standard for evaluating medical knowledge and selecting health care programs for yourself. I believe strongly that the only valid standard you should use is *your own needs*. The ancient Greek philosopher Protagoras said that man is the measure of all things, by which he meant that each man and woman must use him- or herself as the standard of measure. Your body, your requirements, your strengths, your vulnerabilities— these are what you need to consider in deciding whether or not any particular program will improve your health.

This means that you need some way to think about yourself that considers all your systems at once, and that does so in a nontechnical but very precise and accurate way. This is what *The Body Type Health Program* is all about. It gives you a way to consider your total health needs based on a system of classification by metabolic types. You'll learn about yourself and your own body type, and this will give you a standard for designing a health program for your personal and individual benefit.

My first book, *Dr. Abravanel's Body Type Diet and Lifetime Nutrition Plan,* used the body-type concept to make sense out of the conflicting advice given by most experts on weight control. Now, I am broadening the focus from weight to health and showing you how to design a complete program for vitality, energy, and longevity.

BODY TYPES
AND YOU

The body-type concept grows out of the extremely striking fact that *people are not all the same*. Look around you. The people you know need different food, grow strong on different exercises, thrive on different lifestyles, get different diseases, and recover with different treatments. Everyone knows this; but somehow, when it comes to specific health decisions, we forget about it and act as if the same programs will work for everybody.

They won't. We have to measure each and every program against the standard of the individual who will use it. It doesn't make sense to decide categorically for or against any particular health idea. What needs to be done is to put each one into perspective by thinking about the kind of person it will be useful for.

For this, we use the body-type concept as a shorthand way of describing a total metabolic system. I have defined three body types in men—the thyroid type, the adrenal type, and the pituitary type—and four in women—the same three, plus the gonadal type. Each one describes a particular way a body works and lets us consider nutritional needs, exercise requirements, stress tendencies, potential for disease, and many other topics, in a specific physiological context. One of these types describes you, and knowing which type you are will enable you to make decisions from the standpoint of what you, as an individual, should have.

In the pages that follow, we're going to take a close look at the body-type concept and what it means. As a general, organizing concept, it draws on a variety of scientific and clinical evidence, which I've outlined for you in an appendix and bibliography. We'll apply the concept to all the basic areas of your health care needs. You'll learn how to determine your body type (through the Personal Metabolic Inventory in Chapter 4), and how to use it to evaluate *any* new piece of medical information that comes along, not just the ones we'll specifically discuss here.

AN IMPORTANT REMINDER

The use of body types in health care planning is a technique for examining many aspects of current scientific knowledge from a specific viewpoint. It's intended to provide a standpoint for self-examination, not to prove or disprove the validity of any particular treatment.

As you read the book, you may find your thinking about health care taking new directions. DO NOT USE THIS BOOK TO AVOID TREATMENTS OR TESTS PRESCRIBED FOR YOU BY YOUR PHYSICIAN. Rather, use the knowledge you gain about yourself as part of a continuing health program determined by you and the doctors who know you. Use it to increase your choices, not to decrease them.

PERFECT HEALTH: BODY TYPES AND BEYOND

In the course of this book, we're going to be working our way toward a concept of perfect health. I believe that health which is truly perfect is the only goal that makes the practice of medicine—basically a difficult and upsetting profession—worth practicing. To me, perfect health is a state of perfect balance—not just among your glands, but in your total physiology and psychology—that can't be described simply with reference to your body type.

My experience, and a great deal of modern research, strongly indicate that there is a factor in perfect health that goes beyond what can be achieved with any nutrition program, any exercise regime, or any medical treatment, even the very best and most expertly designed ones. This factor is *consciousness*. Consciousness is the integrative factor in our lives, the intangible but undeniable reality that a specific health care program can neither ignore nor overrule. It's the inner light in us that *wants* to live and be healthy. It's what we're striving to improve in ourselves, even when, out of ignorance, we make mistakes. Consciousness alone, when fully developed, is capable of taking us from a state of relative healthiness to perfect health itself.

Perfect health is rare, but it is possible. I have had the privilege of seeing certain individuals who have achieved it, perhaps no more than four or five; but even if there were only one, I'd still think it was achievable and worth striving for. The final chapter of this book concerns consciousness and perfect health, and will show you how developing your consciousness makes all your health efforts far more effective and rewarding.

Perfect health is not just a phrase, useful to spur you to pay more attention to diet or to exercise. To be candid, I don't even think these things are good in themselves— they're just means to a good. Perfect health is the goal that makes the effort worthwhile; it's a concrete reality and not a little one. Beyond disease, beyond cures and treatments, beyond even our usual concept of healthy living lie worlds of energy and effectiveness, clarity and tranquillity, that medicine has only begun to define. These are the worlds we're after, and we won't stop going after them until they are ours.

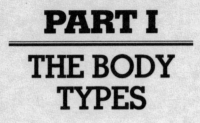

PART I
THE BODY TYPES

1

HEALTH AND THE BODY TYPES

My appointment calendar one morning showed that two patients were coming in for their annual physical examinations. Both were people I had known for many years. The first, a man in his mid-forties, was a smoker, about thirty pounds overweight, tense, and working in a high-pressure job. The second was a woman in her thirties, fairly slim and with a lot of color in her face. She was a nonsmoker and worked out with weights several times a week.

As any doctor, I tried not to go into the exams with too many preconceptions—they make you miss things—but I had my thoughts on the subject of what their exams might turn up. And as it turned out, my predictions were right. When I tested for heart problems, I found that the man's arteries were in pretty good shape, with minimal arteriosclerotic blockage. He had trouble with chronic allergies, but that was nothing new—he'd been having trouble with them for years. The woman, on the other hand, did show arterial blockage, not severe but still significant, and I suggested that she needed treatment or she was going to be in trouble not too far down the road.

Now this is not at all what ordinary medical thinking or common sense would lead you to expect. The man was older than the woman and smoked, and was fatter and tenser as well. So how did I guess he would probably be fairly free of heart disease, while she might well have some? The answer is simple. *I made my predictions because I knew their body types*. I made use of a simple system of classification in which I divide people into three (for men) or four (for women) body types, according to which of their glands is most active in their metabolism.

The man, I knew, was a "pituitary type." The dominant gland in his metabolism was the pituitary gland. The woman was an "adrenal type," whose strongest and most active glands were her adrenals. In pituitary types (or P-types), arteriosclerosis is more likely to appear either very late in life, or not at all; in adrenal types (or A-types), it is something you watch for early on.

WHAT IS A BODY TYPE?

I could have chosen any number of examples where the insight of the body type proved to be of unique predictive value, for knowledge of the body type is an amazingly effective window into the total health potential of the individual. But what exactly is a body type? Basically, it is a simple yet very effective description of the basic structure of the metabolism—that is, of the total body chemistry.

In the years I have been practicing family medicine, I have developed a technique for classifying my patients into one of four metabolic body types on the basis of which of the body's four major glands is most active in their system. The four major glands—the pituitary gland, the thyroid gland, the adrenal glands, and the gonads (or sex glands), produce four distinct and easily recognizable metabolic types.

So your body type is a shorthand way of saying what kind of metabolism you have. Each of the glands, through the chemicals (called "hormones") that they produce, influences your body to react in characteristic ways. Even though we all have the potential to respond to our environment in a variety of ways, we know that there are certain ways that are *typical* for us.

For example, let's say you're faced with the prospect of completing a long, complicated report. You know that you *might* do a little bit of work on it every day for two weeks, or you *might* work on it night and day for three days, or you *might* just work on it whenever you feel like it, sometimes at night and sometimes during the day, but what you *actually will* do is to put in the same four hours every day for six days. This is your typical, your characteristic, reaction. In most situations, your typical reaction is characteristic of your body type. (In this example you're probably a gonadal type, by the way.)

The influence of your dominant gland is very intense on all parts of yourself. So knowing your body type—knowing whether the pituitary gland, the thyroid gland, the adrenal glands, or the gonads (sex glands), is your strongest influence—will give you all kinds of valuable information about your personal and individual style. You'll be amazed to find that so much of your individuality is not a matter of chance, but makes perfect sense when you know your body type.

THE LANGUAGE OF YOUR BODY TYPE

Knowing my patients' body type has proven to be such a valuable predictor of tendencies, both physiological and psychological, that I always consider it part of an overall health profile. And what is perhaps more important, I always give this information to my patients themselves. I have written this book so that you can have the same access to knowledge about your body type as you would have as a patient in my office.

Physicians, by training, have many ways of knowing what's going on in your body. We also have any number of sophisticated machines at our disposal to probe you ever deeper and more thoroughly. You, on the other hand, don't have these techniques for looking at yourself—yet you need to know about your body as much or more than I do. Fortunately, you do have some advantages over me as well.

You have, first, a familiarity with your body I'd never have, even if I were your doctor for thirty years. You live in it, with it, every minute of every day. You know its shape (from the front, anyway), you know its patterns, you know exactly how it feels. (When I call the body "it," I reveal my prejudice—I do think of the body as a vehicle for the spirit.) You also know exactly what childhood and other diseases— even what little aches and pains—your body has undergone. You know your family health history (or you should), and you know your habits, the good ones and the bad ones, in the here and now.

All this information of yours is valuable, but it needs to be organized. *This is what knowing about your body type will do.* It will take the information you have from living with your body and show you its significance. It will teach you the language of your body. All the uncountable messages you've been getting from yourself will begin to make a whole new kind of sense.

You need this information because *it's your body.* If it's sick, *you* hurt. If it gets well, *you* feel better. If it's in perfect health, *you* feel wonderful. Who should have the knowledge of your body type more than you? Who is really going to make it work? And who is going to enjoy the benefits?

FINDING YOUR BODY TYPE

Your body type, as I have already said, is basically a description of your body's style of functioning, as looked at from the angle of your strongest and most active gland. Men and women are divided into body types differently: Men have three body types, the adrenal type, thyroid type, and pituitary type. Women have four types: the same adrenal, thyroid, and pituitary types, and a fourth, the gonadal type. Since only women are gonadal types, the dominant gland of the G-type is the female sex gland, the ovaries. In men, the sex glands are the testes but they do not produce a separate body type. Instead, they work in concert with the adrenal glands, so that a man who is an adrenal type could be called an adrenal/gonadal type.

Discovering which of the body types you are is not difficult and does not call for expensive laboratory tests. It's done by a process of just looking at and thinking about yourself—that is, by using some of the wealth of information you already have. Each of the types has characteristics that are easy to pick out. Some of the easiest to use are body shape, location of any extra weight, food preferences, and energy "highs and lows" throughout the day.

Just to give you an idea how it works, here are some quick characteristics of each body type. (We'll go into this very thoroughly in Chapter 4, the Personal Metabolic Inventory, a self-test to find your own body type.) If you are tall, long-limbed, and fine-boned, put on weight in a "jelly roll" or midriff bulge, love starches and sweets, and tend to work in very intense spurts followed by periods of exhaustion, you are probably a thyroid type.

See how it works? We've looked at body shape, fat distribution, food preferences, and energy patterns, just in brief, and come up with a preliminary body-type determination. Let's do the same thing with the other types.

Suppose you are solid and muscular, put on a "beer belly," love meat and potatoes, and can work all day on a few hours' sleep at night. You're probably an adrenal type. Say you have a child's body and a slightly big head, put on "baby fat" all over your body, love dairy products and fruit, and tend to spend more time thinking about work than working. If so, you're probably a pituitary type. Finally, if you're a woman who is much smaller above the waist than below, who puts on every extra pound in the rear end, loves creamy and spicy food, and has calm, steady energy throughout the day, you're probably a gonadal type.

HOW THE BODY
TYPE CONCEPT
WAS DEVELOPED

I first began to see the important differences in individual metabolism when I became interested in weight control. I determined to find an explanation for one of the most striking facts in this field—that different people have very different results on exactly the same diet.

If I were to go on what I had learned in medical school, I would expect everyone on the same diet to have the same results. If I read any of the various "diet books" I found in the bookstore, I would have imagined that anyone who ate what the author recommended (cottage cheese and grapefruit, high protein, high fiber, whatever it was) would lose weight easily, painlessly, and permanently. But, of course, this isn't what happens. On any given diet there are always people who do beautifully, people who do so-so, people who lose weight and then rebound, and people who don't lose weight at all.

I remember being especially struck by the contrast between two patients of mine, women named Anna and Joanne, who came in to lose weight together. Both were on a then popular high-protein, low-carbohydrate diet. Anna was doing very well. She was losing weight in all the right places, her eyes were bright, her skin was clear, her energy was high. But Joanne was what I would have to call a failure. She lost slowly, sometimes not at all. Some weeks she even gained. She felt hungry all the time, had terrific cravings for spicy foods, and was often irritable and depressed.

At that time, most people would have said that Anna was a "good" dieter and Joanne a "bad" one—and would have blamed the patient for the failure of the diet. I was tempted to do that myself (after all, patients do cheat on diets, it wouldn't be the first time); but they were watching each other for mutual reinforcement, and Anna assured me over and over that Joanne was following her diet faithfully.

So I began to try and peer into the metabolisms of the two women to find out what was going on. I arrived at the conclusion that these two individuals were very different metabolic types and actually needed very different diets in order to succeed.

I now know that Anna was a thyroid type, and that a high-protein, low-carbohydrate diet suits her body type perfectly. Joanne, on the other hand, was a gonadal type, and this same diet is totally wrong for her. It was overstimulating her ovaries, increasing her system's imbalances, creating food cravings, and simply not working. Once she was put on a lighter, lower-protein diet rich in complex carbohydrates— the kind that works for the gonadal-type metabolism— Joanne too began to have the results she wanted. And the concept of body types began to take shape.

THE MEDICAL IMPLICATIONS

This experience, and many others like it, led to the development of the body-type system. I developed nutritional programs for each type, and worked out the Personal Metabolic Inventory (see Chapter 4), which I use to involve my patients in body-type analysis. I can usually tell body types at a glance, but I like my patients to know what I'm looking at.

At first I used body types mainly with my weight control patients, but in time an interesting process of cross-fertilization began. I started noticing correlations between body type and certain patterns of health and disease. I noticed that the adrenal types were the ones I had to watch more closely for vascular disease or diabetes, but that they seldom had colds, flu, or colitis; these were more apt to strike thyroid types. Many patients with allergies turned out to be pituitary types or thyroid types. Women with lumpy breasts were often gonadal types. And so it went with many patterns emerging around the body-type determination.

All this I found extremely intriguing and exciting. I realized that knowing a patient's body type gave me a wealth of information about the metabolism and style of functioning of the entire physiology. I extended my investigations into other areas: I looked at exercise, vitamin and mineral supplementation, nutritional programs for the nonoverweight, and at the new preventive medical techniques becoming available today.

In every field I found that knowing a patient's body type brought into focus the needs of the individual patient, and that I could use this technique to personalize a program for each one. This was a great revelation to me, giving me a way to take individual differences into account in all areas of treatment, in a systematic way. By knowing your body type, you too will be able to design a personal health program for yourself, so that you can get the best results for the least effort in all areas of health care.

DR. SHERLOCK HOLMES AND THE MYSTERY FOUR

Imagine that one day you happen to be in a fast-food restaurant such as McDonald's or Burger King. (I know that, like my patients, you *never* eat fast-food—but in actual fact an occasional stop at one of these chains is not the worst thing you can do, as long as it's not every day.) Anyway, you're there, and you run into four people—two men and two women—you know from work. It's three-fifteen. They've just come from a long, difficult meeting, and they're all very ready for a little snack.

You carefully watch as they place their orders. One man has a milk shake. The second man has a large coffee with sugar, and a Danish. One of the women orders a double cheeseburger. The other woman chooses a rib sandwich.

If I were in that fast-food place with you, from this information alone I could make some pretty good guesses about what job each one does, what kind of health problem each is worried about, what kind of relationship each has with his or her family, and what each will be doing for the rest of the day.

And I'd be right nine times out of ten, too—and here's why. The four people haven't ordered what they did for random reasons. They've chosen their snacks because of the *structure of their metabolisms.*

It might seem to them that they chose just what they liked—but that's only part of it. Where do these preferences come from? Again, they come from the metabolism. A certain kind of individual doesn't just *feel* like having coffee and a Danish—he or she *has* to. If you look at the world with his type of metabolism, only coffee and a Danish look good. With another type of metabolism, you can't conceive of anything but a milk shake. With yet another type of metabolism, you just know that the only things that will revive you after such a meeting are greasy foods like ribs. So knowing what each person chooses to eat tells me something about his or her metabolism; this tells me the body type, and this in turn tells me everything else.

FOOD CRAVINGS AND YOUR METABOLISM

All right, but what is it about the metabolism that makes us want one food over another? It's the fact that we use food not just for nourishment but for its mind-altering effects. What each of us is looking for in food is a *particular change in our state of mind*. We want the food that will make us feel both calmer and more awake. We've all had the experience of eating more than we really want; what's usually going on is that we keep putting food into our mouth, hoping to find the food that will make us feel really good—tranquil but alert, awake and yet calm.

There is a great deal of new evidence in biochemical research to support this. Science is just beginning to understand the relationships between the biochemistry of food, the state of the brain, and the psychological effects we actually experience. It is now possible to verify the idea that the various foods we eat are not all the same in their effects, but actually produce particular states of mind. In the Appendix, "Notes for Scientists," I review some of the recent research that indicates exactly how we use foods to stimulate our various glands and bring out the brain state we want.

This idea, in fact, helps explain not just why we eat things we "know" we shouldn't, but why we do any number of actions that we also "know" are unhealthy. The explanation is that *we're looking for an effect on the way we feel*, and that the desire actually to *feel better* will take precedence every time over what we only believe may be bad for our health.

Each body type, then, is looking for this state of restful alertness from food. But, characteristically, each type of metabolism is set up to create restful alertness in itself by a particular set of biochemical reactions. There are several ways to get to the inner chemistry of energetic tranquility, and each of the four major glands has a way to create it in the system. According to your body type, you'll choose foods that set in motion one particular pathway to restful alertness.

What happens is that each and every food provides stimulation to some part of the glandular system. Some foods have very strong effects indeed on particular glands. Dairy products have a strong, stimulating effect on the pituitary gland. Sweets are thyroid stimulants. Meat and eggs stimulate the adrenals; greasy and spicy foods stimulate the gonads.

Each of us has a built-in tendency to eat foods that stimulate our dominant gland and get us to the state of mind we want in a particular way. If you're a thyroid type, for example, you like to improve your inner state through thyroidal energy, which is quick, immediate, and intense.

You've learned by experience that sweets and starches (and also caffeine drinks) give you a quick, sharp thyroidal "boost," so these are the foods you reach for at times of fatigue or stress.

In the same way, if you're a gonadal type, you reach for gonad-stimulating foods. If you're a pituitary type, you want to stimulate your pituitary; and if you're an adrenal type, nothing looks as good as an adrenal-gland stimulant. Catching those four people at three fifteen, when they are tired, hungry, and most in need of a change in inner feeling, you can be sure that each will be having the food he or she knows will stimulate their dominant gland.

Whenever we do this, we are using foods as mind-altering drugs and not for their nutritional qualities. The purpose of our snacks, whether we realize it or not, is to wake us up and calm us down—to make us feel more comfortable *inside*. Whether we think, intellectually, that a particular food is "good" for us or "bad," we don't really care. Even if we think it's bad, we'll have it when we need it, for the mind takes precedence over the body any day of the week.

GETTING RESTFUL ALERTNESS WITHOUT STIMULATION

All of the four people in the restaurant were affected by the experience of the stressful meeting, and the stress had affected them in characteristic ways. It made the P-type feel spaced-out and anxious; the T-type was nervous and irritable; the A-type felt aggravated and ready to jump down someone's throat, and the G-type felt vaguely frustrated. Naturally, they all wanted to get back to restful alertness—but *the way they chose to do it, through stimulating their dominant gland, was totally wrong*.

What you don't need, in this situation, is more stress to

your system. And eating foods which stimulate your dominant gland (a gland that is already tired from the stress of the meeting), is not at all helpful. What you can do, instead, is to choose foods that nourish and *gently* stimulate a different gland, not your dominant one, so that your system improves in balance and receives less stress.

The thyroid type could get to the state of mind he wants *more effectively* by choosing an adrenal stimulant—an egg sandwich, for instance—rather than a thyroid stimulant like coffee and a sweet. Instead of pumping up his dominant thyroid for one more push, he could stimulate his adrenals in a gentle way to give him steadier energy throughout the afternoon.

The adrenal type can do the same thing by choosing a pituitary stimulant instead of an adrenal stimulant—a milk shake, for instance, rather than a hamburger. The gonadal type can choose a pituitary-stimulating piece of fruit instead of the gonad-stimulating ribs, and the pituitary type can alter his metabolism in a more favorable direction with an adrenal-stimulating hamburger instead of that pituitary-stimulating shake.

All that's necessary is for you to understand the type of metabolism you have, and give yourself what you need—*not what you crave*. You need to learn to trade your "drug" for an actual food.

It's not just food, though, that you can use in this way. You can learn to make use of a whole range of healthy influences—exercise, nutritional supplements, acupressure, preventive medicine programs, and many more—to reach even higher levels of energy, health, and efficiency. Nutrition is the keystone of the Body Type Health Program because it provides the building material from which a new, more efficient system can be formed; but you will be able to go still further and do still more by using these principles in a way that works for your body type.

THE REALITY OF
THE BODY TYPE

Your glands, as I've said, are the basis of your body type. Yet the glandular system is so integrated into your whole system that it is a *reflection* of your body type, not its actual cause. I have chosen to use the dominant gland as a way of describing your body type, but the reality of your body type goes beyond the dominant gland. You aren't an adrenal type because you happen to have terrific adrenals; rather, you have a certain style of metabolism, and strong adrenals are just part of your metabolic style. The dominant gland is the signpost, rather than the cause, of your body type.

The true reason why you have one body type rather than another is probably genetic—that is, you were born with the tendencies of your type. I have observed signs of body-type distinction even in little babies, before a difference in diet or environment would have had a chance to influence it (at that age they drink only milk, anyway).

As to why different body types exist, I can only speculate. The four body types give the impression of being variations of the same basic machinery, perhaps designed for slightly different purposes. Or they may be four possible responses to changes in the environment, which became encoded in the genes over time. In any case, the value of knowing your body type is not in knowing why you happen to be a pituitary type or an adrenal type, but what it *means* to be one, and how to use your given machinery in the best possible way.

HOW WOULD THE
EPA RATE YOU?

Bodies are, in a way, like any piece of machinery—say, an automobile. A more efficient body uses less motion and works less to perform a task. We have all experienced the inefficiency of looking high and low for a set of keys that we were holding in our hand the whole time. We've also experienced inefficiency in the supposedly "good" exercise we've done that in the end made us look and feel worse, not better. Or we've experienced the inefficiency of working so long and hard on a project that our own best selves got lost in the maze.

All these are signs that our machinery—our physical system—is not efficient or is out of balance. We are like gas guzzlers or oil burners. Ask yourself: If the EPA were rating me and my friends, how would we do? One of the purposes of knowing your body type is to improve the efficiency of your own physical–mental–emotional system.

What I mean by efficiency is that mind and body work together well. Having a strong back and a good technique and a very efficient way of digging a hole—but in the wrong place—is not my idea of efficiency. Yet it's what many of us do. In this case, what was missing was the restful alertness, which has to be developed, that would have let us see our foolish mistake.

But efficiency, like metabolism, varies according to your body type. For example, if you're an adrenal type, you are most efficient when your strong adrenals are balanced by an active thyroid and pituitary gland. That's why the A-type having the snack could have improved her efficiency by ordering a coffee for thyroid stimulation. Whereas for a thyroid type, efficiency is highest when a strong thyroid gland is steadied by the influence of well-nourished adrenals. Hence, the efficiency-improving quality of an egg sandwich.

For a gonadal type, efficiency comes about when an active pituitary gland balances the strong sex glands—so a milk shake, by stimulating her pituitary gland, would improve her efficiency. Finally, a pituitary type works most efficiently when he or she has active adrenals and sex glands to increase steadiness and focus. That's why an adrenal-nourishing hamburger would help.

The effect we want to achieve is like the balance of a good orchestra or jazz band. The dominant gland is the soloist, and each one has a different style. But the soloist needs to be supported by a strong set of back-up musicians. There must always be a dynamic sense of interaction and support among all the different parts.

INEFFICIENCIES: THE BODY TYPE WINDOWS OF VULNERABILITY

Let's go back for a moment to that fast-food restaurant. You watched each one of the four people order a food that stimulated his or her dominant gland. This tendency—which we all share—to eat foods that stimulate our dominant gland is the basis of inefficiency in the system and produces what I call "windows of vulnerability" for each body type.

A window of vulnerability develops through *over-stimulation* of the dominant gland. What happens is that, through overuse of stimulating foods, tendencies belonging to the dominant gland become too emphasized or "fixed" in the system. Your body actually develops "habits" of functioning that are hard to break.

For example, one of the effects of adrenal hormones is to raise the blood pressure as part of the "fight or flight" response. If you're an adrenal type, you rely on adrenal energy in times of stress or fatigue. When you stimulate your adrenals with meat or salty foods, your adrenals raise your blood pressure more than is appropriate in a balanced system. Your body tends then to fall into the habit of hypertension. In medicine, the development of this habit of the body has a name. "Labile hypertension" ("labile" means changeable) is the name used while hypertension is developing and the blood pressure is still bouncing up and down. Later, when the pattern is fixed, it is called "essential hypertension," meaning in part that it has become an essential feature, a regular habit of the body.

Each of the body types has a tendency to develop such habits, which become the characteristic body-type windows of vulnerability. If you're a thyroid type, to take another example, the overstimulation of the thyroid gland leads to a habit of too much effective thyroid hormone. Many thyroid types develop skin problems or irritation of the bowels in this way.

Windows of vulnerability can also lead to fixed habits of thought. We get used to relying on a certain style of responding—T-types try to solve everything with a burst of flighty ideas, A-types react with too much stubbornness in situations where stubbornness doesn't help at all, P-types try to think their way out when some honest emotion would be better, G-types try to mother everyone and end up smothering instead. A fixed mental habit, in other words, is as serious a window of vulnerability as a fixed physical reaction.

Another window of vulnerability for each type develops through underactivity of the nondominant glands. Adrenal types, for instance, usually have fairly underactive thyroid glands, and thyroid hormone is needed to regulate blood cholesterol levels. Just as there is a window of vulnerability of hypertension from too much adrenal activity, there's a potential for elevated blood cholesterol related to low thyroid levels.

These windows of vulnerability are not invariable predictors of disease. Just because you're an adrenal type, you needn't *necessarily* develop hypertension or elevated cholesterol. Indeed, with the A-type Health Program, you can take important steps to avoid these problems. They are simply areas to be aware of, to watch out for, and to take care of. In medicine especially, forewarned is forearmed. You can close the windows of vulnerability and latch them shut.

BODY TYPE HEALTH STRATEGIES

The concept of windows of vulnerability helps explain what we want to accomplish for each body type. Since each type has a characteristic pattern of imbalance and a tendency to overuse the dominant gland, the goal of the body-type health strategies I'll be giving you is to remove the imbalance—to balance the metabolism and increase its power and efficiency.

There are many ways to accomplish this, and in Part II we'll go through them systematically. Nutrition is the cornerstone of the process; with the foods you eat, you can reduce stimulation of your dominant gland, support and strengthen your less-active glands, and build a healthier and more balanced body. There are many other strategies that you can use as well. The right exercise, nutritional supplements, and stress reduction techniques, along with the precise preventive medicine programs for your own needs, are all part of a total health plan that will work for you.

But before designing your health plan, I want you to have a better idea of what a body type really is. To make the concept real, I'm going to introduce you to some people and their body types. In the next two chapters you'll get an idea what it means to be a gonadal type, what being a thyroid type feels like, what life is like for a pituitary or adrenal type. This information will then be put to use in Part II, where you'll design your own Body Type Health Program around the needs of your body.

2

YOU AND
YOUR
BODY TYPE

It is fascinating to observe the way the body-type concept clarifies understanding of complex, interrelated problems. For example, let me tell you about a patient of mine named Tina M. When she originally came to me, she just wanted a checkup to try and find out why she felt so tired all the time.

I gave Tina the Personal Metabolic Inventory, but I could see at a glance that she was a thoroughly exhausted gonadal type. She worked in public relations, and although she was well trained for her job and good at it, at the time she walked into my office she felt totally burnt out. She was about twenty-five pounds overweight, and of course in typical G-type fashion, it was all on her rear and outer thighs. Her chest was sunken and her eyes had bags under them. She looked as though she hadn't slept in weeks.

One thing I noticed about Tina was that she actually smelled toxic. I don't want to make anyone who has ever been a patient self-conscious, but the fact is that a doctor can get quite a bit of information about you when he or she walks into the examining room, after you've changed into a gown and your body smell has been released from your clothes. The skin and sweat glands are escape routes for toxic overload, and in Tina's case the toxins smelled strong, sharp, and rather spicy—indicating a body that wasn't working efficiently.

Also, the room was noticeably warmer than the last time I'd been in it. Tina's body was wasting heat because it wasn't running well—like an overheated engine. I was dealing with a person whose gonadal-type metabolism was severely unbalanced, even though Tina was basically healthy and had nothing you would really call disease.

TINA'S STORY

I asked Tina to tell me about herself, starting with her diet. It turned out she was living on Mexican and Thai food, and was drinking two to three alcoholic drinks per day. She jogged and took a vitamin supplement. I asked about stress, and she mentioned that she was under a lot of pressure at work—she felt she wasn't performing well and that her boss wasn't pleased. A moment later she added that there was another problem. Her boyfriend was into sexual practices she wasn't comfortable with and that went against her upbringing, but being a modern woman in Los Angeles, she felt she should be openminded. She was doing what her boyfriend wanted, but felt terrible and longed for a simpler, more homey brand of sexual affection.

I now knew the basis of Tina's problem. All the influences she had described—food, sex, job pressures, even her jogging and her vitamin pill—had led Tina down the garden path of G-type imbalance. Every single influence I've mentioned turned out to be contributing to her exhaustion because of the structure of her gonadal-type metabolism.

A G-TYPE HEALTH PROGRAM

Tina's diet was the first thing to change. All the Thai and Mexican foods were overstimulating her dominant gland, her ovaries, which are much affected by spice, by grease, and also by alcohol. I put her on the G-type Balancing Diet right away, knowing that this change alone would go a long way toward taking care of her fatigue. It is also important as preventive medicine for gonadal types. A low-fat diet has been associated with decreased risk of uterine cancer, and this is something I want to see G-types take full advantage of.

Next I looked at her vitamin pill to see precisely what she was taking. It turned out to be a good start; but as a G-type, she needed more antioxidants, especially vitamins A and E, to offset her toxic tendencies. I put her on the G-type Nutritional Supplement Program (see chapter 9) and made sure she was getting just what she needed.

Her exercise was the next thing to scrutinize. I told Tina that jogging was the wrong exercise for her. It is mainly a lower-body exercise, and what she needed was both an aerobic program and an exercise that would improve upper-body/lower-body coordination. I suggested jazz dancing.

Tina's relationship was also contributing to her problems, especially the sexual aspect. The last thing this woman needed was any more stimulation of her exhausted sex glands. Her inner conflicts over sex were probably also causing congestion in her uterus and ovaries. However, I only mentioned this point to her lightly because it was already a subject of stress between Tina and her boyfriend, and I didn't want to add pressure to her life at this point.

Her job stress, though, I could look at. I found that she was going in to work very early and leaving early because this was the way her boss liked to work. However, G-types tend to have more and better energy in the later portions of the day. I suggested Tina try adjusting her hours and see what happened. This one simple change was very helpful—she began arriving at ten and leaving at six—and the quality of her work improved dramatically.

A month later I had Tina try the Long Weekend of Rejuvenation for gonadal types. This is a special weekend I've designed with the specific needs of each body type in mind, a sort of spring cleaning to make the metabolism more balanced and efficient (see chapter 12). The results were a revelation to Tina, and she was inspired to continue reordering her life in accordance with her needs as a gonadal type.

I was thrilled to see how Tina looked after about ten weeks. She appeared fully ten years younger, with the fat gone from her hips and the bags vanished from under her eyes. She told me that with her improved performance at work, she'd been given a raise, and then added that even her sex life had smoothed out. It turned out that when she started feeling better herself, Tina was able to communicate her own wishes more easily to her boyfriend. And she discovered to her amazement that he was quite willing to adjust. They found something both were happy with.

THE SCOPE OF CHANGE

One of the most interesting points about Tina's case is how *little* she actually had to do to make such great and positive changes. I think we often imagine that to improve our lives we must revamp them from top to bottom, and we shrink from the effort and do nothing. Actually, it often turns out that the changes we need to make are relatively small and involve only *adjusting* what we are doing anyway to the exact needs of our body type.

Tina was already taking vitamins—she just needed to take a little more of the *right* vitamins to make a major difference. She was exercising—but needed to change to the *right* exercise for her particular metabolic needs. She didn't need to change jobs or boyfriends—just make some adjustments in the way she related to them. She had to change only her diet, and there again it was more a question of emphasis than of total change. Once the metabolism is in better balance, even a G-type can eat *some* spicy food!

This is just one example of the way the body-type concept works. Tina's example shows the way you can use the knowledge of your body type to make dramatic improvements in your life as well. It's a matter of *personalizing* what you do and adjusting your actions to the needs of your body type.

If Tina had been a thyroid type, we might have looked at the same areas, but the program we would have come up with would have been entirely different. What worked for Tina won't necessarily work for you—but the principles that Tina and I used will help you set up the exact health program that *will* give you the results you want.

THE "AHA!" EXPERIENCE

One interesting experience of Tina's I've found applies to almost everyone. Once she understood her body type, she herself was able to begin making the right changes in her life to give her the results she wanted. In fact, knowing about her body type gave her a way of using a lot of information she already had about herself, but hadn't put together in quite that way.

Like Tina, you'll probably find that the moment of discovering your body type is a real "aha!" experience. You discover that you're a thyroid type or a pituitary type, an adrenal type or a gonadal type, and suddenly all kinds of perceptions you've had about yourself fall into place. You think, so *that's* why I always need to sleep two hours less than my husband! Or, no *wonder* I crave potato chips at four in the afternoon! Or, now I know why I feel so good all morning when I jog and eat yogurt for breakfast! Whichever your type, there's always a shock of recognition—yes, right, that's me, that's how I am.

Knowing your body type helps you trust your intuition about yourself. For example, it's part of good nutrition for T-types to eat eggs for breakfast regularly. Some T-types I've had as patients have already discovered this about themselves and tell me that the eggs make them feel much better. But they go on to ask anxiously, "*Should* I have them? Aren't they bad for me?" They have the experience of their own better feeling but aren't confident enough to trust it in the face of expert advice to the contrary. So I tell them that their perception is valid and explain the value of eggs by describing the dynamics of their T-type metabolism.

By contrast, adrenal-type patients, who are more liable to be affected by eating too many eggs, never say that eggs make them feel *better*. They make them feel pumped up and full, but not better. They usually crave eggs (and bacon as well) for breakfast and resist giving them up because of the craving, but they are aware that this is their situation. Like T-types, most A-types are aware of the way eggs make them feel.

There are many things you know about yourself in this way, and when you know your body type, you find the reasons they are so and learn to work with your body with assurance that what you're doing is right.

What it comes down to is learning to trust what you know about yourself. This self-knowledge is just as important as the *new* information I'm going to supply you with about your body type. You're going to find that you know more about yourself than you imagine, and once you know how your body type works, you'll see how your own perceptions fit in to your own Body Type Health Program.

OTHER PEOPLE'S BODIES

Yours is not the only body in your life. It's the one that's your primary responsibility, but if you live with, work for, exercise with, cook for, employ, or just plain relate to anyone else, you'll benefit from knowing that person's body type as well. In fact, once you get the idea of body types, you'll find yourself checking out the type of all the people around you, just for the information it gives you about the way they work. Soon you'll find yourself including a person's body type in your description of him or her as a matter of course. "Oh, yes, I know Fred. Works in my building. Good looking, dark hair, sharp dresser, a T-type. You know who I mean?" That sort of thing.

Wouldn't it be terrific to know what time of day your boss is most likely to be feeling expansive, optimistic, and generous? If you know about body types, you can avoid going in to ask for a raise just when the body-type "low" comes around and your boss is sure the company's going to go broke any second. You'll be able to choose the time when you're most likely to get a positive response.

If you're familiar with body types you'll also know the most effective time to schedule meetings with just about anybody, where the best place would be to take a client to lunch, and what topics make the quickest ice-breakers in a sales talk. By the way, I'm not talking about manipulation. I'm talking about working with other people's metabolic realities so that everyone's comfortable and able to perform at his or her best.

At home, you can use your knowledge of body-type rhythms to improve family interaction. Understanding the various body types in your family can make the difference between a home life of relaxation and creative growth, or one of friction and mutual misunderstanding. If you know your wife is a thyroid type, for example, you'll know the signs of thyroidal letdown to be aware of—as well as the signs of an oncoming burst of great, thyroidal creativity and exuberance—and believe me, the knowledge will help you.

If you're aware that your husband's an adrenal type you'll have arguments to marshall against his workaholic habits and the insight to appreciate why he acts the way he does. You'll know what kind of relaxation to suggest for him *and* what kind of meals to prepare to cool him off after a hard day. In a relationship, this kind of knowledge is worth a lot.

YOUR FAMILY AND THEIR DIFFERENCES

If you and your spouse have different body types, you'll be able to plan your health programs so that you both get what you need. And if you have the same body type, you'll be able to avoid reinforcing one another's weaknesses. I've seen families of all thyroid types eating thyroid stimulants together, getting more and more wired on sugar and coffee until they all crash. I've seen adrenal-type families growing obese and dull together on huge meals of meat, potatoes, and gravy. But this can be avoided. If you know your body types, you can all counteract your body-type vulnerabilities together and grow stronger and healthier as a family.

Your kids can benefit, too. Let's say you have two children: one adrenal and one pituitary type. If you know what this means, you'll have the information you need to help them both do well in everything, from sports to school to perfect health. You'll also be able to let them know why you treat them individually—as opposed to constantly dealing with, "Pam had a milk shake after school, why can't I?" Children love knowing their body type; it's part of their sense of individuality. And because their minds are so quick, with a little practice they often become better at picking out body types than you are!

WHAT IF YOU AREN'T FAT?

One of the most obvious features of each body type is the place on the body where fat accumulates. If you see an overweight woman with most of her excess weight on the derriere, you can be quite confident she's a gonadal type. An overweight adrenal type can be picked out by the presence of a potbelly, an overweight thyroid type is noted for the midriff "jelly roll," and the pudgy pituitary type is always found with baby fat all over. If you've read the *Body Type Diet*, you already have some experience in picking out body types by location of excess weight.

But what if you're not overweight? And what if you're interested in finding the body type of someone who hasn't an ounce of excess fat on his or her body? Don't worry—it can be done. But it takes a little closer look than if you have those extra pounds to go on.

Overweight is an *unbalanced* condition, and like all unbalanced conditions, it carries with it the signs of an exaggerated body type. An overweight thyroid type will actually look *more thyroidal* than a healthy thyroid type who is at the ideal weight, because the condition of overweight means that the body has some imbalance and is overworking the dominant gland. He or she is in a sense a caricature of the ideal T-type. Since each type loses weight by reducing stimulation of the dominant gland and increasing stimulation of the less-active glands, a person who isn't overweight must have a more balanced metabolism than an overweight one.

However, even if the person you're curious about (yourself or someone else) has the most balanced metabolism in the world, it's still possible to discover the body type. Overweight isn't the only indication—there are many other clear signs you can use.

VERY BALANCED
PEOPLE

Let's say you just met a very balanced person—someone who's slender and energetic and doesn't seem to crave any particular food. You think, he's (or she's) cute; but what's his (or her) type? How are you going to pick it out?

First, you have to assume that this person must have

worked out a way to maintain balance in his system by himself. Maybe he's figured out, by trial and error or by trusting his own instincts, a diet that works for his body type. Maybe he's evolved an exercise program that stimulates balance for their type, or perhaps his job has a balancing effect. There are various possibilities, but there will be *something,* and a little bit of probing into his lifestyle will usually bring it out.

For instance, suppose you meet a tall, long-legged, well-muscled man and, over the course of an afternoon, have the chance to observe that his energy is remarkably stable. You can't quite figure out his type. From his height and his long legs you had immediately sized him up as a thyroid type, but what about those muscles? Good muscles usually mean an adrenal type. And then there's his energy—it's more stable than you'd expect a T-type to be.

You're still wondering when you go out to dinner, but there you get your answer. He orders a meal of broiled chicken, salad, and green vegetables, has only a half a piece of bread, and tastes your dessert but doesn't order one for himself. Over a cup of decaffeinated coffee, he tells you that he swims laps four times a week and plays basketball with his buddies every Saturday morning.

Now the light dawns. You realize that he's a thyroid type who balances his body by diet and regular aerobic exercise, and avoids the excessive thyroidal stimulation of coffee and carbohydrates. No wonder he looks and works so well. He's well balanced—but you can still find his body type.

In the next chapter we're going to go through the characteristics of each body type. I'll give you at least one clue for each type that works regardless of weight. Basically, what you're looking for is what is called "bone structure"— the underlying body shape that persists whether or not you put on weight. Usually it can be seen in the face, and almost always it can be seen in the hands.

Many times people come up to me dressed in clothes that aren't exactly revealing—a down parka and baggy pants, for instance—and ask what body type they are. I can see their faces, of course, and I ask to see their hands. I can usually make a determination, which I later confirm by checking their body outline once they get out of the down coat. I'll show you how to do this yourself. It's quite easy once you know what to look for.

Now let's go ahead and take a look at the four body types. The next chapter examines many of their characteristics, both physical and psychological. As you read through it, you'll learn to pick out each of the types, whether in men or women, children or adults. You'll learn the distinguishing characteristics and the little "giveaways" that each type can't hide.

Because it's so helpful to know about all the body types, I've given you this information *before* the Body Type Personal Metabolic Inventory, which follows in Chapter 4. I don't want you only reading about your own type! Remember, opposites attract. So if you're a thyroid type, chances are your spouse, lover, or best friend is an adrenal; if you're a pituitary, you're sure to have at least one close associate who is a gonadal type; if you're an adrenal type you surely have a great, if rather baffling, attraction to those thyroid and pituitaries you know.

3

THE FOUR
BODY TYPES

THE
CONTRADICTORY
THYROID TYPE

He's a dynamo of energy in the office from nine until ten-thirty; then he's a wreck until he's had another cup of coffee.

She's brilliant, witty, and lively until three in the morning, but the next day she's too depressed to get out of bed.

He's one of those people who can eat anything in the world and never gain an ounce—until the day comes when he gains forty-five pounds in three months and you hardly recognize him.

She's the overweight lady whose face and hands are slender and delicate, and whose energy, concentrated to the point of hysteria, defies you to look at her below the neck.

They're energetic and lethargic, creative and destructive, confident and insecure, upbeat, downbeat, and deadbeat by turns. They're thyroid types, and if you're one of them, you know it.

The thyroid type has a metabolism that is dominated by the thyroid gland, the gland located at the base of the throat just above the notch you can feel in the front of the breastbone. The thyroid gland is in charge of the function of the metabolism called *oxidation*—the burning of food in the

31
—

tissues. It works by secreting chemicals called thyroid hormones into the bloodstream. The amount of thyroid hormone secreted by this gland, and how it acts in the cells, are what determine the rate at which the body burns its food. Thyroid hormones also control the flow of energy from the liver to the blood. The liver is the body's storehouse of glycogen, a storage form of blood sugar, and it releases it into the blood when directed to do so by the thyroid gland. Thyroid hormones also act to increase the heart rate and improve muscle tone.

What this means is that the thyroid gland is the gland of quick, lively energy. It is the gland of speed, of the burst of activity as opposed to the sustained flow. It is the gland of the sprinter, not the long-distance runner. It is capable of remarkable output, but the gland, and the body type it produces, require a period of recovery after each energy burst. These are the characteristics of the person whose system is dominated by the thyroid gland.

THE T-TYPE WINDOWS OF VULNERABILITY: STIMULATION INSTEAD OF REST

When a T-type is "on," there's no one livelier—but like the thyroid gland itself, T-types need a period of rest after each period of activity. They don't always take it; characteristically, they'll take stimulation instead of rest. If you're a thyroid type, failure to recognize your need for rest, and to rest when you need to, is the single most important factor in your health problems.

If you're overweight, you got that way by using food as a stimulant for your thyroid gland. You were trying to combat fatigue and to get your mind into a more alert, tranquil state—but without resting or balancing your metabolism. Remember the man in the fast-food restaurant at three fifteen in the afternoon after a long, stressful meeting? The one who ordered a large coffee and a Danish? He's a typical thyroid type, and he's using carbohydrates and caffeine to stimulate his thyroid gland, whip his body, and arouse his brain.

I don't doubt that this man was the star of the meeting. He was undoubtedly entertaining and forceful, the kind of person who carries all before him. By the end of the meeting, though, he was probably wired and glassy. He should have gone back to his office, closed his eyes, and rested for half an hour. Or, if he really had to go on to the restaurant with the others, he should have ordered a chicken sandwich and thrown away the top bread.

Instead, his tendency is to stretch his reserves, get another half hour of pseudo-energy out of the thyroid stimulants, and then "crash" into fatigue and depression at half past four. At that point he'll probably reach for a candy bar or a cola drink for the energy to get home. Can overweight be far away? Perhaps it's already here, for that matter.

And not only overweight, for fat isn't the only hazard lurking here. The tendency to overstimulate the system can lead to many other problems as well. The thyroid is the most delicate gland in the endocrine system—the one that goes out the most easily. There are a hundred people with exhausted, nonfunctioning thyroid glands for every one who has worn out the adrenals. After a certain amount of the persistent stimulation to which T-types subject their thyroid glands, thyroid collapse often follows.

A low- or nonfunctioning thyroid gland leads to many other problems, such as skin irritations, a lowered resistance to minor infections and diseases, and even more serious problems. Physicians will prescribe thyroid hormones to be taken in pill form, and many thyroid types are taking supplemental thyroid pills, but it is obviously much better to take good care of the thyroid gland you have and keep it healthy.

THE THYROID TYPE IDEAL

Everything in the T-type Health Program is designed to teach you to close this window of vulnerability. It provides strength and support for the thyroid gland, nourishes the less-active adrenals, and structures your system to respect its need for both activity and rest. With this sort of support, you can get back to the ideal of the thyroid type—sparkling without being "hyper," calm without looking sedated.

The ideal T-type is a beautiful sight. Those T-types who have learned their body-type rhythm, who alternate activity and rest, exercise and recreation, and support their thyroid with the right nutrition, enjoy all the advantages of a superb body type.

The thyroid-type body is built for speed with delicacy and strength. T-types have fine bones, delicate faces, bright smiles with generally straight, white teeth, and very fine, glowing skins. The hands are always a good feature, with fine bones, tapering fingers, and flexible and precise motion.

T-type women who are in good balance have supple, greyhound bodies, with fairly wide shoulders, definite waists, and rounded but slender hips. Their breasts can be fairly substantial and tend to get a little bigger with age. Balanced T-type men also have wide shoulders, and their bodies taper to narrow waists and hips. T-type men usually have almost no rear end. In both men and women, the limbs are proportionally long and slender. To picture a T-type in typical form, picture Victoria Principal or Jeremy Irons.

T-type personalities display the same liveliness-with-strength that makes their ideal bodies so terrific. No one in the world adds the wit, perceptiveness, and liveliness that a T-type does. And it's not necessary to burn out doing it, either. I'm a T-type, and I know. You *can* preserve your liveliness and health, even in this crazy world.

THE POWER OF THE ADRENAL TYPE

The difference between thyroid types and adrenal types is one on which the world turns. The two types are utterly different, yet they balance one another; and whether in work or play, they need each other for a sense of completeness.

Adrenal types are the steadiest, hardest workers in the world—and so hearty and warm that everyone gathers around them after work to joke, relax, and talk about football. They're the first ones to show up in the morning and the last to leave at night, and if their families sometimes complain that they never see them—well, that's part of what it means to love an adrenal type.

At play, adrenal types are ready, willing, and able—whatever you have in mind. They have a digestion like a coal furnace and an appetite for all things; and since they need less sleep than any other type, they always feel the night is young and inviting. Take a camping vacation with an A-type, if you get the chance. They'll pack the car, do most of the driving, set up the tent, and get the campfire going. Later, in bed, they're the ones everybody wants to be close to—their bodies give out heat on the coldest night and will always keep your feet warm too!

The adrenal type carries through with ideas, where the thyroid type initiates projects and then loses interest. When a thyroid type is already fatigued from a burst of creativity, the adrenal type is just getting started and will see possibilities in a project that the thyroid type never suspected. A philosopher once said that people are either foxes or hedgehogs: foxes know many things and hedgehogs know one big thing. If this is so, then adrenal types are hedgehogs and T-types are foxes. While T-types are all over the place going from idea to idea, A-types concentrate on one thought and carry it from idea to actuality. Powerful and consistent, steady, even, and often inflexible, the adrenal type dominates his or her world by sheer persistence—and enjoys every minute of it, as well.

The metabolism of this body type is dominated by the adrenal glands—plural, because there are two, one located on top of each kidney. These small glands, no bigger than two lima beans, are the most powerful glands in the system and the ones with the most diverse roles to play in the metabolism.

The various chemicals secreted by the adrenals, which go by the general name of adrenal hormones, perform many functions. They assist the liver in the manufacture of glycogen, a reserve form of blood sugar, which is later brought into the bloodsteam by the thyroid gland. They assist the kidneys in purifying the "internal ocean" of bodily fluids. They control the formation of fat and muscle, and affect the balance between them. Adrenal hormones stimulate the appetite, raise the blood pressure, and give a sense of power and fullness to the body. You couldn't survive more than a few days without them. In short, the adrenals are the glands of balance, power, and steadiness of energy, and the characteristics of the adrenal type come from these qualities of their dominant gland.

THE ADRENAL TYPE WINDOW OF VULNERABILITY: OVERDOING IT ALL

The problem with your system, oddly enough, is that in a way you're *too* steady, *too* powerful, *too* balanced. Like a diesel truck, once you get going you like to keep going. Once you start eating, you don't like to stop. Once you lose your temper and start shouting, you like to keep on until everyone around you is thoroughly cowed (adrenal hormones are the instigators of the "fight or flight" reaction, and on the whole, fight is your preference). Once you get into a project at work, you hate to come home—and once you start partying and drinking, you hate to quit.

Your system is given to excess, and because you are so strong you think you can take anything. You almost can—but not quite. Remember the movie *North Dallas Forty* about professional football? It gave almost a textbook illustration of adrenal types driving themselves on and on, to and past the point of exhaustion and collapse, absorbing and ignoring punishment.

The adrenal type we last saw taking a fast-food break was having a double burger and, in her heart, looking rather askance at the thyroid type who had just ordered coffee and a Danish. The A-type was thinking that her T-type colleague was having something unhealthy, just as a "pick-me-up," whereas she, the A-type, was having something healthy and nourishing. This is just an amusing self-delusion; nothing could be further from the truth. The hamburger is just as much an adrenal stimulator as the carbohydrates and caffeine are thyroid stimulants, and the A-type is doing exactly the same thing to her body with meat and salt as the T-type does with coffee and sweets. Both are using their own chemical pathways to get the brain/mind effect they want. The desired effect of arousal with calmness is the same—only the stimulant they use is different.

In both cases, they are using food to stimulate the dominant gland. But whereas the thyroid type stimulates the thyroid, which then collapses into fatigue and exhaustion, the adrenal type stimulates the adrenals, which keep on pumping out the power and creating more and more appetite. In each case the punishing effect on the body is disregarded while you concentrate on the way the food makes you *feel*. This is truly the drug effect of food.

T-types may go home after work and be too tired to cook, but you A-types will go home hungry and with the energy to cook yet another heavy, meaty, salty meal. The result: You can get not only fat, but amazingly obese, and because you have the energy to carry it, you can fool yourself into thinking that there's nothing wrong with the way you are.

On the contrary, an all-too-common sight in a doctor's

office is the overweight, overtired adrenal type, whether man or woman, who is suffering from high blood pressure, hardening of the arteries, and diabetes. Because one of the functions of adrenal hormones is to raise the blood pressure and the blood sugar, and because both your high-salt and high-fat diet and your generally high-pressure lifestyle encourages this response, you A-types are prone to get diseases of the cardiovascular and circulatory systems, and also diabetes—a serious combination.

Picture, if you will, an A-type in his or her mid-thirties to forties. A solid frame carries what I call "hard fat" in a "beer belly" in front and another layer across the back and neck. From the inside the person is "larded," like rich meat. The face is rather flushed-looking, perhaps with a few broken veins in the nose or cheeks. The energy is still high, but there's an underlying sense of fatigue or strain, and a sense that the person is somehow about to burst.

The recent research showing the relevance of blood cholesterol to arteriosclerosis and cardiovascular disease are particularly relevant to A-types—*you are the ones most at risk*. It even makes sense for you to be a vegetarian if you wish—for your body type this diet works beautifully. There are many other strategies I'll give you in the following chapters—from supplements to exercise to preventive health programs. These dietary changes will immediately lighten up your excessive adrenal function, and you'll start to look and feel better right away.

THE ADRENAL TYPE IDEAL

Once you've closed this window of vulnerability, you will enjoy the full value of your body that's built to last. You've got strong arms and very good legs, a compact, solid torso, and a squarish head with a round or square face. Your skin has good color, and being generally a bit oilier than T-type skin it wears well and is not particularly inclined to wrinkles. Your hair is strong and has good body.

Adrenal-type men have a tendency to become bald, in a very virile and attractive way. A-type men look very masculine, in the style of football rather than basketball players. You have well-muscled arms and legs, a solid body, not much of a waist, a rounded rear end—like Nick Nolte, Carrol O'Connor, or Mr. T.

Adrenal-type women—with large, rounded breasts, flat rears, and great legs—are classically voluptuous and often the envy of their friends. You don't have a very emphasized waist, but tend to taper more from chest to hips. The flatness of the rear is your characteristic tip-off, for no other body type has this feature. To picture an A-type woman, think of Linda Evans or Bette Davis.

In personality, the same power and warmth that your body has in such abundance shine through in your personal vividness and strength. And you can learn to enjoy change, to take it easier, and have all the flexibility and liveliness that anyone could ask. You're an A-type for life, but you don't have to be totally "type A." You can have it all without overdoing—with the A-type Health Program.

THE FINE BALANCE
OF THE
PITUITARY TYPE

Which is the ideal body type? It's a question I'm occasionally asked and don't really like to answer because I don't think in those terms: I like to think in terms of the ideal for each type. But if I had to say, in my opinion the ideal would be a pituitary type—as long as he or she had good, strong functioning from all the other glands. The balanced P-type looks like the person of the future—with a large head, clear face, and healthy body.

This P-type would be a lively, intelligent person, with all

the fluid curiosity of a young child. He or she would also have the flash and creativity of a thyroid type, the power of an adrenal type, and all the warmth and sensuality of a gonadal type. Sounds terrific, don't you think?

But for this ideal to be realized, all the glands, not just the pituitary, need to be developed. What happens more often is that the pituitary is strong, but the other glands aren't well developed at all. The typical P-type is *all* pituitary: the curiosity and lively intelligence are there, along with a head that is characteristically just a bit bigger than usual and a rather childish-looking body, but the qualities that come from the other glands just aren't there. Many P-types give the impression that they live in their heads only, with the body existing mainly to carry the head around.

P-types are relatively rare in the United States—in my experience only ten percent of the population or less—and there seem to be even fewer women in this body type than men. Yet the P-types I know are memorable people. There's always something unusual, elusive, and intriguing about them. They're always ready for a deep discussion of the nature of life and invariably have an opinion to offer, no matter how abstract the topic. You P-types are the ones who listen to other people's emotional crises, but never seem to have one of your own. You're highly imaginative and can picture yourself doing anything in the world—as long as it doesn't involve leaving your room. If and when you do finally step out into the world of action, what you do is often very unusual. You are, in short, very interesting people.

The world might be a better place if it had more people in it like you. Why, then, are P-types such a rarity? Business and sports are highly adrenal, communication and the arts are extremely thyroidal, and most of advertising works directly on the gonads. Maybe it's because pituitary ideas are so potent. The creative thought of one P-type computer designer, say, creates work for a thousand A-type salespeople and T-type entrepreneurs and changes everybody's life while doing it.

THE P-TYPE WINDOW OF VULNERABILITY: NEGLECTING THE BODY

The P-type in the fast-food place was the one who ordered the milk shake. P-types are no different from other types in that they try to get their tranquil alertness through foods that stimulate their dominant gland. Dairy products are pituitary stimulants, and when you P-types are tired or stressed and want to feel better you usually reach for something that will give you the kind of energy you're most used to—the cool, detached energy of the pituitary gland. Your downfall are foods like yogurt and ice cream, for these foods act to overstimulate your pituitary and leave your other glands underactive.

What happens when your dominant gland is overstimulated is that you become *too pituitary,* and this means that you don't take the care you should take of your body. A dangerous detachment is created, and you don't pay nearly the attention to your physical liabilities that you should.

For example, if your digestion is weak (as it often is), you ignore it; you decide that probably everyone feels slightly nauseous or has gas after eating. Your sexual function may also be weak, but again, you think that everyone's *really* like you, just pretending to be interested in sex. Rather than doing something about these physical problems, you tend to ignore them and just "think about something else."

I have found that allergies are common in P-types— often extreme allergies, the sort of situation where almost anything can set off a reaction. This is partly a result of the weak adrenal function, and partly just an effect of P-type detachment. You can get so out of touch with the outside world that your body just doesn't know how to react. Allergy is a sort of furious rejection and denial of the world. Frequent colds are another result of your neglect of the body.

Another related problem is mental obsession. Your mind goes round and round on some problem—and because there's rarely any action taken which might resolve the situation, the obsession just goes on and on. This can be a truly debilitating situation for many pituitary types.

I can see the picture of an overweight, unbalanced P-type I know as clearly as though he were standing before me in my office. He looks almost exactly like a big, pudgy baby. There's a round, childlike face with a bright expression and a body that hasn't essentially changed, except to put on weight, since the age of twelve. His extra pounds are on the hands and arms, back and chest, and his stomach is rounded like a child's. There is no one area that is noticeably fatter than another; all areas of the body are equally pudgy.

This man (let's call him James) is a vegetarian, lives alone, and works as an architect (a typically P-type occupation, as it is intellectual and slightly detached from the "real world" of building). I was not surprised to learn, on his first visit to my office, that before coming in he'd worried about his weight for nearly a year, had been obsessed about his exam for three months, and *thought about* trying at least ten different diets, but hadn't actually tried any of them. Thinking about dieting made him tense, and he would smoke and eat whipped-cream treats to "calm his nerves." The only diet he'd actually tried featured a great deal of cottage cheese and left him more out of balance than ever.

This same patient was the man I mentioned before, whose arteries were in such surprisingly good shape but who was troubled by allergies. After a thorough history, physical, and lab work had determined that he had no potential heart problem, I told James that the way to bring his system back into balance was to stimulate his adrenals and sex glands with red meat and organ meats.

"That's what I feed my dog," he replied indignantly. "Does your dog have allergies?" I shot back. "No." "Well, then."

On this diet, I assured him, his allergies would be better, he'd lose weight and have more energy. Like most P-types, he thought his digestion wouldn't be able to handle this much meat, but he agreed to try it. And by the next week I already saw remarkable improvements. When he came in he looked so hearty I almost expected an A-type slap on the back. He didn't slap, but did pat my shoulder—and from him the acknowledgment that I even had a shoulder was great progress.

In the course of his treatment James was able to transform his system from an almost purely pituitary one to an *ideal* P-type body, with all the secondary glands playing their roles in a coordinated way. His allergies cooled off, and he started to look less childish, more manly. His architectural style even changed, becoming slightly less intellectual, warmer, and more relevant.

It's amazing how beautifully the P-type metabolism responds to the Balancing Diet for this body type. All the various aspects of the P-type Health Program—exercise, supplements, antistress program, life extension and preventive medicine—work with the nutritional program in bringing about a vastly improved integration of mind and body.

THE PITUITARY TYPE IDEAL

When a P-type becomes perfectly developed and achieves balanced functioning, he or she is really unbeatable. Many P-types seem to believe that their best bet is to write off the body and concentrate on the mind. You know—never get undressed in public, wear shoes and socks on the beach, play aerobic chess. But this is not the way to go. If you can get every part of your system to work—body as well as mind—you can acquire a physical glow to match the mental and spiritual one you already have.

The P-type body at its best is supple and flexible, and keeps a youthful appearance far longer than calendar years would suggest. You have very fine hair, delicate hands and feet, and a slender, well-shaped body. With the right diet P-type women *can* have a shape, although they will never have the sensual roundness of an adrenal type or the sharp voluptuous curves of a thyroid type. P-type women have small, childlike budding breasts, with a smooth, nongrainy texture, not actually like the breast tissue in women of other types. But with your radiant P-type glow, you have your own brand of sexuality that is every bit as attractive. Just picture an angel with sexuality—that can be you.

Your key words for ideal development are integration of mind and body. You need to get that energy out of your head—not to become merely physical, but to integrate your physical nature with your excellent mind. When you do, you get the best of both worlds—the excellent P-type intellect with a beautifully functioning and coordinated body. You will leave people with the impression that you know more than you do. When your whole system works together, you really are the man or woman of the future. The P-type Health Program will make it happen for you.

THE WARMTH AND RADIANCE OF THE GONADAL TYPE

The G-type woman is highly distinctive, but in some ways every woman has some gonadal-type characteristics. In the years from puberty to the menopause, every woman's metabolism is deeply influenced by the ovaries, the female sex glands, and cannot help acquiring some G-type characteristics.

Female sex hormones are among the most powerful chemicals in the system, as witnessed by the fact that some women are all but enslaved by the vicissitudes of their menstrual cycle. In fact, these are the ones that first come to mind when we say the word "hormone." But for the gonadal-type woman, the influence of these powerful hormones sets the tone and style of her entire metabolism, and gives her a set of unique physiological characteristics.

G-type women have the most distinct appearance of all body types and are the easiest to recognize. As I've already mentioned, the key area is their derriere. One patient of mine says she thinks of it as "big tush syndrome." A G-type farm lady from Iowa says she reminds herself of a backhoe—big treads and a little bucket on top—when she looks in the mirror.

I've occasionally surprised women who want me to determine their body type by asking them to turn around, but it's really necessary to glance, ever so discreetly, at that part of the anatomy. For even in the most slender and well-balanced G-type, there will always be an *emphasis*, at least, on the derriere. And if there are any extra pounds at all, here and on the "saddlebags" is where they will be.

Some people think that the term "gonadal type" is a judgment on their sexiness. The truth is that one's sexuality is a complex phenomenon, and not just the province of one's body type. Every type is sexy in its own way and attracts on different terms. (If you think P-types aren't sexy, reflect that there are a billion Chinese, most of whom are pituitary types!) This is one of the things that makes the world interesting, not to mention populous.

Some G-types are sexier than others; some G-types are sexier than some T-types or A-types or P-types—but not all. However, being a G-type does mean that sex in its fullest sense, especially warmth, love, and nurturing will always play an important part in your life. You will always be aware of yourself as being at one end of the male–female duality, whatever else you may be as well.

The G-type metabolism is the steadiest of all body types in the sense that it gives out energy in a controlled, persistent way. It's the body's way of asserting that mothering is a full-time and serious occupation. Your system is well designed for the rigors of childbearing and nursing, activities that require more physical reserves than any other natural event. The storage of fat in the rear end is specifically for this purpose. As you probably know, if your body drops below a certain percentage of fat, you will stop menstruating (as sometimes happens to women athletes in strict training).

This occurs because a certain level of fat needs to be held in reserve before your body feels confident enough to conceive.

If you're not a mother, or if you also work at an outside job, your G-type metabolism extends these natural qualities into the workplace. You're steady, helpful, magnetic, a reliable team player, and you take responsibility as a matter of course.

Because of the steadiness of your metabolism, you have the hardest time of any body type in starting to lose weight if you are overweight. But once you get started, you lose weight comfortably and steadily; and when you reach your ideal weight, you keep it. Where thyroid types will tend to balloon up quickly, and drop weight quickly, you *maintain* your weight, whatever it may be. This is another way your G-type steadiness shows itself.

THE G-TYPE WINDOW OF VULNERABILITY: THE EXTREME OF ENJOYMENT

The G-type we last saw eating fast-food had just ordered a rib sandwich (with extra barbecue sauce, please). You can practically see that sandwich head straight for the saddlebags. The spices and the grease provide a full dose of gonadal stimulation. One effect of eating fats and spices is pelvic congestion—increased blood flow to the lower intestines, uterus, and ovaries. This causes increased and unbalanced hormone production from the ovaries. This overstimulation of the sex glands leads in turn to more congestion in the pelvic organs. The medical problems that a G-type is most likely to have are related to this tendency.

Spicy (and also salty) foods affect the brain to arouse

and tranquilize the person by way of the brain's "nesting" areas. This, combined with the additional hormones, confers the motherly calm alertness that is the effect G-types are trying for with their food cravings. On the other hand, when you stop eating these foods and start balancing your system with pituitary and thyroid stimulants, you can get the restful alertness you want *without* the big tush! You're lucky, for when you change your diet and certain other aspects of your lifestyle, you start to get better really fast and keep going. The protective effect of your ovarian hormones is such that your natural tendency is toward radiant health.

Making your diet consciously low-fat will go a long way. You are the very people for whom the advice about the benefits of a low-fat diet is most useful. Staying away from very spicy foods helps you stay on a lower fat diet, by the way— it's not just something I've come up with to make your life less interesting. Spicy foods actually create cravings for fats in you, and the two together, as in a rich, spicy dish, really overstimulate the ovaries and encourage your body to form cellulite. If you make an effort to use more herbs in cooking and fewer spices, you'll find you can come away from those encounters with the french onion dip with your dignity intact.

THE GONADAL TYPE IDEAL

Do you know what I would like? I would like it if no G-type woman ever again got mad at her body. Your shape is unique, distinctive, your own. You're supposed to have a curvy rear end. It's attractive, so stop slamming it against the wall. Do you want to look like a twelve-year-old boy? You look like a woman, and you should appreciate yourself in that light.

The perfect-looking G-type woman is quite small above the waist and more solid-looking below. Your waist is always pronounced and remains small even if you put on a lot of weight. Your stomach, too, stays quite flat. If you feel you have a pronounced rear but aren't sure if you're a T-type or a G-type, look at your stomach. If it stays flat whether you lose or gain, you're a G-type.

G-type breasts are small but hormonally active. You can feel it in the tissue: it has a very distinctive contour. Both your chest and cup size are small, but your breasts don't feel childish or baby-fat, like the small breasts of P-type women. You have pronounced nipple glands.

Your key words for health and beauty are purification and upward motion of energy. By purification I mean that you need to overcome your body's tendency to become congested and fail to throw off impurities. The thyroid is in charge of this kind of elimination, so a big part of your balancing strategy is to encourage thyroid activity in your system. Upward motion of energy is a concept that includes stimulating your pituitary for better balance, moving your system away from passivity, encouraging better circulation, and improving your mind–body coordination.

All this can be accomplished with the G-type Health Program—a coordinated program of diet, nutritional supplements, exercise, and lifestyle adjustments. You will be amazed at the increased freshness and energy you'll feel. You won't lose your G-type persistence, but you'll gain a whole world of lightness, creativity, and participation that will make you feel brand new.

NOW LET'S FIND
OUT FOR SURE

You have now gained a basic insight into the characteristics of each of the four body types. If you're like most people, you've already recognized yourself among them— but you would like to be sure. The Personal Metabolic Inventory, which makes up the next chapter, goes through every part of finding your body type in an easy, check-off-the-answers, way. After that, you'll be ready to go on to your own personal Body Type Health Program. So now let's go ahead and find out about *you*.

4

THE BODY TYPE PERSONAL METABOLIC INVENTORY

In the following pages you are going to make a survey of your own metabolism. The Personal Metabolic Inventory, or PMI, is the same one I use with my own medical patients to help them determine whether their metabolism is dominated by the adrenal glands, the thyroid gland, the pituitary gland, or (in women) the gonads or ovaries.

The PMI surveys nine areas of your life. Section one looks at your body's basic shape, apart from any extra weight you may have; section two, the location of your extra pounds, if you have any; section three, your eating patterns, with special attention to the foods you crave; section four, your energy patterns; section five, the kind of exercise you like to do; section six, your health history; section seven, your work habits; section eight, your personality; and section nine, your relationships.

Each of these areas is *strongly influenced* (but not totally determined) by your dominant gland. Any one of them by itself may not tell me everything about your metabolism, but when I consider them all together, I find that I can determine your metabolic style with great accuracy.

LAB TESTS: WHY YOU DON'T NEED THEM

My patients are often surprised to find that it's possible to determine which of the four major glands is most active inside the body—which seems like a rather mysterious thing—without resorting to blood tests. However, it is not only possible, it's *preferable* to look at these areas of influence, because laboratory tests of blood hormone levels are surprisingly unreliable in determining your body type.

Suppose (as is often done) your physician wants to find out if your thyroid gland is producing the "right amount" of thyroid hormone. He takes a blood test, sends it to the lab, and gets back a number that may or may not be called "normal." But there are many questions left unanswered. Hormone levels normally vary throughout the day; is this level normal for that time, or high, or low? To help get around this problem, your doctor will usually specify what time of day to take the test. Much more important, how *effective* is the thyroid hormone that is present? Is it having the desired effect on the tissue, or not? If the amount of hormone present seems low, is that because the individual does not require as much thyroid hormone to function, or because the gland is actually depressed, or because of the varying effects of age, or for any of a large number of other possible reasons?

All these questions can be answered, but the answer lies in the way your metabolism is actually working, not in the amount of any hormone which happens to be present in your blood at the time of any one test. By looking at your overall picture, as the PMI lets you do, you can obtain a far better impression of the strength of your four glands than you can do through laboratory tests.

HOW TO TAKE THE PMI

Sections 1 and 2 are concerned with your body's shape and the location of your extra pounds, if you have any. These sections must be completed while standing before a full-length mirror in your underwear or, preferably, nude. If possible you should enlist the aid of a friend or spouse in answering the questions, since another person can view from angles that are difficult to see on yourself. Besides, we usually tend not to see ourselves very objectively; a "second opinion" helps keep us honest.

For the remaining sections, you are the authority on yourself, but many of my patients find that it's helpful to answer all the questions with a close friend or spouse. On questions like what kind of events you find most stressful, or on what your reactions are in certain situations, you may not have thought about yourself much, while someone who knows you well often can tell you exactly how you react! You'll learn a lot about yourself just taking the PMI.

When I was a medical student I used to go with a nurse who would give me coffee and cookies whenever I visited her. Sometimes I would drink two cups of coffee and eat four cookies, sometimes one cup and two cookies. One day she astonished me by announcing to me which brand of coffee and which kind of cookies I liked best. I didn't even realize it. She'd done an experiment on me because she wanted to please me—she'd observed my preferences and bought what I "liked," even though I didn't know what I liked myself. (Unfortunately, those days were the beginning of my jelly roll. Diane, thank you for the cookies and the lesson, but not for the jelly roll!)

Keep in mind while completing the Inventory that there are no "right" or "wrong" answers to any of the questions. Especially in the questions about body shape, I find that many people are overly influenced by certain cultural standards of what a body "should" look like. These standards are extremely variable—just look at an old movie on late-night TV. Try to see how much our ideal of beauty has changed just in the last forty years! So try to put all preconceived ideas out of your mind, and just think about yourself.

I'm not just saying this—it's really true that there is no one "perfect" type. The adrenal type is *different* from the thyroid, pituitary, or gonadal types, not better or worse. Each type has the potential for perfect health; but to realize that potential, you must know what you are working with. In the past you may well have been doing things that would be good for other people, but now I'm only concerned that you find out what's good for *you*.

THE PERSONAL METABOLIC INVENTORY FOR WOMEN

SECTION 1: BODY SHAPE AND APPEARANCE

1. If you are not overweight, look at your body as it is now. If you have extra pounds, think of your body as it would be at your best weight. At your ideal weight you would be:

a.	Slim, but with curvy hips and rear.	Two checks for G: _____ _____
b.	Slender, but full-figured and strongly built.	Two checks for A: _____ _____
c.	Very slender and fine-boned.	Two checks for T: _____ _____

   d. Slender,
childlike,
and un-
developed.   Two checks for P: _____ _____

2. Now turn sideways to the mirror and focus on the line of
your back. Again, if you're overweight, imagine that the extra pounds aren't there and you're at your ideal weight.

   a. My back is
slightly
"swayed"
and my rear
end sticks
out promi-
nently.   Two checks for G: _____ _____

   b. My back is
straight and
my rear ap-
pears to be
flat and
"tucked un-
der."   Two checks for A: _____ _____

   c. My rear is
round but
not ex-
tremely
pronounced;
my back is
straight.   Two checks for T: _____ _____

   d. My rear is
small and
childish, my
shoulders
are round,
and my
head comes
forward
from the
line of my
back.   Two checks for P: _____ _____

3. Next, focus on your head—its shape and its relation to your body as it would be at your best weight.

a. My head is slightly small for my body size.   Two checks for G: _____ _____

b. My head is square and I have a square or round face.   Two checks for A: _____ _____

c. My head is long and I have a slender face.   Two checks for T: _____ _____

d. My head is slightly large for my body size.   Two checks for P: _____ _____

4. Next, focus on your chest and breasts. You have:

a. Small chest, small breasts, with noticeable texture to breast tissue and prominent nipple glands.   Two checks for G: _____ _____

b. Large chest, large rounded breasts.   Two checks for A: _____ _____

c. Small chest, medium to large breasts

(breast size
has in-
creased with
your age).   Two checks for T: _____ _____

   d. Medium
chest, small
"budding"
breasts with
silky tex-
ture.   Two checks for P: _____ _____

5. Examine your hands and feet. They are:

   a. Average in
size, small
fingers and
toes.   Two checks for G: _____ _____

   b. Square,
with small
fingers and
toes.   Two checks for A: _____ _____

   c. Long, with
tapering fin-
gers and
toes.   Two checks for T: _____ _____

   d. Small, deli-
cate.   Two checks for P: _____ _____

6. Focus on your teeth. They are:

   a. White, me-
dium-sized,
slightly
crowded
and uneven.   Two checks for G: _____ _____

   b. Large,
slightly yel-
lowish, with
prominent
ridges.   Two checks for A: _____ _____

   c. Small,
white, even,
prone to
cavities.   Two checks for T: _____ _____

   d. Large, es-
pecially
front center.   Two checks for P: _____ _____

7. Look at the shape of your mouth. It is:

   a. Thin, well-
shaped, "se-
rious."   Two checks for G: _____ _____

   b. Full, often
"set" or
pursed.   Two checks for A: _____ _____

   c. Wide,
mobile, ex-
pressive.   Two checks for T: _____ _____

   d. Rosebud,
childlike.   Two checks for P: _____ _____

8. Look at your skin. It is:

   a. Smooth,
oily.   Two checks for G: _____ _____

   b. Oily, slightly
coarse, with
a tendency
to flaky
patches.   Two checks for A: _____ _____

   c. Smooth, of
normal
oiliness,
with a ten-
dency to red
areas and
easy bruis-
ing.   Two checks for T: _____ _____

   d. Dry, deli-
       cate, with a
       tendency to
       hives.   Two checks for P: _____ _____

Total Score for Section 1:

G: _____ A: _____ T: _____ P: _____

SECTION 2: LOCATION OF EXTRA POUNDS

Answer the questions in this section if you have any extra pounds, or *if you have ever had any*. If you don't have extra pounds now, refer to the location where you have put on weight in the past.

9. Focus on the overall outline and shape of your body.

   a. My body is
       at least a
       full size
       smaller
       above the
       waist than
       below.   Two checks for G: _____ _____
   b. My body is
       stocky and
       full-figured,
       without a
       pronounced
       curve at
       waist or
       hips.   Two checks for A: _____ _____
   c. My body is
       curvy but
       much fuller
       through the
       middle
       (waist, hips,

and upper thighs) than at the extremities (neck and head, lower arms, calves and ankles).   Two checks for T: _____ _____

d. My body is childlike in outline, with small breasts and "baby fat" all over.   Two checks for P: _____ _____

10. Look at yourself in the mirror, focusing on your excess weight. Where is *most* of your fat?

a. On the rear end.   Two checks for G: _____ _____

b. Across the stomach and upper back.   Two checks for A: _____ _____

c. Around the middle— spare tire, wide hips, heavy upper thighs.   Two checks for T: _____ _____

d. All over, no single location.   Two checks for P: _____ _____

11. Look at yourself from the back, or ask your friend to look. Look at your *total fat*. Do you have more fat:

a. Below the waist.   Two checks for G: _____ _____

b. Across the upper back.   Two checks for A: _____ _____

c. Around the
waist.   Two checks for T: _____ _____

d. All over—
not more
above or be-
low.   Two checks for P: _____ _____

12. Still looking at yourself from the back, do you have "saddlebags" (pockets of fat on the outer thighs)?

a. Yes. (check
both)   One check for G: _____
                          One check for T: _____

b. No. (check
both)   One check for A: _____
                          One check for P: _____

13. Turn back to look at yourself from the front again. Do you have a "spare tire" (a roll of fat around the middle)?

a. Yes. (check
both)   One check for A: _____
                          One check for T: _____

b. No. (check
both)   One check for G: _____
                          One check for P: _____

14. Focus on your hands and feet. Do they have an accumulation of fat? If they do, the bones won't be too prominent.

a. Yes. (check
both)   One check for A: _____
                          One check for P: _____

b. No. (check
both)   One check for T: _____
                          One check for G: _____

The next eight questions are on the location of cellulite, or "cottage cheese" fat. Even if you are not overweight, you probably do have some cellulite on your body. To check for cellulite, first examine the area in question. Does the fat there appear to be wrinkly? If so, the area has cellulite. If the area appears to have fat, but the fat is not wrinkly, then gently squeeze about an inch or so of the fat between two fingers, or have your friend do so. When you examine the fat in this way you may find wrinkles that were not apparent just from looking at it. If you do, the area does have cellulite, although it is cellulite at an earlier stage than cellulite you can see without squeezing it between your fingers, and you should count yourself as having cellulite in that location. If you find you have no cellulite now, but have had it in the past, answer the questions as if you have the cellulite now.

15. First, check your upper arms. Do you have cellulite?

   a. Yes. (check
      both)   One check for A: _____
                      One check for T: _____

   b. No. (check
      both)   One check for G: _____
                      One check for P: _____

16. Check your upper hips—meaning the place where you put your hands when you've got your hands on your hips. Do you have cellulite there?

   a. Yes.   Two checks for T: _____ _____
   b. No. (check
      all three)   One check for G: _____
                      One check for A: _____
                      One check for P: _____

17. Check your lower hips—the place where you smooth your skirt. Do you have cellulite?

   a. Yes. (check
      both)   One check for G: _____
                      One check for T: _____

   b. No. (check
      both)   One check for A: _____
                      One check for P: _____

18. Check the front of your upper thighs. Do you have cellulite?

   a. Yes.   Two checks for T: _____ _____

   b. No. (check

        all three)   One check for G: _____

                   One check for A: _____

                   One check for P: _____

19. Check the inside of your knees. Do you have cellulite in this area on the upper (not the lower) leg?

   a. Yes.   Two checks for P: _____ _____

   b. No. (check

        all three)   One check for G: _____

                   One check for A: _____

                   One check for T: _____

20. Check over your shoulder blades. Do you have cellulite?

   a. Yes.   Two checks for A: _____ _____

   b. No. (check

        all three)   One check for G: _____

                   One check for T: _____

                   One check for P: _____

21. Check your rear end—the buttocks proper. Do you have cellulite?

   a. Yes.   Two checks for G: _____ _____

   b. No. (check

        all three)   One check for A: _____

                   One check for T: _____

                   One check for P: _____

22. What is your *main* area of cellulite—the place you consider to be your biggest figure problem?

   a. Rear, outer

        thighs.   Two checks for G: _____ _____

   b. Stomach,

        back.   Two checks for A: _____ _____

   c. Upper
      thighs.   Two checks for T: _____ _____
   d. Knees,
      breasts.   Two checks for P: _____ _____

Total Score for Section 2:

G: _____ A: _____ T: _____ P: _____

SECTION 3: EATING PATTERNS

23. Of the following foods, which do you love the most?

   a. Rich or
      spicy foods.   One check for G: _____
   b. Steak, salty
      foods.   One check for A: _____
   c. Bread,
      sweets.   One check for T: _____
   d. Dairy prod-
      ucts, fruit.   One check for P: _____

24. At an afternoon party, which of these foods would you find hardest to resist?

   a. The creamy
      dips.   One check for G: _____
   b. The hot
      dogs, sa-
      lami, or
      peanuts.   One check for A: _____
   c. The cakes
      or candies. One check for T: _____
   d. The ice
      cream.   One check for P: _____

25. How much coffee, tea, or cola do you drink each day total, adding up all the cups, cans, and glasses?

   a. One or two. One check for G: _____

b. Three or
   four.   One check for A: _____
c. Five or
   more.   One check for T: _____
d. None or
   one.   One check for P: _____

26. Which of the following would you prefer for breakfast?

a. French
   toast.   One check for G: _____
b. Bacon and
   eggs.   One check for A: _____
c. Toast and
   jam.   One check for T: _____
d. Fruit and
   yogurt.   One check for P: _____

27. Ideally, when would you like to have your biggest meal?

a. Breakfast.   One check for G: _____
b. Dinner.   One check for A: _____
c. Lunch.   One check for T: _____
d. Prefer no
   big meal,
   just lots of
   snacks.   One check for P: _____

Total Score for Section 3:

G: _____ A: _____ T: _____ P: _____

SECTION 4: ENERGY PATTERNS

28. Ideally, how many hours do you sleep each night?

a. 8–9 hours.   One check for G: _____
b. 4–6 hours.   One check for A: _____
c. 5–6 hours
   when ener-
   getic, 9–10

	hours when tired.	One check for T: _____
d.	7–8 hours.	One check for P: _____

29. When does your highest energy period occur?

a.	Late in the day.	One check for G: _____
b.	Energetic all day.	One check for A: _____
c.	Following meals.	One check for T: _____
d.	First thing in the morn- ing.	One check for P: _____

30. Do you have trouble sleeping at night?

a.	Rarely.	One check for G: _____
b.	Often.	One check for A: _____
c.	Occasion- ally, but only for one night at a time.	One check for T: _____
d.	Occasion- ally, but when I do it happens every night for a while.	One check for P: _____

Total Score for Section 4:

G: _____ A: _____ T: _____ P: _____

SECTION 5: EXERCISE PATTERNS

31. *Why* do you exercise? (Refer to whatever exercise program you do now.)

a. Because moving feels good.   One check for G: _____

b. To burn off my excess energy.   One check for A: _____

c. So I can eat more later.   One check for T: _____

d. To get an exercise "high."   One check for P: _____

32. What is your favorite aerobic exercise?

a. Jazz dancing.   One check for G: _____

b. Pumping iron.   One check for A: _____

c. A very varied workout.   One check for T: _____

d. Long-distance running.   One check for P: _____

33. How do you feel if you miss your regular exercise?

a. Heavy, tired.   One check for G: _____

b. Angry.   One check for A: _____

c. Irritable, or depressed.   One check for T: _____

d. My thoughts go round and round.   One check for P: _____

Total Score for Section 5:

G: _____ A: _____ T: _____ P: _____

SECTION 6: YOUR HEALTH HISTORY

34. What is your *most typical* small health problem?

a. Bladder in-
fections.   One check for G: _____
b. Con-
stipation.   One check for A: _____
c. Tiredness,
fatigue.   One check for T: _____
d. Colds.   One check for P: _____

35. Which of these larger health problems do you feel you are most likely to get (or, if you have any of them, which one do you now have)?

a. Breast
lumps.   One check for G: _____
b. High blood
pressure.   One check for A: _____
c. Ulcers.   One check for T: _____
d. Chronic al-
lergies.   One check for P: _____

36. Are you prone to upset stomach or diarrhea?

a. No. (check
both)   One check for G: _____
                   One check for A: _____
b. Yes. (check
both)   One check for T: _____
                   One check for P: _____

37. Are you prone to headaches?

a. No. (check
both)   One check for G: _____
                   One check for A: _____
b. Occasion-
ally.   One check for T: _____
c. Yes, quite a
bit.   One check for P: _____

38. Do your hands and feet feel cold at night?

a. Sometimes.
   (check both)   One check for G: _____
                     One check for P: _____
b. Rarely or
   never.   One check for A: _____
c. Often.   One check for T: _____

39. Do your feet tend to swell up?

a. Yes, mostly
   when over-
   weight.   One check for G: _____
   (check both)   One check for A: _____
b. No.   One check for P: _____
c. Yes, mostly
   in hot
   weather.   One check for T: _____

40. Do your hands tend to swell up?

a. No. (check
   both)   One check for G: _____
                    One check for P: _____
b. Yes, when I
   eat salty
   food.   One check for A: _____
c. Yes, mostly
   in hot
   weather.   One check for T: _____

41. When you are ill, which parts of your body are most likely to ache?

a. Hands and
   feet.   One check for G: _____
b. Lower back.   One check for A: _____
c. Neck and
   shoulders.   One check for T: _____
d. Knees.   One check for P: _____

42. How much do you perspire?

a.	Moderately.	One check for G: _____
b.	Quite a bit.	One check for A: _____
c.	Variably. Very lightly when slim, more when heavy.	One check for T: _____
d.	Lightly.	One check for P: _____

43. Which of your senses do you feel is your most acute one?

a.	Touch.	One check for G: _____
b.	Hearing.	One check for A: _____
c.	Taste/smell.	One check for T: _____
d.	Sight.	One check for P: _____

44. Which of your senses do you feel is your least acute one?

a.	Sight.	One check for G: _____
b.	Taste/smell.	One check for A: _____
c.	Hearing.	One check for T: _____
d.	Touch.	One check for P: _____

45. Are you prone to cramps during your menstrual period?

a.	First day only.	One check for G: _____
b.	Rarely.	One check for A: _____
c.	Yes, quite badly.	One check for T: _____
d.	Very little.	One check for P: _____

46. If you have been pregnant, which of these best describes your experience?

a.	Delightful— enjoyed it.	One check for G: _____
b.	Easy, comfortable.	One check for A: _____

  c. Felt heavy
       and uncom-
       fortable.   One check for T: _____

  d. Didn't like it
       much.   One check for P: _____

Total Score for Section 6:

G: _____ A: _____ T: _____ P: _____

SECTION 7: CREATIVITY AND WORK

47. If you had your choice of any work in the world—money aside—what would you do?

  a. Teaching
       something I
       love.   One check for G: _____

  b. Selling
       something I
       believe in.   One check for A: _____

  c. Creating
       something I
       feel for.   One check for T: _____

  d. Designing
       something
       essential.   One check for P: _____

48. If you could work in any situation at all, where would you work?

  a. In my
       home.   One check for G: _____

  b. In a giant,
       wonderful
       workplace.   One check for A: _____

  c. Out in the
       world, trav-
       eling.   One check for T: _____

   d. In a serene,
beautifully
designed of-
fice.   One check for P:　_____

49. Of these real-life jobs, which one would you choose?

   a. Service per-
son (health
care profes-
sional,
secretary,
teacher).   One check for G:　_____

   b. Production
person
(salesper-
son,
engineer, ex-
ecutive).   One check for A:　_____

   c. Marketing/
creative per-
son
(designer,
marketing
person).   One check for T:　_____

   d. Technical
person
(computer
programmer,
accountant). One check for P:　_____

Total Score for Section 7:

G: _____　A: _____　T: _____　P: _____

SECTION 8: PERSONALITY

50. Is it easy for you to laugh at yourself? (Be honest, now!)

   a. It's possible
if I don't

feel threat-
ened.   One check for G: _____
  b. Yes—I ac-
cept my
kookiness.   One check for A: _____
  c. No—I'm
not kooky.   One check for T: _____
  d. I don't ex-
actly
laugh—I'm
amused.   One check for P: _____

51. Which of these subjects do you most enjoy discussing or thinking about?

  a. Sex, home,
family, food.   One check for G: _____
  b. Business,
money,
practical
things.   One check for A: _____
  c. The arts,
current
events, your
latest proj-
ect.   One check for T: _____
  d. Philosophy,
ideals, the
broader
questions of
life.   One check for P: _____

52. Which of the following best describes your disposition?

  a. Sensuous,
warm, and
comfort-
able.   One check for G: _____
  b. Friendly,
open, and
practical.   One check for A: _____

   c. Artistic,
lively, and
changeable.   One check for T: _____

   d. Intellectual,
cool, and
detached.   One check for P: _____

53. When you're "up," you're:

   a. Radiant,
welcoming
to all.   One check for G: _____

   b. A "hail fel-
low well
met."   One check for A: _____

   c. Sparkly and
funny.   One check for T: _____

   d. Giggly as a
happy child.   One check for P: _____

54. When you feel "down," you become:

   a. Weepy.   One check for G: _____

   b. Angry and
hollering.   One check for A: _____

   c. Depressed,
irritable,
even cruel.   One check for T: _____

   d. Neurotic,
obsessed,
withdrawn.   One check for P: _____

55. Which of the following best describes your temper?

   a. Quick-tem-
pered but
easily dis-
tracted from
your anger
by flattery
or apolo-
gies.   One check for G: _____

b. Slow to get angry, but once you are, you stay mad for a while.   One check for A: _____

c. Quick-tempered over small matters, inclined to get depressed when thwarted.   One check for T: _____

d. Slow to get angry and quick to get over it, once you have a chance to think things over.   One check for P: _____

Total Score for Section 8:

G: _____ A: _____ T: _____ P: _____

SECTION 9: RELATIONSHIPS

56. What do you feel is most important in a relationship?

a. Nurturing of one another.   One check for G: _____

b. A stable relationship, home base.   One check for A: _____

c. Variety, stimulation, interaction.   One check for T: _____

d. Compan-
ionship.   One check for P: _____

57. How do you feel your work relationships should be organized?

a. I like a
sense of
friendly
teamwork
with my co-
workers.   One check for G: _____

b. I like
friendly but
competitive
relationships
at work.   One check for A: _____

c. It varies. I
like to keep
changing—
sometimes
work alone,
then with
others.   One check for T: _____

d. I'm an
"ivory
tower" sort
of worker,
like to keep
a certain
distance.   One check for P: _____

58. How many close personal friends do you like to have?

a. I need a lot
of warm re-
lationships
to feel good.   One check for G: _____

b. I prefer a
"crowd" of
friends, all

equally
close.   One check for A: _____

c. I like to
have lots of
friends, and
each one
different.   One check for T: _____

d. Few, but I
need deep
intensity.   One check for P: _____

59. In your love relationship, how often do you like to have sex?

a. Every day.   One check for G: _____

b. Twice a
week or so.   One check for A: _____

c. In spurts. A
lot for a
while, then
not at all for
a while.   One check for T: _____

d. Once a
week or
less.   One check for P: _____

Total Score for Section 9:

G: _____   A: _____   T: _____   P: _____

Scoring Instruction:

Go through your Total Scores for all nine sections and add them together. Write the total for all sections here:

G: _____   A: _____   T: _____   P: _____

Now look at your score. Your highest number indicates your body type.

If your highest number of answers is G, you are a gonadal type.

If your highest number of answers is A, you are an adrenal type.

If your highest number of answers is T, you are a thyroid type.

If your highest number of answers is P, you are a pituitary type.

SPECIAL INSTRUCTIONS IF YOU HAVE A TIE:

A tie indicates that your body type is well balanced. However, you do have a dominant gland that will determine your type. In this case you should use *only* your answers from Sections 1, 2, and 3, since appearance is more clearly indicative of body type than any of the other factors.

SPECIAL INSTRUCTIONS FOR GONADAL TYPES:

If your score indicates that you are a G-type but your ovaries are no longer active (either because you have passed the menopause or because of surgery), you should consider yourself as being the body type with the *next* highest number of answers. However, if you are taking female sex hormones, you should still consider yourself a G-type, since the supplementary hormones you are taking take the place of your body's natural hormones and this enables you to retain the metabolism of a G-type.

THE PERSONAL METABOLIC INVENTORY FOR MEN

SECTION 1: BODY SHAPE AND APPEARANCE

1. Look at yourself straight on in the mirror, focusing on the overall outline and shape of your body.

    a. My body is square, sturdy, and looks as if I played football.   Two checks for A: _____ _____

    b. My body is long-limbed and looks as if I played basketball.   Two checks for T: _____ _____

    c. My body is boyish and looks much as it did when I was fourteen.   Two checks for P: _____ _____

2. Now turn sideways to the mirror and focus on the line of your back.

    a. My back is slightly swayed and my rear appears

   slightly
   rounded.　　　　Two checks for A: _____ _____
   b. My back is
   straight and
   I have prac-
   tically no
   rear.　　　　　Two checks for T: _____ _____
   c. My back is
   curved and
   my head
   comes for-
   ward from
   my neck.　　　Two checks for P: _____ _____

3. Next, focus on your head—its shape and relation to body
size.

   a. My head is
   square and I
   have a
   round or
   square face.　 Two checks for A: _____ _____
   b. My head is
   long and I
   have a
   slender
   face.　　　　　Two checks for T: _____ _____
   c. My head is
   slightly
   large for my
   body size.　　 Two checks for P: _____ _____

4. Examine your hands and feet. They are:

   a. Square,
   with short
   fingers and
   toes.　　　　　Two checks for A: _____ _____
   b. Long, with
   tapering fin-
   gers and
   toes.　　　　　Two checks for T: _____ _____

   c. Small, deli-
cate.   Two checks for P: _____ _____

5. Focus on your teeth. They are:

   a. Large,
slightly yel-
lowish.   Two checks for A: _____ _____
   b. Small,
white, even.   Two checks for T: _____ _____
   c. Large, es-
pecially
front center. Two checks for P: _____ _____

6. Look at the shape of your mouth. It is:

   a. Full.   Two checks for A: _____ _____
   b. Wide,
mobile.   Two checks for T: _____ _____
   c. Curved,
well-shaped. Two checks for P: _____ _____

7. Look at your skin. It is:

   a. Oily, slightly
coarse.   Two checks for A: _____ _____
   b. Smooth, of
normal
oiliness.   Two checks for T: _____ _____
   c. Dry, deli-
cate.   Two checks for P: _____ _____

8. If you are overweight, think back to when you were at your ideal weight, or try to imagine how you would look at your normal weight based on what you have already observed about your present shape. At your ideal weight you would be (or are):

   a. Slender but
strong look-
ing.   Two checks for A: _____ _____
   b. Rangy and
fine-boned.   Two checks for T: _____ _____

   c. Boyish and
        slender.   Two checks for P: _____ _____

Total Score for Section 1:

A: _____ T: _____ P: _____

SECTION 2: LOCATION OF EXTRA POUNDS

9. Look at yourself in the mirror, focusing on your excess
weight. Where is *most* of your fat?

   a. Across the
        stomach and
        upper back.   Two checks for A: _____ _____
   b. Around the
        middle in a
        "roll."   Two checks for T: _____ _____
   c. All over, no
        single loca-
        tion.   Two checks for P: _____ _____

10. Look at yourself from the back, or ask your friend to
look. Do you have more fat:

   a. Across the
        upper back?   Two checks for A: _____ _____
   b. Around the
        waist?   Two checks for T: _____ _____
   c. All over—
        not more
        above or be-
        low?   Two checks for P: _____ _____

11. Turn back to look at yourself from the front again. Do
you have a "spare tire" (a roll of fat around the middle)?

   a. Yes. (check
        both)   One check for A: _____
                    One check for T: _____
   b. No.   One check for P: _____

12. Focus on your hands and feet. Do they have an accumulation of fat?

   a. Yes. (check
      both)   One check for A: _____
                            One check for P: _____
   b. No.   One check for T: _____

Total Score for Section 2:

A: _____ T: _____ P: _____

SECTION 3: EATING PATTERNS

13. Of the following foods, which do you love the most?

   a. Steak, salty
      foods.   One check for A: _____
   b. Bread,
      sweets.   One check for T: _____
   c. Dairy prod-
      ucts.   One check for P: _____

14. At an afternoon party, which of these foods would you find hardest to resist?

   a. The hot
      dogs, sa-
      lami, or
      peanuts.   One check for A: _____
   b. The cakes
      or candies. One check for T: _____
   c. The ice
      cream.   One check for P: _____

15. How much coffee, tea, or cola do you drink each day? Combine all for a single number.

   a. Three or
      four cups.   One check for A: _____

   b. Five cups or
       more.   One check for T: _____

   c. None, one
       or two cups.   One check for P: _____

16. Which of the following would you prefer for breakfast?

   a. Bacon and
       eggs.   One check for A: _____

   b. Toast and
       jam.   One check for T: _____

   c. Fruit and
       yogurt.   One check for P: _____

17. Ideally, when would you like to have your biggest meal?

   a. Evening to
       late night.   One check for A: _____

   b. Early to
       mid-day.   One check for T: _____

   c. Prefer no
       big meal,
       just lots of
       snacks.   One check for P: _____

Total Score for Section 3:

A: _____ T: _____ P: _____

SECTION 4: ENERGY PATTERNS

18. Ideally, how many hours do you sleep each night?

   a. 4–6 hours.   One check for A: _____

   b. 5–6 hours
       when ener-
       getic, 9–10
       hours when
       tired.   One check for T: _____

   c. 7–8 hours.   One check for P: _____

19. When does your highest energy period occur?

   a. Energetic all
      day.   One check for A: _____

   b. About an
      hour after
      meals.   One check for T: _____

   c. First thing
      in the morn-
      ing.   One check for P: _____

20. Do you have trouble sleeping at night?

   a. Often.   One check for A: _____

   b. Occasion-
      ally, but
      only for one
      night at a
      time.   One check for T: _____

   c. Occasion-
      ally, but
      when I do it
      happens
      every night
      for a while.   One check for P: _____

Total Score for Section 4:

A: _____ T: _____ P: _____

SECTION 5: EXERCISE PATTERNS

21. *Why* do you exercise? (Refer to whatever exercise program you do now.)

   a. To burn off
      excess en-
      ergy.   One check for A: _____

   b. To calm my-
      self down.   One check for T: _____

c. To get an ex-
ercise
"high." One check for P: _____

22. What is your favorite type of exercise?

a. Pumping
iron, or a
strenuous
competitive
game. One check for A: _____

b. Tennis, or
something
with a lot of
variety. One check for T: _____

c. Long-dis-
tance
running. One check for P: _____

23. How do you feel if you don't exercise?

a. Heavy or
angry. One check for A: _____

b. Irritable or
depressed. One check for T: _____

c. Obsessed
with my
problems. One check for P: _____

Total Score for Section 5:

A: _____ T: _____ P: _____

SECTION 6: YOUR HEALTH HISTORY

24. What is your *most typical* small health problem?

a. Con-
stipation,
minor
aches. One check for A: _____

b. Tiredness,
   fatigue.   One check for T: _____
c. Colds.   One check for P: _____

25. Which of these larger health problems do you feel you are most likely to get (or, if you have any of them, which one do you now have)?

a. High blood
   pressure or
   hardening of
   the arteries.   One check for A: _____
b. Ulcers or
   colitis.   One check for T: _____
c. Chronic al-
   lergies.   One check for P: _____

26. Are you prone to upset stomach or diarrhea?

a. No.   One check for A: _____
b. Yes. (check
   both)   One check for T: _____
                     One check for P: _____

27. Are you prone to headaches?

a. No.   One check for A: _____
b. Occasion-
   ally.   One check for T: _____
c. Yes, quite a
   bit.   One check for P: _____

28. Do your hands and feet feel cold at night?

a. No.   One check for A: _____
b. Often.   One check for T: _____
c. Rarely.   One check for P: _____

29. When you are ill, which parts of your body are most likely to ache?

a. Lower back.   One check for A: _____

    b. Neck and
        shoulders.   One check for T: _____

    c. Knees,
        armpits.   One check for P: _____

30. How much do you perspire?

    a. Quite a bit,
        even at rest.   One check for A: _____

    b. Variably.
        With exer-
        cise, very
        lightly when
        slim, more
        when heavy. One check for T: _____

    c. Lightly, all
        over the
        body.   One check for P: _____

31. Which of your senses do you feel is your most acute one?

    a. Hearing.   One check for A: _____
    b. Taste/smell. One check for T: _____
    c. Sight.   One check for P: _____

32. Which of your senses do you feel is your least acute one?

    a. Taste/smell. One check for A: _____
    b. Hearing.   One check for T: _____
    c. Touch.   One check for P: _____

Total Score for Section 6:

A: _____ T: _____ P: _____

SECTION 7: CREATIVITY AND WORK

33. If you had your choice of any work in the world—money aside—what would you do?

a. Selling something I believe in.   One check for A: _____

b. Creating something I feel for.   One check for T: _____

c. Designing something essential.   One check for P: _____

34. If you could work in any situation at all, where would you work?

a. In a large, excellent corporation with space to "move up."   One check for A: _____

b. Out in the world, traveling.   One check for T: _____

c. In a serene, beautifully designed office.   One check for P: _____

35. Of the following jobs, which one would you choose?

a. Production type (salesperson, engineer, executive).   One check for A: _____

b. Marketing/creative type (designer, marketing person).   One check for T: _____

c. Technical
   type (com-
   puter
   programmer,
   accountant).　　One check for P: _____

Total Score for Section 7:

A: _____ T: _____ P: _____

SECTION 8: PERSONALITY

36. Is it easy for you to laugh at yourself? (Be honest, now!)

a. Yes—I ac-
   cept my
   kookiness.　　One check for A: _____
b. No—I'm
   not kooky.　　One check for T: _____
c. I don't ex-
   actly
   laugh—I'm
   amused.　　One check for P: _____

37. Which of these subjects do you most enjoy discussing or thinking about?

a. Business,
   money,
   practical
   things.　　One check for A: _____
b. My latest
   project—it
   varies.　　One check for T: _____
c. Philosophy,
   the arts, the
   broader
   questions of
   life.　　One check for P: _____

38. Which of the following best describes your disposition?

  a. Friendly, open and practical—a cool mind in a hot body.   One check for A: _____

  b. Artistic, moody, and change-able—a warm mind in a cool body.   One check for T: _____

  c. Intellectual and de-tached—a hot/cold mind in a hot/cold body.   One check for P: _____

39. When you feel at your best, you're:

  a. Warm and full of infectious energy.   One check for A: _____

  b. Lively and very funny.   One check for T: _____

  c. Happy as a child.   One check for P: _____

40. When you feel negative, you are most apt to become:

  a. Angry and hollering.   One check for A: _____

  b. Depressed, irritable, sometimes even cruel.   One check for T: _____

  c. Neurotic, obsessed, withdrawn.   One check for P: _____

41. Which of the following best describes your temper?

    a. Slow to get angry, but when I do I stay mad for a while.   One check for A: _____

    b. Quick-tempered over small matters, inclined to get depressed when thwarted.   One check for T: _____

    c. Slow to get angry and quick to get over it, once I have a chance to think things over.   One check for P: _____

Total Score for Section 8:

A: _____ T: _____ P: _____

SECTION 9: RELATIONSHIPS

42. What do you feel is most important in a relationship?

    a. Permanence, a home and family.   One check for A: _____

    b. Variety, stimulation, interaction.   One check for T: _____

c. Compan-
ionship.   One check for P: _____

43. How do you feel your work relationships should be organized?

a. I like
friendly but
competitive
relationships
at work.   One check for A: _____

b. It varies—I
like to keep
changing
things at
work, some-
times
working
alone,
sometimes
with others.   One check for T: _____

c. I am an
"ivory
tower" sort
of worker
and like a
certain dis-
tance.   One check for P: _____

44. How many close personal friends do you like to have?

a. I prefer a
"crowd" of
friends, all
equally
close.   One check for A: _____

b. I like to
have lots of
friends, and
each one
different.   One check for T: _____

    c. Few, but in-
tense and
deep.   One check for P: _____

45. How are you most likely to fight with spouse or friends?

    a. I show my
anger
openly.   One check for A: _____

    b. I use strat-
egy to get
my way.   One check for T: _____

    c. I tend to
withdraw.   One check for P: _____

46. In your love relationship, how often do you like to have
sex?

    a. Pretty often.   One check for A: _____

    b. In spurts. A
lot for a
while, then
not at all for
a while.   One check for T: _____

    c. Not too
often.   One check for P: _____

Total Score for Section 9:

A: _____ T: _____ P: _____

Scoring Instruction:

    Go through your Total Scores for all nine sections and
add them together. Write the total for all sections here:

    A: _____ T: _____ P: _____

    Now look at your score. Your highest number indicates
your body type.

If your highest number of answers is A, you are an adrenal type.

If your highest number of answers is T, you are a thyroid type.

If your highest number of answers is P, you are a pituitary type.

SPECIAL INSTRUCTIONS IF YOU HAVE A TIE:

A tie indicates that your body type is well balanced. However, you do have a dominant gland that will determine your type. In this case you should use *only* your answers from Sections 1 and 2, since appearance is more clearly indicative of body type than any other factor.

ILLUSTRATION 4–1:
P-type man

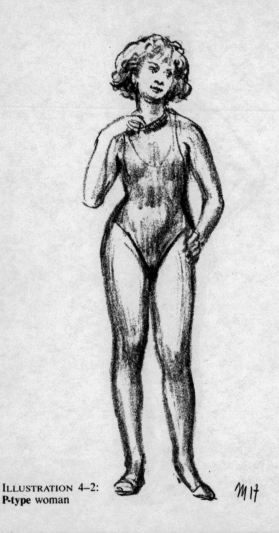

ILLUSTRATION 4–2:
P-type woman

ILLUSTRATION 4–3:
G-type woman:

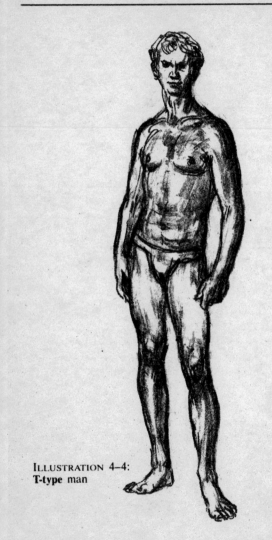

ILLUSTRATION 4–4:
T-type man

ILLUSTRATION 4–5.
T-type woman

ILLUSTRATION 4–6:
A-type woman

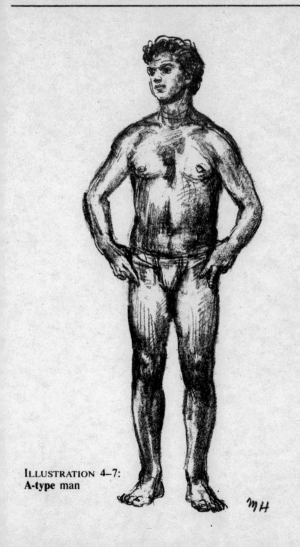

ILLUSTRATION 4–7:
A-type man

PART II

THE BODY TYPE HEALTH PROGRAM

INTRODUCTION

Now that you've completed the Personal Metabolic Inventory and know which body type you are, you know a great deal about yourself. In the following chapters, you begin to put your knowledge to work for you. Part II explores all the important aspects of your health program beginning in Chapter 5 with the all-important subject of nutrition: what you eat, what you *should* eat, and why. For each of the four body types there is a three-stage program: the Balancing Diet, the Purification Diet, and the Health and Weight Maintenance Program. Chapter 6 gives the Balancing Diet for each type, Chapter 7 the Purification Diet, and Chapter 8 the Health and Weight Maintenance Program.

Then, in Chapter 9, we'll go on to look at the nutritional supplements that are vital for each body type. Chapter 10 examines exercise—what each type can do to get the most from exercise with the least strain. Chapter 11 is about stress reduction for each type. Chapter 12 explains the remarkable Body Type Long Weekend of Rejuvenation—an ideal way to start the Body Type Health Program and increase your momentum toward perfect health. Chapter 13 explains the secrets of self-acupressure massage—an easy and effective technique to strengthen and balance your metabolism.

5

LIFETIME NUTRITION FOR YOUR BODY TYPE

What would you eat if you had only yourself to please? Would you secretly like to feast morning and night on your favorite "bad" foods—like chocolate, potato chips, or ice cream? Maybe you're not one for junk food; maybe you privately wish only for the discipline to stick to a terrifically healthy and virtuous regime. Or you might long for a nostalgic combination of childhood and ethnic treats.

What your honest answer to this question would tell me is that you want many things from food besides physical nourishment. You want sensual pleasure, social communion, aesthetic enjoyment, a feeling of self-respect ("I am in control of my eating"), variety, stimulation, and relaxation. You *should* have them! What you eat ought to make you feel totally nourished—sensually delighted, socially satisfied, full of that sense of well-being that only food can give.

Unfortunately, satisfaction like this is the very opposite of the idea conjured up by the word *diet*. You might even be forgiven for supposing that a "lifetime nutrition plan" is just a subtler way of getting you "on a diet" for life—restricted, deprived, and bored. Why shouldn't you, then, go into it full of unspoken reservations: "Sure, I'll try it. For a while. I can always go back to lasagna and chocolate bars when it doesn't work, which it won't."

In fact, if you're like most of my patients and most of the people I know, you're divided in two over food. On the one side you have your "good" self, the "dieter," who's full of discipline, willpower, and virtue. On the other side is your "bad" self, who wants only to feel good and to enjoy.

Most people are quite capable of spending their lives yo-yoing between their two selves. "I can follow any diet like an angel for two weeks," one of my patients once said. "Then I think, 'What am I killing myself for? I work hard. I deserve a little pleasure.' And I go out and eat everything in sight." Does this sound as though it could be you?

FULFILLMENT, GOOD HEALTH, LONG LIFE

But dividing yourself in two over food is a mistake! The two selves—the one who wants to be "good" and the one who wants to enjoy—aren't really enemies. They're *both right* in their way, and they both deserve attention if you want to find a way of eating that will really work.

The good dieter in you is right in thinking that you must be aware of your nutritional needs in order to maintain balance in your diet and to keep your weight at a healthy level. But your "bad" self has a point, too. Nutrition may be basic to health and longevity, but fulfillment is more basic yet. Actual fulfillment—nothing else will do.

Remember your favorite uncle, the one who lived to be ninety-five and attributed it to a glass of bourbon and a cigar every day? It isn't that bourbon and cigars are "good for you"—you know that. It's that your Uncle Jim enjoyed every minute of his life, and lived it to the end. While your aunt—let's call her Aunt Mabel—who forced herself to eat prunes and bran and all the rest of it, didn't necessarily live that long—it just *seemed* like a long time to her and to everyone else.

The Body Type Lifetime Nutrition Program is designed to introduce the Uncle Jim and the Aunt Mabel inside each of us to one another. I don't mean prunes in your bourbon, or cigars with your bran flakes. I mean that we have to start from the beginning and come up with something really new. The Body Type Lifetime Nutrition Program is that new thing; it's not a diet at all, but an entirely new set of *principles of eating* that both Jim and Mabel will love. It's a way of eating that lets you choose and enjoy your food on the basis of understanding your own personal needs. The same principles that apply in the whole Body Type Health Program are here applied to your diet and you.

WHY JUST DIETING WON'T WORK

"This all sounds absolutely marvelous," said one of my most assertive patients when I began to explain body-type nutrition. "But let me tell you why it won't work."

This patient, a woman named Barbara H., told me that she'd been trying to lose fifteen pounds for the last five years—with no success. Her pattern was a typical one. She'd start a diet with high hopes on the Monday after a big eating holiday. Since she was still full from the night before, she felt that she had plenty of will power. The diet would be strict and stringent—a favorite one involved mainly salads, grapes, and four ounces of chicken a day. Soon, once the holiday dinner was finally digested, she'd be starving, so she'd keep herself going with black coffee and diet cola.

On this regime Barbara would drop four pounds (mainly water) the first week, but there was a problem: as each day went by, her craving for chocolate would increase. On day eight, more or less, after being "good" over the weekend, she'd go to a bakery, buy a cake, bring it home, and eat the whole thing. Though secretly relieved to feel like "herself" again, she'd also feel defeated and horribly guilty, call herself every bad name she could think of, and then go back to her old eating habits. After all, she'd rationalize, she couldn't diet—so she might as well eat and enjoy herself.

"Who wouldn't love to eat what's good for her and enjoy it too?" she concluded after telling me this story. "But I can't, because I have uncontrollable cravings for chocolate and sweets. If I eat what I want, it's chocolate, and I get fat. If I stay away from it, I get all depressed and deprived and end up eating it anyway. Food is too much of a trip. I can't handle it. Obviously, it's my destiny to be fat, unhealthy, and out of balance. I'd better just develop my personality."

I couldn't help laughing—her personality was pretty well developed already—but the problem Barbara described is very, very real. Cravings—those strong, almost irresistible desires for particular foods—are so difficult to deal with and so destructive to healthy eating. As I explained in earlier chapters, we all do many things that we "know" are bad for us because they make us feel better *in our minds*. We eat the foods we crave—even when we know they're making us fat and unhealthy—because they do create a biochemical pathway to what seems like a calmer and more alert state of mind. We'll do anything to feel like that—because the mind takes precedence over the body.

So long as we don't know any other way to create the state of mind we want, we remain tied to the foods we crave. They're the only way we know to feel the way we want to feel, so we just eat them anyway! Our cravings are, in fact, what makes it so hard to stay on a diet *or* to enjoy eating freely. Our first goal, then, in Body Type Nutrition, is to activate new biochemical pathways to feeling satisfied. Then and only then do *cravings become just a memory*.

When I told Barbara that she'd feel completely different once she got rid of her cravings, I don't think she believed me. I said she'd be able to get the satisfaction of eating chocolate, but without the fat. But for so long she'd felt that only the foods she craved would really satisfy her, and she could hardly conceive of the reality of getting that satisfaction from "healthy" foods. To convince her it might be possible, I had to tell her more about how cravings come about.

STAGE ONE: BREAKING CRAVINGS

In Chapter 1 of this book, I talked about the connection between cravings and your body type. Whichever type you are, you have a particular biochemical pathway that you're used to using to get to the brain state of calm alertness. In each body type, you get that state through reactions set off by your dominant gland, and so you develop *cravings* for stimulant foods for your dominant gland. Barbara H. is a thyroid type, and her cravings are for thyroid stimulants—in her case chocolate. Other thyroid types have cravings for candy, bread, pasta, rolls, or other carbohydrates.

Adrenal types, by contrast, crave rich, salty foods—red meat, salami, ripe cheeses—and, often, alcohol. Of course, any body type *can* come to crave alcohol, but with A-types it is especially tempting. Even though they "know" it's bad for them—it may even be killing them!—if it gives them the feeling they want, and they don't know any other way to get that feeling, they'll go right on drinking.

A-types don't usually care that much about desserts. Even though they say they love steak and potatoes, half the time the potato will still be on their plates when they're finished eating, unless it was mainly a blotter for butter and salt. These foods are stimulants to the adrenal glands—so they give A-types the feeling that they want.

Pituitary types, again by contrast, crave dairy products, which are pituitary-gland stimulators. Interestingly enough, I have known quite a few P-types who are actually allergic to milk products, but who have terrific cravings for them all the same. You wouldn't think that anyone would crave something that gave him headaches and hives, yet this is what happens. The explanation is simple—dairy products activate a *brain state* that feels good, so the body's bad reactions take a back seat.

Gonadal-type women, finally, have their typical cravings

for fats and spices, which are stimulating to the sex glands. If you've ever seen a G-type woman at a party trying to resist the creamy dip, you know how difficult it is to deal with a craving. She'll try to have just the carrot stick, but ends up scooping it into the sour cream anyway. And again, it's not that she's weak! It's that she needs to feel calmer and more alert (especially at a party), and knows that a dominant-gland stimulator is what she needs to feel that way.

All of the body types, in their various ways, are doing the same thing: using the food as a drug. And when I say that, I'm not just being melodramatic. It is a fact that all these foods do have specific brain effects, one of which is to stimulate production of beta-endorphins. Beta-endorphins are natural morphine-like substances that are actually physically addictive, just as morphine is. (There is an explanation of the brain effects of food in the Appendix, "Notes for Scientists," page 347.) So when you crave your own particular gland-stimulator—be it sweets, salt, fats, or dairy—you're not just fighting a "bad habit," you're fighting an actual physical dependency.

Barbara happened to be fifteen pounds overweight, but it isn't only overweight people who have cravings. Some thin and apparently well-balanced people have their lives made miserable by them too. One patient of mine, a slender woman of Italian background, told me she was fighting against a craving for pasta every day of her life. This is a sad situation, because it's no longer necessary to fight cravings. Rather, knowing what we now know about the way food works on the brain, we can actually *eliminate*, rather than fight, cravings.

HOW TO BREAK CRAVINGS: FOOD AS MEDICINE

The technique to eliminate cravings, which works whether you're overweight or not, is *systematically to sub-*

stitute foods that stimulate your less-active glands for foods that stimulate your dominant gland. This will have a balancing effect on your system. Instead of relying on just one biochemical pathway to the brain state you want, you'll find a variety of pathways. By cutting back on stimulators of your dominant gland, you'll be breaking the physical dependency you have on these foods; and by nourishing your less-active glands, you'll be developing new ways to get the satisfaction you need. In these ways you'll actually be using *food as medicine* to eliminate cravings and produce balance in your system.

According to your body type, you'll be using different foods to stimulate your less-active glands. If you're an adrenal type, you'll be eating more carbohydrates and dairy products to stimulate the thyroid and pituitary glands. If you're a thyroid type, you'll be eating food like eggs and meat to stimulate your adrenal glands. Pituitary types will be increasing their eggs and meat, especially organ meats, in order to stimulate the adrenals and sex glands. Gonadal types need to increase dairy and carbohydrates for thyroid and pituitary stimulation.

USING THE THREE-STAGE NUTRITION PROGRAM—FOR WEIGHT LOSS OR WEIGHT MAINTENANCE

The Body Type Nutrition Program is not just for losing weight. The original Body Type Diet, which I described in *Dr. Abravanel's Body Type Diet and Lifetime Nutrition Plan*, was designed for weight loss, but the Nutrition Program goes beyond weight loss and is a total nutritional package to balance, purify, and maintain the system, whether you are overweight or not.

If you have extra pounds you'd like to lose (that is, more than three to five pounds), then you can use the Balancing Diet for your body type precisely as a weight-loss diet. Your schedule should be to follow the Balancing Diet for three weeks, or until you are within three to five pounds of your weight goal, whichever comes first.

At this point you should then change to the Purification Diet for your type and follow it for a week. If after a week on the Purification Diet you still have weight to lose, go back to the Balancing Diet for another three weeks. Again, if you come within five pounds of your weight goal, switch back to the Purification Diet for a week.

Continue in this way to alternate three weeks on the Balancing Diet with a fourth week on the Purification Diet until you have reached your ideal weight. You are then ready for the Body Type Lifetime Maintenance Program.

If you are using the Balancing Diet for weight loss, you may find that you have additional questions on the subject of weight control. I had too much ground to cover for the Body Type Health Program to cover weight control completely. If your primary goal is weight loss and you have significant weight to lose, I suggest you get hold of a copy of the *Body Type Diet*. You'll find such topics as how to eat out on the Body Type Diet, menus, recipes and meal plans as well as a complete explanation of the role of all parts of the program, the influence of weight on health, and the way that overweight develops in each body type.

THE THREE-STAGE PROGRAM FOR THE NONOVERWEIGHT

On the other hand, suppose you aren't overweight at all, but would still like to get the benefits of Body Type Nutrition; you shouldn't go right to the Health and Weight Maintenance Program. The Maintenance Program is not a diet; it prescribes no set amount of foods, but rather gives *guidelines* in the form of lists of "Plenty Foods," "Moderation Foods," and "Rarely Foods." Experience with my patients has taught me that even in nonoverweight people, the metabolism still requires balancing and purification before you can realistically make the choices involved in the Maintenance Program.

Also, most people who are at or even below their ideal weight do have cellulite (wrinkly, "cottage cheese" fat) somewhere on their bodies. The presence of cellulite indicates a need for balancing and purification. It also suggests that being at your ideal weight and being in perfect balance are not *necessarily* the same thing. It's not just the pounds— it's the *quality* of the pounds that really counts. (There's more about cellulite in Chapter 7, where I explain the Purification Diet.)

For all these reasons, when you begin the Body Type Nutrition Program, you should start with a week on the Balancing Diet for your body type. Then, ideally, follow this week with a week on the Purification Diet for your type. I say ideally because the Purification Diet is fairly strong stuff. Experience with my patients has been that unless they are on weight control and are using the Purification Diet as part of a weight-loss regime, many of them like to do the Purification Diet when they are less busy and have a chance to eat more of their meals at home. So I offer an option. If you're just starting the program, you can follow your initial week on the Balancing Diet *either* with a week on the Purification Diet (this is the better choice), or with a second week on the Balancing Diet if your schedule requires you to eat out a great deal. But do this with the understanding that you'll do a week on the Purification Diet when your schedule lightens up a bit.

What happens next depends upon you. If you find that you feel comfortable with the nutrition guidelines that you're learning from stages one and two, and are free of cravings and at your best weight, then you can try the Health and Weight Maintenance Program. Try it for a week or two and see how it goes. If you have cravings—or if you have any trouble with the program at all—go back to the Balancing Diet. The Maintenance Program works for people who are truly in balance, and if you have any cravings or any problem with choosing food, you're just not ready for it yet. The Balancing Diet will get you ready, and you can stay on it for as long as you like, just increasing the amounts slightly if you don't want to lose any more weight.

As for those of you who are actually underweight, you too need the Balancing Diet. If you've been trying unsuccessfully to gain weight, this is also a sign that your system is out of balance. Reducing stimulation to your dominant gland and nourishing the less-active glands will result in better utilization of the food you eat, and your weight will tend to normalize. What you should do is to follow the Balancing Diet *in terms of what foods to eat,* but eat *as much as you want* of all the foods. Just be sure you don't fill up on one food and skip the rest. Eat at least the designated amount of all foods and then add more of whichever ones you wish.

THE SUBTLE EFFECTS: WHY QUALITY MATTERS

It is very rewarding to me as a physician to have my patients reach the point of perfect balance, when they really can eat *whatever they want* and still be in full control of their own eating. When you reach this point, you'll find that you can help yourself to feel better with food in all kinds of ways.

The fact is that through stimulating or nourishing your various glands, you can bring about tremendous effects on the way you feel. Biochemical studies definitely show that our minds are affected by complex chemical processes. You can make the biochemistry of food work for you, but in a more conscious way than ever before. Instead of trying to feel better with your cravings foods, you'll be able to feel just the way you want to feel by using the right foods as medicine.

When I see a certain patient of mine who is an attorney, and she tells me that she's worked out the exact breakfast for a day at court, so she'll feel just aggressive enough to win; when I see a patient who's an author and he tells me he can adjust his diet so that he writes all day without either getting tired or losing his creativity; when a busy young mother tells me she has found the mid-afternoon snack that keeps her from yelling at her two-year-old, I am deeply gratified.

But even these effects, based on biochemical understanding, do not tell the whole story of the influence food has on our lives. When we digest food, our bodies are breaking down and releasing the *binding energies* that hold food elements together. These are energies that are studied by physicists, not biochemists—and they are subtle, difficult to measure, but perfectly real for all of that.

Again, we *do* experience the differences in food on this subtle level—even though we don't always credit our experience. We feel differently, for example, after eating a good, crisp Washington apple or a ripe tropical mango, even though on a strictly biochemical level there is not very much difference in the fruit sugars they contain. We even feel differently after a meal prepared by someone who loves us, and one made by an indifferent person or a machine. And I'm not being "mystical" when I say this. I am convinced that we do sense the intangible factors that create our food, and that these factors aren't trivial. They are important and real, whether we currently possess the technology to measure them or not.

D.H. Lawrence wrote about the experience of eating an apple:

> An apple becomes *mystic* when I taste in it
> the summer and the snows, and wild welter of earth
> and the insistence of the sun.
>
> All of which things I can surely taste in a good apple.
> Though some apples taste preponderantly of water,
>   wet and sour,

and some of too much sun, brackish sweet
like lagoon-water, that has been too much sunned.

If I say I taste these things in an apple, I am called
  mystic, . . .

But if I eat an apple, I like to eat it with all
  my senses awake.

I would like you to approach your lifetime nutrition program in precisely this spirit, with all your senses awake. Everything about your food does matter. The freshness of it, the way it was grown, the way it was prepared, the surroundings in which you eat it, and, just as important, your own state of mind while you are eating. All these are part of your life and should be part of your lifetime nutrition plan.

Of course, none of these things ought to overwhelm you. *No single event should be taken too much to heart.* You won't be destroyed by a bad meal, an occasional upset at dinner, a rotten apple; but the trend of your eating should be toward good, fresh food, eaten in a relaxed way among pleasant surroundings and with people you love. All your positive experiences are actually *nourishing*. And I want you to be nourished—in every part of yourself. This way lies perfect health.

Now, let's take a look at the three stages of the Body Type Nutrition Program. Each of the following three chapters describes one of the stages and then gives the actual diet or eating program for that stage. In each chapter you'll find the gonadal-type program first, the adrenal-type program second, the thyroid-type program third, and the program for pituitary types fourth.

6

THE BODY TYPE BALANCING DIET

The Balancing Diet is the first step in the Body Type Nutrition Program. Whether you want and need to lose weight, or are primarily interested in fine-tuning your metabolism and balancing your glandular system, the Balancing Diet for your body type is the way to start.

This is a restricted calorie diet—about 1200 calories per day. If you are overweight, the Balancing Diet will be the backbone of a weight-control program, and you will be following it (along with the Purification Diet) on a specific schedule until you have reached your ideal weight. (The precise schedule for each type is given below.)

If you aren't overweight, you should follow the Balancing Diet for your body type for a week; then follow the Purification Diet for your type (see Chapter 7) for another week. Experience with my patients has taught me that even if the scales show they weigh the correct number of pounds, these may not be the right pounds. Your weight may not be distributed in exactly the way you'd like. There might be little pockets of fat here and there—on your hips or outer thighs, around the middle, or on your upper arms—depending on your body type. Other parts of your body might not be quite filled in enough. The Balancing Diet will start these extra pockets of fat moving, and the Purification Diet will get them off. Then, when you go on the Health and Weight Maintenance Program, you'll fill back in exactly where you should, not in the old pockets.

Each of the four Balancing Diets is designed carefully for the needs of the particular body type. The diets each have some special features: the Body Type Herbal Teas, the Body Type Vegetable Soups, and the Body Type Snacks. *Be sure to take advantage of these features*. I developed them for my weight-control patients, and each one is invaluable in making what is really the hard work of dieting much easier. Each one also fulfills a very definite purpose in balancing the metabolism and eliminating cravings.

Be sure, also, to eat *all* the foods prescribed at each meal and to observe the full interval *between* meals. These intervals aren't designed to torture you; they are based on the activity cycle of your dominant gland. Each of the four glands does have its own particular rhythm, which means it has times when it is very active and times when it rests. The foods I've prescribed for specific meals for each type are designed to work with the cycle of the gland during the interval between the meals. So you must be very sure to eat exactly what is prescribed in each meal and wait the prescribed time before you eat again. Remember, at this stage of your program you are using food as medicine—and you must follow your prescription carefully if you want the best results.

THE BALANCING DIET FOR GONADAL TYPES

BREAKFAST

Choice of 1 apple OR: 2 apricots, ½ banana, 1 cup of berries, ¼ cantaloupe, 10 cherries, 2 fresh figs, ½ mango, 1 nectarine, 1 peach, 1 pear, ½ cup of fresh pineapple, 2 plums, 1 cup of strawberries, or 1 cup of watermelon

Coffee, tea, or red clover tea (with ½ teaspoon of sugar or honey if desired)

WAIT FOUR HOURS

LUNCH

Large green salad of any combination of lettuce, cucumber, mushrooms, celery, sprouts, radishes, bell pepper, tomato, and onion

1 teaspoon of any *clear* diet dressing (not creamy or spicy)

Choice of ½ cup of beets, carrots, cauliflower, peas, pumpkin, squash, or turnip

2 ounces of lowfat firm cheese OR 1 cup of yogurt OR 1 cup of lowfat cottage cheese OR 1 egg (soft- or hard-boiled, or fried in 1 teaspoon of vegetable oil or, preferably, spray shortening)

1 slice of whole-grain bread (rye bread is recommended), without butter

1 glass of skim milk

1 piece of fruit (from the same choices offered at breakfast)

Coffee, tea, or red clover tea (with ½ teaspoon of sugar or honey if desired)

WAIT FIVE HOURS (G-type Snack only if necessary)

DINNER

Choice of 4 ounces of chicken OR 4 ounces of turkey OR 4 ounces of fish OR 2 eggs. (The eggs may be soft- or hard-boiled, or fried in 1 teaspoon of vegetable oil. You should not have eggs if you had an egg for lunch.) Exotic, nongreasy fowl such as quail or pheasant or partridge is allowed, but duck and goose are definitely out

1 teaspoon of vegetable oil (may be used in preparation of the poultry or fish, on the vegetables, or to cook your eggs)

Steamed vegetables (your choice, as much as you like), or G-type Vegetable Soup (recipe below)

Choice of 1 slice of whole-grain bread OR ½ cup of bulgur wheat OR ½ cup of brown rice OR ½ cup of millet—no butter

1 piece of fruit (from the same choices offered at breakfast)

1 glass of skim milk

Red clover tea (with ½ teaspoon of sugar or honey if desired)

SPECIAL NOTES:

The G-type Herbal Tea is red clover tea. It is best made with teabags (available at most health-food stores), because red clover tops tend to have tiny little bits that are hard to strain out if you use loose tea. To make red clover tea, bring water to a boil, pour over a teabag in a cup, and allow to steep 3–5 minutes. Red clover is a purifier and is tremendously restorative to your overworked ovaries.

The G-type Snack is a small piece of fruit—for example, a small plum or a small handful of grapes, or ½ cup of strawberries, or half an apple. The fruit will give you a mild thyroid boost and help you resist the tendency to go for a creamy snack later on.

G-type Vegetable Soup is made as follows: Cut up ½ zucchini, ¼ cucumber, 2 leaves romaine lettuce, one small handful each of parsley and watercress, and 2 beet tops. Place in a saucepan and cover with water. Bring to a boil and simmer about five minutes. Remove from heat and blend briefly in the blender (you want small pieces, not a fine puree). Eat as is or add ½ teaspoon chicken-flavored boullion.

THE BALANCING DIET FOR ADRENAL TYPES

BREAKFAST

Choose either: 1 cup of lowfat yogurt OR 1 cup of lowfat cottage cheese OR 1 cup of cereal with ½ cup of skim milk

Coffee, tea, or parsley tea (½ teaspoon of sugar or honey permitted)

WAIT FOUR HOURS

LUNCH

Large green salad made with any combination of lettuce, cucumber, mushrooms, celery, sprouts, radishes, bell pepper, tomato, or onion

1 teaspoon of any *clear* (not creamy) diet dressing

Choice of ½ cup of beets, carrots, cauliflower, peas, pumpkin, squash, or turnips

Choice of 1 cup of yogurt OR 1 cup of lowfat cottage cheese OR 4 ounces of lowfat firm cheese (such as Mozzarella) OR 4 ounces of fish (but not shellfish)

Choice of 1 apple OR: 2 apricots, ½ banana, 1 cup of berries, ¼ cantaloupe, 10 cherries, 2 fresh figs, ½ mango, 1 nectarine, 1 peach, 1 pear, ½ cup of fresh pineapple, 2 plums, 1 cup of watermelon, or 1 cup of strawberries

Coffee, tea, or parsley tea

WAIT SIX HOURS (A-type Snack only if necessary)

DINNER

Choice of 4 ounces of chicken OR 4 ounces of turkey OR 4 ounces of fish OR 2 eggs

Steamed or raw green vegetables (as much as you like), or A-type Vegetable Soup (recipe below)

2 teaspoons of vegetable oil (may be used in preparation of the poultry, fish, or eggs, or on the vegetables)

1 cup of skim milk

Choice of the same fruits as offered at lunch OR small dessert (150 calories maximum)

Parsley tea

SPECIAL NOTES:

The A-type Herbal Tea is parsley tea, made from dried (not fresh) parsley leaves (available at most health-food stores). Parsley tea has a refreshing astringency and is purifying to the adrenal glands. To make parsley tea, bring a cup of water to a boil. Pour over 1 teaspoon of leaves and allow to steep 3–5 minutes. Strain and serve.

The A-type Snack is ½ cup of plain, lowfat yogurt or ½ cup lowfat cottage cheese. Actually, you don't need to snack. Your strong adrenals make you the best of all dieters, and you can sail through the afternoon without getting hungry; but if you have a craving for something salty, have the A-type Snack instead. It will drive off the craving.

A-type Vegetable Soup is made as follows: Cut up ½ zucchini, ¼ green pepper, 1 stalk celery with leafy top, 1 tomato, and about 5 Chinese snow peas. Place in a saucepan with water covering them. Bring to a boil and simmer about 5 minutes. Run briefly through a blender (you want small pieces, not a fine puree). Serve as is or add ½ teaspoon chicken-flavored bouillon powder.

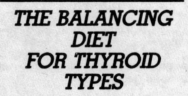

THE BALANCING DIET FOR THYROID TYPES

BREAKFAST

2 eggs, any style

1 teaspoon of butter or oil (use either to cook the eggs, or on the toast)

½ slice of whole-grain bread or toast

1 cup only of decaffeinated coffee, decaffeinated tea, or raspberry leaf tea

WAIT FOUR HOURS

LUNCH

Large green salad of any combination of lettuce, cucumber, mushrooms, celery, sprouts, radishes, bell pepper, tomato, and onion

1 teaspoon of any *clear* (not creamy) diet dressing

1 teaspoon of butter or mayonnaise

Choice of either: 4 ounces of poultry OR 4 ounces of fish (not shellfish)

Choice of either: 1 slice of whole-grain bread OR ½ cup of bulgur wheat OR ½ cup of brown rice OR ½ cup of millet

1 cup of skim milk

Raspberry leaf tea

WAIT SIX HOURS (T-type Snack only if necessary)

DINNER

Choice of 4 ounces of chicken OR 4 ounces of turkey OR 4 ounces of any seafood OR 4 ounces of lamb with fat cut off OR 4 ounces of organ meat (liver, kidneys, or heart) OR 4 ounces of lean beef (NOTE: Have beef 2–3 times a week only)

Raw or steamed vegetables (your choice, as much as you wish), or T-type Vegetable Soup (recipe below)

Choice of 1 slice of whole-grain bread OR ½ cup of bulgur wheat OR ½ cup of brown rice OR ½ cup of millet—no butter

1 cup of skim milk

Raspberry leaf tea

SPECIAL NOTES:

The T-type Herbal Tea is raspberry leaf tea. It is made as follows: Bring 1 cup water to a boil. Pour water over 1 teaspoon raspberry leaves (available at most health-food stores). Allow to steep five minutes. Strain and serve. Remember, no sugar or honey. Drink this tea as often throughout the day as you wish—it is very strengthening to the thyroid and will help ward off your cravings for starches and sweets.

The T-type Snack is a ½ hard-boiled egg. *Always* keep a hardboiled egg ready in the refrigerator. You are the body type most likely to feel you must have a snack, and the thought of hard-boiling an egg at that moment will seem impossible. So if you don't want to succumb to the cookie monster, keep that egg ready.

T-type Vegetable Soup is made as follows: Cut up 1 carrot, 1 carrot top, 1 stalk of celery with green leafy top, 1 yellow squash or zucchini, and 6 green beans. Place in a saucepan with water to cover. Bring to a boil and simmer 5 minutes. Run briefly through a blender (you want small pieces, not a fine puree). Serve as is or add ½ teaspoon chicken-flavored bouillon powder.

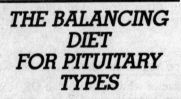

THE BALANCING DIET FOR PITUITARY TYPES

BREAKFAST

Choose either: 4 ounces of lean beef OR 4 ounces of lean pork OR 4 ounces of dark poultry meat OR 4 ounces of lamb OR 4 ounces of liver OR 4 ounces of kidney OR 4 ounces of heart

Choose either: ½ cup of brown rice OR ½ cup of bulgur wheat OR ½ cup of millet OR 1 cup of whole-grain cereal OR 1 slice of whole-grain bread

1 cup of decaffeinated coffee, decaffeinated tea, or fenugreek tea

WAIT FOUR HOURS

LUNCH

Large green salad made with any combination of lettuce, cucumber, mushrooms, celery, sprouts, radishes, bell pepper, tomato, or onion

1 teaspoon of any *clear* (not creamy) diet dressing

One 4-ounce serving of either beets, carrots, cauliflower, peas, potatoes, pumpkin, or squash

4 ounces of shellfish or water-packed tuna

One piece of whole-grain bread

Choice of 1 apple OR: 2 apricots, ½ banana, 1 cup of berries, ¼ cantaloupe, 10 cherries, 2 fresh figs, ½ mango, 1 nectarine, 1 peach, 1 pear, ½ cup of fresh pineapple, 2 plums, 1 cup of strawberries, or 1 cup of watermelon

Fenugreek tea

WAIT SIX HOURS (P-type Snack only if necessary)

DINNER

Choice of 4 ounces of light poultry meat OR 4 ounces of fish or shellfish OR two eggs (three times a week maximum)

Fresh vegetables (steamed or raw, as much as you wish), or P-type Vegetable Soup (recipe below)

One piece of fruit (same choices offered at lunch)

Fenugreek tea

SPECIAL NOTES:

The P-type Herbal Tea is fenugreek seed tea. It is made as follows: Bring 1 cup water to a boil. Add 1 teaspoon fenugreek seeds (available at most health-food stores). Boil the seeds for about five minutes. Strain and serve. Remember, no sugar or honey. Drink this tea as often throughout the day as you wish. It is very purifying and a good defense against cravings.

The P-type Snack is a small amount of cooked meat—for example, an ounce or two of cooked hamburger well drained of fat. You should always keep a small amount of cooked meat ready in the refrigerator. Beef jerky is a good handbag or pocket item. Then, when the urge to eat ice cream strikes, you're ready.

P-type Vegetable Soup is made as follows: Cut up ¼ beet, 2–3 okra (if available), 6 green beans, 1 stalk of celery, ½ zucchini, 1 green onion, 3 mushrooms, and 2–3 beet tops. Place in a saucepan with water to cover. Bring to a boil and simmer 5 minutes. Run briefly through a blender (you want small pieces, not a fine puree). Serve as is or add ½ teaspoon chicken-flavored bouillon powder.

7

THE
BODY TYPE
PURIFICATION
DIET

The Body Type Purification Diet is strong stuff. It's the most stringent and powerful diet in the Body Type Nutrition Program and has been designed to give your whole metabolic system a powerful boost toward balance, integration, and health.

If you're overweight, you'll be using the Purification Diet as part of your weight-control program in alternation with the Balancing Diet. Follow the Balancing Diet for the first three weeks and then change to the Purification Diet for the fourth week. Continue changing to the Purification Diet every fourth week until you have reached your ideal weight.

The Purification Diet is also designed to be used for the last five pounds of extra weight. This means that if you happen to get within five pounds of your weight goal on the Balancing Diet, you change at that point to the Purification Diet—*even if you haven't finished three weeks on the Balancing Diet*. At any point that you are five pounds from your weight goal, the Purification Diet is the one to use.

If you aren't overweight, use the Purification Diet after an initial week on the Balancing Diet. As I say, it's a powerful program; if you were to try it before you'd been on the Balancing Diet, you'd find it difficult and you might not be able to complete it. But after the Balancing Diet, you'll find it refreshing and invigorating—just what your metabolism needs.

Finally, you use the Purification Diet as a key element in the Long Weekend of Rejuvenation (see Chapter 12 for details).

WHAT HAPPENS ON THE PURIFICATION DIET

The Purification Diet has a number of different goals. Which of the goals is primary for you depends on the timing of the diet—at what point in your program you pick it up. If you use it as part of a weight-loss program, you will gain one set of benefits; as a vital ingredient in your health, fitness, and life-extension program, it will give you even more.

One result of the Purification Diet is to break plateaus. Plateaus are those periods when weight loss unaccountably slows down or stops, even though you are craving-free and following your nutrition program to the letter. Plateaus most commonly occur every fourth week. They are, in fact, related to glandular cycles and reflect periods of extra rest, when the dominant gland is recuperating from past overstimulation. Plateaus also come about because your body becomes more efficient and needs fewer calories to do the same work.

Second, the Purification Diet is used for the most stubborn plateau of all: the plateau that occurs when you are down to your last five pounds of excess weight. As anyone who has ever dieted to this point knows, these pounds are the hardest of all to lose, much harder than the ten, twenty, or fifty that came before. This is because the last five pounds are mostly composed of *cellulite,* commonly known as wrinkly or "cottage cheese" fat.

CELLULITE AND THE PURIFICATION DIET

Some diet "experts" dispute the existence of cellulite and say that it is just ordinary fat in slightly different form. However, I have been convinced by much experience that cellulite is very different indeed from ordinary fat. If it's just ordinary fat, why does it come up in such unusual places? Why is it so hard to lose? I have seen patients who are actually underweight, but who still have cellulite (many models are in this situation).

Cellulite is so difficult to lose because it is highly toxic—it acts as a storage place for unwanted materials that the body has not been able to eliminate. Your body, wisely, resists freeing these toxins from their hiding places if it is not strong enough to eliminate them. This means that it is impossible to lose cellulite until your system has come into sufficient balance to be able to deal effectively with cellulite itself.

The Purification Diet is highly effective in eliminating cellulite—this is one of the main purposes for which I have developed it. When you reach your last plateau and are down to your final five pounds of excess weight, you should switch to the Purification Diet and stay on it for a week. If a week on the Purification Diet does not eliminate all of the last five pounds, you may go back to the Balancing Diet for four days and then finish off the last pounds with the Purification Diet.

Finally, the Purification Diet really comes into its own when you are at your ideal weight. It plays a major role in the Long Weekend of Rejuvenation (see Chapter 13), a special weekend I have designed for each body type. As part of the Long Weekend, the Purification Diet works to set your entire metabolic system on a course of dramatic improvement, toward health and long life.

Remember, whether you are using the Purification Diet for plateaus, for the last five pounds, or for health and revitalization, you will never be on it for more than a week at a time. It is a very powerful, very purposeful diet and is not intended to be followed for any longer period.

THE PURIFICATION DIET FOR GONADAL TYPES

Important: Do not begin this diet until you have followed the G-type Balancing Diet for *at least* a week. The sequence of diets is vital for bringing your metabolism into balance and preparing you for your lifetime nutrition program.

BREAKFAST

Choice of 1 apple OR: 2 apricots, ½ banana, 1 cup of berries, ¼ cantaloupe, 10 cherries, 2 fresh figs, ½ mango, 1 nectarine, 1 peach, 1 pear, ½ cup of fresh pineapple, 2 plums, 1 cup of strawberries, or 1 cup of watermelon

Coffee, tea, or red clover tea (with ½ teaspoon sugar or honey if desired)

WAIT *FIVE* HOURS (Note difference from Balancing Diet)

LUNCH

3 ounces lowfat firm cheese OR lowfat string cheese

1 slice of whole-grain bread

1 teaspoon of butter or mayonnaise

1 piece of fruit (same choices as breakfast)

G-type Vegetable Soup (as much as you want)

Red clover tea (with ½ teaspoon of sugar or honey if desired)

WAIT *SIX* HOURS (no snack at this stage)

DINNER

Choice of 1 cup of plain lowfat yogurt OR 4 ounces of lowfat cheese OR 2 eggs OR 1 egg and 2 ounces of lowfat cheese

G-type Vegetable Soup (as much as you want)

1 teaspoon of vegetable oil or butter (you may cook your egg in this or use it on your bread or rice)

½ cup of white rice OR 1 slice of whole-grain bread

1 piece of fruit (same choices as breakfast)

Red clover tea (with ½ teaspoon of sugar or honey if desired)

THE PURIFICATION DIET FOR ADRENAL TYPES

Important: Do not begin this diet until you have followed the A-type Balancing Diet for *at least* a week. The sequence of diets is vital for bringing your metabolism into balance and preparing you for your lifetime nutrition program.

BREAKFAST

Choice of 1 cup of plain lowfat yogurt OR 1 cup of lowfat cottage cheese OR 1 cup of whole-grain cereal with ½ cup skim milk

Coffee, tea, or parsley tea (1 teaspoon of sugar allowed if desired)

WAIT *FIVE* HOURS (Note difference from Balancing Diet)

LUNCH

A-type Vegetable Soup (as much as you want)

1 slice of whole-grain bread (without butter)

Choice of 1 apple OR 2 apricots, ½ banana, 1 cup of berries, ¼ cantaloupe, 10 cherries, 2 fresh figs, ½ mango, 1 nectarine, 1 peach, 1 pear, ½ cup of fresh pineapple, 2 plums, 1 cup of strawberries, or 1 cup of watermelon

Parsley tea (with 1 teaspoon of sugar if desired)

WAIT *SIX* HOURS (no snack at this stage)

DINNER

Choice of 4 ounces of chicken OR 4 ounces of turkey OR 4 ounces of fish (not shellfish) OR 2 eggs (eggs no more than twice per week)

1 teaspoon of vegetable oil or butter

½ cup of white or brown rice OR ½ cup of bulgur wheat OR ½ cup of millet OR 1 slice of whole-grain or fiber bread

A-type Vegetable Soup (as much as you want)

Parsley tea

THE PURIFICATION DIET FOR THYROID TYPES

Important: Do not begin this diet until you have followed the T-type Balancing Diet for *at least* a week. The sequence of diets is vital for bringing your metabolism into balance and preparing you for your lifetime nutrition program.

BREAKFAST

2 eggs, any style

1 teaspoon of vegetable oil

T-type Vegetable Soup (as much as you want)

Raspberry leaf tea

WAIT *FIVE* HOURS (Note difference from Balancing Diet)

LUNCH

4 ounces of fish OR shellfish

T-type Vegetable Soup (as much as you want)

Raspberry leaf tea

WAIT *SIX* HOURS (no snack at this stage)

DINNER

Choice of 4 ounces of poultry OR 4 ounces of fish OR 4 ounces of shellfish

T-type Vegetable Soup (as much as you want)

Choice of ½ cup of millet OR ½ cup of brown rice OR ½ cup of bulgur wheat OR 1 slice of whole-grain bread

Raspberry leaf tea

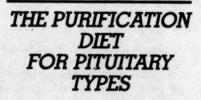

THE PURIFICATION DIET FOR PITUITARY TYPES

Important: Do not begin this diet until you have followed the P-type Balancing Diet for *at least* a week. The sequence of diets is vital for bringing your metabolism into balance and preparing you for your lifetime nutrition program.

BREAKFAST

2 eggs, any style (raw is best, lightly cooked is next best)

1 teaspoon of vegetable oil

1 slice of whole-grain toast

1 cup of decaffeinated coffee or tea, or fenugreek tea (no sugar or honey)

WAIT *FIVE* HOURS (Note difference from Balancing Diet)

LUNCH

Choice of 1 apple OR: 2 apricots, ½ banana, 1 cup of berries, ¼ cantaloupe, 10 cherries, 2 fresh figs, ½ mango, 1 nectarine, 1 peach, 1 pear, ½ cup of fresh pineapple, 2 plums, 1 cup of strawberries, or 1 cup of watermelon

Choice of 4 ounces of lean beef OR 4 ounces of lean pork OR 4 ounces of lamb (but drain the fat thoroughly) OR 4 ounces of dark poultry meat OR 4 ounces of organ meat (liver, heart, or kidneys)

P-type Vegetable Soup (as much as you want)

Fenugreek tea

WAIT *SIX* HOURS (no snack at this stage)

DINNER

4 ounces of fish OR shellfish

1 slice of whole-grain bread

P-type Vegetable Soup (as much as you want)

Fenugreek tea

8

THE BODY
TYPE
HEALTH AND
WEIGHT
MAINTENANCE
PROGRAM

Suppose, for a moment, that you've completed stages one
and two of Body Type Nutrition. You've been on the Balancing Diet and Purification Diet, and if you were overweight,
you've reached your ideal weight. Your cellulite's gone, your
cravings are controlled, and your metabolism is in balance.
Where are you now? What does it feel like?

It will probably feel more or less the way it felt to my
patient, Barbara H., so I'll let her tell you her experience.
"What I feel now," she said after completing her last round
on the Purification Diet, "is *normal*. I mean, I feel about
eating the way I used to when I was a kid—nine or ten, I
guess—before I started to worry so much about my body
and whether or not I was fat.

"If I feel hungry," she went on, "I eat. I ask myself
what it is I want—not so much what food I want, as what
feeling I want in myself. I know I want to feel satisfied, and I
realize now that chocolate won't really satisfy me. So I reach
for something that *will* satisfy my body, usually an egg or

some chicken with salad or vegetables. And I feel so much more energy, it's unbelievable. Do you think, Doctor, that all that chocolate was actually draining my energy from me?"

I told Barbara that the foods we crave aren't necessarily harmful to us; a craving is just a symptom of imbalance. Some people crave "healthy" foods like whole-wheat bread or cheese; others crave foods more obviously unhealthy for them, such as chocolate or potato chips. It's not important. The craving is just a way for your body to tell you it needs some help, and with the Body Type Programs you've given it the help it needs. Getting rid of cravings has really only been a by-product of our real goal: creating balance in the system. We are bringing about a situation where you use the energy of all four of your glands, not just your dominant one—a metabolism that runs on all four cylinders, not just one.

The third stage of Body Type Nutrition begins when you are at this point, when you change to your Health and Weight Maintenance Program. This is a program and *not* a diet: You are really now in a position to make choices about what you eat, choices that are intelligent and informed, and that will work for you.

The Maintenance Program only works because you're ready for it. Your metabolic system is ready, and you have a real understanding of the effects of food on your body. By the time you reach this stage, you are ready to make use of this information. So let's take a look at the way you will be using food to produce precisely the results that you want for yourself.

BODY TYPE MAINTENANCE: THE THIRD STAGE

The Body Type Health and Weight Maintenance Program is not a diet, so it does not tell you what or how much to eat. Instead, it provides *guidelines of emphasis*. You are now at a point where you need only be aware of which foods to emphasize and which ones to eat only under special, limited circumstances, depending on the results you want.

For each body type the Maintenance Program contains three classes of food. The first is called Plenty Foods. These are the backbone of your diet, the foods you should eat regularly, every day. Second, there are your Moderation Foods. These are foods that you can eat within reason. They are foods that have some stimulating qualities for your dominant gland, and that you'll have to watch a bit to check their effects. If you find yourself getting cravings again, it's a sign to cut back on your Moderation Foods.

Finally, there are your Rarely Foods. These are foods that will definitely create cravings and imbalance if you eat them more than once in a while. On the other hand, you can use your Rarely Foods to produce specific effects in yourself—to increase endurance, creativity, or relaxation—depending on what your specific requirements are. I'll show you precisely how to do this in Chapter 15, "Signposts to Change."

On the Maintenance Program you learn how to select foods for yourself properly. You don't just choose them for their "food value"—protein, carbohydrates, or fats—but for the total effect that they will have on your metabolic and glandular systems.

THE FEELING EFFECT OF FOOD

In some ways, you've always used food in just this way. It seems that we "know" that different foods give us different effects, and we can be quite adept at selecting the right foods for each job. We know, for example, that turkey is just what the doctor ordered for a holiday dinner. We may never have heard that turkey is rich in the amino acid tryptophan, which has a relaxing and stress-reducing effect, but we know there's *something* in turkey that makes it right for a big festive occasion when having the whole family around can produce just a little bit of stress and strain.

In the same way, you know that on a day when you have to be especially strong—an important meeting at the office or a stressful meeting at your child's school—you need to fortify yourself with a good breakfast of bacon and eggs. You may not realize that what you're doing is increasing your sodium intake, which increases the production of adrenal hormones (and, in men, sex hormones). These hormones actually produce measurable increases in aggressive behavior—which is just what you want.

You know, too, that there's a difference between the way you're going to feel after a meal in which the main course is fish or chicken, or pork or beef. The popular wisdom says that "chicken is lighter than meat" or "fish is brain food," but what we're really sensing are the distinct chemical properties of these foods and the different effects they have on our metabolisms. All are dense, complete proteins of animal origin, but their effects are vastly dissimilar. That various fruits and vegetables will make us feel different—a corn tortilla isn't the same as a flour one, butter gives a different effect from margarine—is again, something we actually do know.

Yet if we think about it, we know these things *despite* everything we've ever heard or read about nutrition! We read in school that protein is protein, and it *simply doesn't matter* whether we get it from fish, fowl, cow, pig, grains, or beans. We're taught that starch is starch and saturated fats are saturated fats, regardless of where they come from. We learn that our bodies digest food so thoroughly and break it down into such simple elements that the distinction between different *sources* is totally obliterated.

We're taught to think of our bodies as highly efficient chemical factories. We supply them with forkfuls of the complex chemicals we call food, and they extract from the raw materials the nourishment they need. There are certain requirements that must be satisfied. The standard thinking goes on: we need a certain number of calories, a certain amount of protein, carbohydrates, and fat, and certain minimum quantities of vitamins and minerals. Given these requirements the chemical factory will tick along just the same, thank you.

But this is one case where we the people intuitively know what nutritionists are only just finding out. When we adjust our diet automatically, picking certain foods for certain effects, we're actually much closer to the latest scientific thinking than the majority of people who write and speak on nutrition. The truth is that standard nutritional statements have lagged far behind the latest scientific knowledge from other fields.

A great deal of research exists showing the ways food does influence the way you feel. (A list of references to some of this research appears in the Bibliography to the Appendix.) But you don't have to read the research to know the truth of what's going on. All you really have to do is know your own body and be alert to the way food makes you feel.

This alertness is important if you want to make best use of the Health and Weight Maintenance guidelines. Eat your Plenty Foods as the basis of your diet, vary them with Moderation Foods, use Rarely Foods when you need their effects. But *watch what happens*. Keep in mind that all food is chemical and can act as a drug or as a medicine. Use it well, with yourself in mind, and it will always be a medicine for total health.

THE GONADAL TYPE HEALTH AND WEIGHT MAINTENANCE PROGRAM

The formula for keeping the balance you've achieved through stages one and two is to keep a continuing awareness of your body type and its special needs. The G-type Balancing Diet and Purification Diet have brought about a state of balance in your metabolism; the G-type Health and Weight Maintenance Program is designed to make it easy for you to *maintain* that balance, to keep your ideal weight, and to move toward perfect health.

1. YOUR PLENTY FOODS:	Fruit Fresh vegetables Whole grains Yogurt Cottage cheese Red clover tea
2. YOUR MODERATION FOODS:	Poultry Fish Skim milk Light cheese Vegetable oils Light desserts Coffee or tea
3. YOUR RARELY FOODS:	Red meat Spices Cream, sour cream, ice cream Butter Rich desserts
4. YOUR IDEAL EATING SCHEDULE:	A very light breakfast—or even no breakfast at all A light lunch—salad and a sandwich Your main meal at night Watch out for evening and late-morning snacking!

THE GONADAL TYPE HEALTH AND WEIGHT MAINTENANCE EATING PROGRAM

BREAKFAST

A large piece of fruit (with ½ cup of plain yogurt on very busy days) OR 1 cup of whole-grain cereal with skim milk

Coffee, tea, or red clover tea (with a teaspoon of sugar if you wish)

LUNCH

A large green salad with your favorite vegetables and just a little dressing

A serving of lowfat cottage cheese or hard cheese

2 slices of whole-grain bread OR ½ cup of brown rice OR ½ cup of bulgur wheat OR ½ cup of millet

A glass of skim milk

A piece of fruit

Coffee, tea, or red clover tea (with a teaspoon of sugar if you wish)

DINNER

A serving of fish or poultry, OR 2 eggs. Eat meat once a week or less. Avoid pork and "variety meats" (salami, cold cuts, organ meats, poultry "rolls")

A serving of whole grain 4 times a week
(You may have refined grains 3 times a week if you wish)

Vegetables, cooked or raw, as much as you like

A glass of skim milk (optional)

A piece of fruit or a small, light dessert—but avoid creamy desserts and whipped cream

Coffee, tea, or red clover tea (with a teaspoon of sugar if you wish)

THE ADRENAL TYPE HEALTH AND WEIGHT MAINTENANCE PROGRAM

The formula for keeping the balance you've achieved through stages one and two is to keep a continuing awareness of your body type and its special needs. The A-type Balancing Diet and Purification Diet have brought about a state of balance in your metabolism; the A-type Health and Weight Maintenance Program is designed to make it easy for you to *maintain* that balance, to keep your ideal weight, and to move toward perfect health.

1. YOUR PLENTY FOODS:	Lowfat Yogurt
	Fish
	Lowfat cheese
	Cottage cheese

Skim milk
Fruit
Fresh vegetables
Whole grains
Parsley tea

2. YOUR
MODERATION FOODS:

Poultry
Coffee or tea
Desserts
Vegetable oils

3. YOUR
RARELY FOODS:

Salty foods
Highfat cheese (cheddar, Swiss, etc.)
Red meat
Butter

4. YOUR
IDEAL EATING SCHEDULE:

A light breakfast of dairy products or whole grains

A fairly light lunch, with only a small amount of protein

Your main meal at night

THE ADRENAL TYPE HEALTH AND WEIGHT MAINTENANCE EATING PROGRAM

BREAKFAST

A serving of lowfat yogurt or cottage cheese OR a bowl of whole-grain cereal with skim milk

Coffee, tea, or parsley tea (with a teaspoon of sugar if desired)

LUNCH

A large green salad with all your favorite vegetables, and dressing in moderation

A small serving of chicken or fish. Lamb or shellfish may be substituted once a week if you like

2 slices of whole-grain bread OR an equivalent serving of other whole grain

A glass of skim milk

A piece of fruit

Coffee, tea, or parsley tea (with a teaspoon of sugar if desired)

DINNER

A serving of fish, poultry, or meat. Fish can be eaten 5 times a week but at least 3 times; poultry twice and red meat no more than twice. Eggs or cheese dishes may be substituted for meat meals only—no more than twice a week

Vegetables, cooked or raw, as much as you like

A serving of grain, which should be whole grain at least 4 times a week

A piece of fruit or small light dessert

Coffee, tea, or parsley tea (with a teaspoon of sugar if desired)

THE THYROID TYPE HEALTH AND WEIGHT MAINTENANCE PROGRAM

The formula for keeping the balance you've achieved through stages one and two is to keep a continuing awareness of your body type and its special needs. The T-type Balancing Diet and Purification Diet have brought about a state of balance in your metabolism; the T-type Health and Weight Maintenance Program is designed to make it easy for you to *maintain* that balance, to keep your ideal weight, and to move toward perfect health.

1. YOUR PLENTY FOODS:	Eggs Poultry (chicken, turkey, game hen) Fresh vegetables Raspberry leaf tea Fish
2. YOUR MODERATION FOODS:	Red meat Cheese

Yogurt
Whole grains
Fruit
Decaffeinated coffee and tea
Butter, vegetable oils

3. YOUR
RARELY FOODS:

Refined starches (white
flour, white sugar, pasta)
Coffee
Tea
Desserts

4. YOUR
IDEAL EATING SCHEDULE:

Eggs for breakfast (a good
lifetime habit for T-types)

Your total food intake divided more or less evenly
among your meals

Protein at each meal

A protein snack (e.g., half a
hard-boiled egg) in the late
afternoon if you feel tired

THE THYROID TYPE HEALTH AND WEIGHT MAINTENANCE EATING PROGRAM

BREAKFAST

2 eggs, any style

1 slice whole-grain toast with butter

Decaffeinated coffee, tea, or raspberry leaf tea

LUNCH

A large green salad with plenty of your favorite vegetables, clear dressing used in moderation

A serving of hard cheese, yogurt, or cottage cheese OR a serving of meat or fish

2 slices of whole-grain bread OR an equivalent serving of other whole grains

A glass of milk

A piece of fruit

Decaffeinated coffee, tea, or raspberry leaf tea

DINNER

A serving of meat, poultry, or fish. Plan to eat meat about twice a week, fish or poultry on the remaining nights.

Vegetables, cooked or raw, as much as you like.

A glass of milk (optional)

A piece of fruit or a small light dessert (but not more than twice a week total)

Raspberry leaf tea

THE PITUITARY TYPE HEALTH AND WEIGHT MAINTENANCE PROGRAM

The formula for keeping the balance you've achieved through stages one and two is to keep a continuing awareness of your body type and its special needs. The P-type Balancing Diet and Purification Diet have brought about a state of balance in your metabolism; the P-type Health and Weight Maintenance Program is designed to make it easy for you to *maintain* that balance, to keep your ideal weight, and to move toward perfect health.

1. YOUR PLENTY FOODS:	Beef, lamb, and pork (without visible fat) Organ meats (liver, kidneys, heart) Fresh vegetables Poultry Fish Fenugreek tea
2. YOUR MODERATION FOODS:	Fruits Whole grains Skim milk Vegetable oils Eggs Decaffeinated coffee and tea
3. YOUR RARELY FOODS:	Yogurt Ice cream

Sour cream
Cheese
Butter
Desserts
Coffee, tea

4. YOUR
IDEAL EATING SCHEDULE:

A substantial, protein-rich
breakfast

A moderate lunch, with
salad and some protein

A light dinner

Avoid late-night eating

THE PITUITARY TYPE HEALTH AND WEIGHT MAINTENANCE EATING PROGRAM

BREAKFAST

2 eggs, any style, OR a small minute steak, broiled, OR a slice of liver, kidneys, or heart, broiled

1 slice of whole-grain bread

Decaffeinated coffee, tea, or fenugreek tea

LUNCH

A large green salad with plenty of your favorite vegetables, and dressing used in moderation

2 slices of whole-grain bread, or an equivalent serving of other whole grains

A serving of fish, poultry, or meat. You may substitute yogurt or cottage cheese *occasionally* (about every 2 weeks) if you feel good and are not overweight

1 piece of fruit

Decaffeinated coffee, tea, or fenugreek tea

DINNER

A serving of fish, poultry, or meat. Plan to eat meat 2–4 times a week, fish or poultry on the remaining nights

Vegetables, cooked or raw, as much as you like

4 ounces of skim milk

1 piece of fruit or a small dessert

Fenugreek tea

9

BODY TYPE NUTRITIONAL SUPPLEMENTS

Judith P. sat across from me in my office looking like who she was—a T-type with a problem. When I had last seen her, several months before, she had wanted to lose just five pounds. I put her on the Thyroid Type Balancing Diet, and she had lost the pounds easily. They'd been gone about a month, but Judith still wasn't happy.

"It's my energy level," she complained. "It's a lot better than it was before the diet. I can jump out of bed in the morning feeling pretty good now—that's progress for me. But I can't keep going. By the time I've made breakfast for my three kids, gotten them off to school, done a wash, organized the slow cooker for dinner, found my husband's clean socks, battled traffic to the office, and straightened out the five or six emergencies that have blown up in my advertising business overnight, I'm exhausted. And it's still only nine-thirty in the morning!"

She looked so desperate it was almost funny—except, of course, that it isn't funny at all. It's the plain, grinding truth of modern life. Like Judith, most of us are living our lives at such an incredible pace, subjecting ourselves to so much pressure and making so many demands on ourselves, that it's surprising we have any energy left at all.

I told Judith that the T-type Lifetime Nutrition Program

would give her everything a diet could possibly give, but she had to realize that she probably needed more nutritional support than *any* modern diet could provide. After all, she was doing two full-time jobs, both of them difficult and demanding. Her next scheduled vacation was in 1992. She was demanding a lot from her body, and she needed to make sure it had *everything* it needed to perform at capacity. What she needed was additional help from nutritional supplements.

There was a time not so long ago when taking supplements—pills or powders providing extra vitamins and minerals, or exotica like extra amino acids and metabolic precursors—was still quite unusual. The average person *might* take a one-a-day vitamin pill from the supermarket, or might not—most people didn't. Those who took a fancier vitamin from the health-food store were considered slightly fanatical; those who actually organized a handful of tablets and capsules for themselves—maybe a multi-vitamin, a mineral supplement, and some extra A, C, and E—were looked on as out-and-out health nuts. The lineup of vitamin bottles along the sink was a sort of modern "organic" joke. Remember those days?

VITAMINS TODAY: NOT WHETHER, BUT HOW MUCH

This is no longer the way it is. Nutritional supplements are big today—big business, big news, and for many people, a big question. You as a consumer are bombarded with ads on TV and in print telling you to buy this pill becase it "has zinc," or that one because, as a woman, you "need iron." Bestsellers tell you what each vitamin "does," what illnesses it "cures," and what quantities you "need."

There are some advisers who want you to take truly astronomical amounts of everything, including vitamins you've never heard of and substances you thought were just put in the cereal to keep it from getting old. Health-food stores are stocked from floor to ceiling (whatever happened to the health *food* they used to sell?), and almost all of us today are either taking something or wondering if we should.

How do you decide? On the spectrum from "I don't need pills, I eat right" to "My body needs all the help it can get," how do you know where the truth is located? The medical profession ought to be helpful, but it really isn't. Most physicians are, themselves, unclear on what to advise. We were taught in medical school that vitamins were mainly for pregnant women, so the only vitamin supplement many doctors feel comfortable with is the prenatal one. Yet many doctors also sense uneasily that their patients have legitimate questions. They just don't know what answers to give.

The official position is still to say that we need vitamins only in the quantities specified in the RDA (Recommended Daily Allowances)—a collection of "minimum daily requirements" put together by the government in the dim and distant past. A number of substances now considered vital, such as the mineral selenium, have no recommended amount, and for those that do the quantities recommended are extremely low. This does have the advantage of making it appear easy to satisfy the requirements with food alone. Officially, and especially in print, physicians still subscribe to the RDA standards. In private, many doctors will agree that the RDA are in need of scrupulous scientific reevaluation, and that the medical profession should be providing much better guidelines than we are today.

THE BODY TYPE SUPPLEMENT GUIDELINES

However, this doesn't help you much now. You can't wait until the scientific machine moves, in its ponderous way, to evaluate the body's precise needs. You probably suspect, and rightly, that needs vary from person to person. So you need some guidelines that you can use, starting now, that will make sense for you personally. Let's face it, there's a lot at stake here.

The Body Type Supplement Program provides you with these guidelines. But please be aware of the fact that there is still quite a bit of controversy in this field, even among true experts. As our knowledge improves, so will our recommendations. Also keep in mind that many claims made for nutritional substances in the popular press are scientifically unfounded. The Body Type Nutritional Guidelines will give you only what makes sense as of today.

When I gave Judith P. the list of supplements I recommended for her as a T-type, she asked me how I had arrived at the recommendations—since I'd already explained to her that the RDA were woefully out-of-date, and that a consensus didn't exist about what, and how much, was really needed. I told her that the recommendations I was giving her, and that I will give you, were based largely on my experience with tens of thousands of individuals in an innovative material weight-control program called Skinny School.

THE INNOVATION OF SKINNY SCHOOL

In 1980 I became a consultant for the Skinny School Medical Clinics, a large group of weight-control centers and franchises in Southern California. Skinny School was founded by an old friend and physician, Murry Buxbaum, M.D. Dr. Buxbaum had a bold, innovative concept of controlling weight exclusively through the use of nutritional supplements (he also thought up the name Skinny School, so don't blame me!). Dr. Buxbaum did a great deal of work developing his concept that weight control could be achieved *without dieting,* by controlling cravings through specific supplements. His genius shows in the fact that the Skinny School program does work.

I became more closely associated with Skinny School when Dr. Buxbaum left to pursue other interests, and I was impressed with the research and thought that had gone into his program. According to Buxbaum, specific cravings—for example, the craving for sweets—came from the effects of specific nutritional deficiencies on the brain. The sweets craving was related to deficiencies in magnesium, chromium, and zinc, or all three. Similarly, the cravings for starches, alcohol, or oils came from other deficiencies of vitamins, minerals, or amino acids. The idea was that once you'd taken care of your brain and body by taking extra quantities of the missing nutrient, you simply wouldn't *want* to eat the foods you used to crave. When you'd corrected your brain metabolism, the desire, which was created by the deficiency, would simply go away—and you'd lose weight without having to diet.

I was immediately interested in this work because of my own long-standing interest in the subject of cravings. I saw that while Buxbaum ascribed cravings to nutritional deficiencies, I related them to body type—but I wondered how far apart the two concepts really were. Buxbaum dealt with the sweet craving, for instance, but I knew from my own work that where there was a sweets craving, I could be pretty sure that I was dealing with a thyroid type. So it works out in practice that the supplements that work to break the craving for sweets are usually the very ones that are most helpful for T-types.

There is one problem with the Skinny School concept, at least as Dr. Buxbaum developed it. Using only supplements simply isn't the most efficient way to balance the metabolism and bring cravings under control. The Body Type Nutrition Program—eating right for your body type—has to be part of it. You *can* lose weight with the really intelligent use of supplements—Dr. Buxbaum's and my thousands of Skinny School students who lose literally tons of fat every month prove that. The success of the Skinny School program shows how much help you can get from improvement in your body chemistry through supplementation. But to get the maximum benefit, the supplements should be *supplementary* to a nutritional program that's right for you and your body type.

As for losing weight without dieting, again, Dr. Buxbaum was both right and wrong. To lose weight, you *do* have to eat less. You can't eat whatever you want and still stay at your right weight until *after* you've brought your cravings under control. But to control cravings fully you still have to rest your dominant gland and strengthen your less-active glands with the right diet. Only then can you eat purely for enjoyment and fulfillment.

THE BODY TYPES AND NUTRITIONAL SUPPLEMENTS

Skinny School and the Body Type concept have now joined together for your benefit. The supplementation program—originated by Dr. Buxbaum and refined by myself and the excellent nutritionists at the Skinny School—is now an integral part of the Body Type Health Program.

In *Dr. Abravanel's Body Type Diet and Lifetime Nutrition Plan*, I gave the impression that supplements weren't strictly necessary. Based on the successes chalked up by Skinny School, and on the demands created by the intensity of modern life, I now know that they are. (As Abraham Lincoln once said, when reminded that he had changed his mind completely about some issue, "Yes, I have, and I thank God that I am wiser today than I was yesterday.")

At Skinny School, the nutritionists now use the Body Type Diets and the Body Type Supplement Guidelines. We've combined the best of both worlds, and now you can get the combined experience of both with the Body Type Supplement Program.

Being associated with Skinny School has been tremendously valuable for what I've learned about supplements. At Skinny School we see a large number of students—thousands each week—who all take vitamins and minerals, along with other selected nutrients. We always use the best, purest, strongest, and most complete products we can find anywhere and keep careful records of our students' progress. What we have gathered as a result is probably one of the largest bodies of practical knowledge currently available about nutritional supplements and the specific needs of different types of people.

As you'll see, the Body Type Supplement Program falls somewhere between the extravagant (where you take so much of every nutrient, you have to buy vitamin powders in bulk) and the very conservative (the RDA). I am convinced that supplements are extremely valuable, but know that you don't have to spend a hundred dollars a week to get the benefits. The Body Type Supplement Program recommends the adroit, personalized use of supplements to satisfy your needs safely, effectively, and realistically.

WHAT NUTRITIONAL SUPPLEMENTS ARE REALLY FOR

My recommendations to patients like Judith, who are living lives of noisy desperation, consist of a list of nutrients with the ideal quantities of each. The total package works together and does many things at once—which means that you can't think about the supplement program in bits and pieces. It's not the case that, for instance, the B vitamins are for the thyroid and vitamin A is for the adrenals. All the parts of the program work interdependently, and the quantities of each are designed to work together to give you the best results.

What you'll notice after a week or two of taking the supplements is that your energy will be better. You should feel more resistant to stress. You'll be better able to keep going if you have a long, demanding day (or even if you don't!). Your cravings, if you still have trouble with them at fatigue or stress times, will definitely be much reduced.

After several months on the program you should be experiencing significant health benefits. Many Skinny School students have reported that they have fewer small illnesses—colds, sore throats, flu—and you may find this as well. This is a sign that the supplements are helping to balance your metabolism, and are working with your Body Type Health Program to optimize your functioning in all parts of your body.

What about long-range benefits—reduction in major illnesses, less aging, longer life? With the lack of long-range studies I've already warned you that it's unscientific to make claims. Yet the effects of these nutrients on the factors that accelerate aging—cross-linkage and superoxidation—are known, and it's reasonable to assume that if they improve health in the present, longevity will be part of the effect. (For a complete discussion of the theories of aging, see Chapter 14.)

To me taking nutritional supplements is certainly a worthwhile investment. There is no danger that we know of, and you're taking the better course: giving yourself *every opportunity* to feel better and live longer.

It's the choice I've made—I take the entire T-type supplements program and feel better than I ever have. And my patients love it. Three months after our first conversation about supplements, Judith told me, "It's working. I'm making it all the way through the morning without collapsing—I don't even feel the need for a cup of coffee at eleven anymore. I haven't had a cold since we talked, and there haven't been any of those awful days when I truly understand why some people abandon their children. One more step to Superwoman!"

THE TRACE MINERALS

One area where my work at Skinny School has impressed me is the importance of trace minerals in controlling cravings and in balancing the metabolism. Interestingly enough, most of the trace minerals do not even have RDA established, yet the experience with thousands of patients has made it clear to me that including these minerals in a supplementation program is extremely helpful in any health or weight program. I strongly recommend that your vitamin and mineral supplements contain all these minerals, in the amounts given under your body type.

The minerals are not very popular, somehow; everyone knows about B vitamins, but who ever talks about molybdenum or vanadium? For your information, here's a quick rundown on the important trace minerals and what they do for you.

Selenium is a trace mineral found to have important protective properties against various cancers and against aging through its antioxidant and antimutation effects.

Chromium is a critical constituent of GTF (glucose tolerance factor), an important chemical for helping your cells respond to the carbohydrates you eat. It also helps the body's insulin do its work.

Magnesium is an important mineral in nerve and brain function. Magnesium deficiency is often related to sweets cravings. It works with chromium.

Manganese is an essential mineral for normal carbohydrate, sex, and adrenal hormone metabolism. Deficiency in manganese can cause sexual dysfunction, as well as produce a craving for starches.

Vanadium is a trace mineral involved in the stabilization of all blood fats (cholesterol and triglycerides), reproduction, and the chemical balance of bones and teeth.

Silicon is a mineral which gives structural stability to connective tissue and helps the body deposit calcium in bones.

Molybdenum is a trace mineral important in preventing kidney stones and dental caries.

Zinc, finally, is a very important mineral in healing, reproduction, blood flow, and helping the body's insulin respond properly to carbohydrates.

HOW TO TAKE YOUR BODY TYPE SUPPLEMENTS

To put together the supplements I've recommended, you're going to have to do some careful label reading. *Not all vitamin and mineral pills are alike.* Though many of the vitamins and minerals for each body type can be obtained in a really good multivitamin combination, with an extra B vitamin pill and an additional mineral supplement, you must get a first-rate vitamin made by a responsible laboratory, or you will not get some of the supplements you need. The "special extras" for each type, plus the extra minerals for the thyroid and pituitary types, are in addition to this basic material.

The trace minerals discussed above are very important, and most grocery-store vitamin pills or even most health-food-store pills just don't have them. For a quick check, look first on the label for molybdenum, vanadium, or silicon. If the pill you're looking at has these, keep reading—there's hope. If not, just put it back on the shelf and keep looking.

Putting together the supplements takes a certain amount of effort, but you'll find that it's worth it. Once you have your sources of supply organized, you can often get discounts by buying two bottles at a time; ask about it.

Except when I say that you need to take something twice a day, you can take all the pills together at any convenient time. Some people find that taking so many vitamins together on an empty stomach can actually upset the stomach, and if you have this problem, simply take your pills right after a meal.

You can use Skinny School as your source for the Body Type Supplements if you wish, for the convenience of receiving your complete program through the mail and all put together for you. The G-type, A-type, T-type, and P-type supplement packets that we use with our patients are available through mail order. Also, the special extras—Brain

Food, Go-55, Prolon and Lipocal, the Body Type Chinese Herbal Formulas—are available through Skinny School. To receive information, write to Skinny School, 6511 Van Nuys Blvd., Van Nuys, California 91401, or call (818) 994–2701.

THE GONADAL TYPE SUPPLEMENT PROGRAM

This supplement program is designed to work with the G-type diet and exercise plans to offset your potential weaknesses and increase your strengths. Interestingly, when it comes to supplements you need a *combination* of the A-type and T-type programs because of the difference between your upper and lower body. Above the waist, your slenderness gives you the needs of a thyroid type—you require stabilization and strength. Below the waist, you have the A-type problems of congestion and lack of flexibility. Your supplement program, therefore, works to give you the benefits necessary for your entire body, both upper and lower.

I have given you the two sets of supplements that, in the other types, increase the effectiveness of exercise. The growth hormone releasers—L-arginine and L-ornithine—will increase the effectiveness of upper-body exercise in building up your strength. Caffeine—which can be either a cup of tea or coffee just before exercising, or the preparation called Go-55, which provides natural caffeine—increases the effectiveness of aerobic exercise in terms of cardiovascular conditioning.

In the area of aging, you are prone to superoxidation above the waist, like T-types, for which I have given you extra vitamin C, vitamin B_{12}, vitamin A, vitamin E, zinc, L-cysteine, and superoxide dismutase (SOD). Below the waist, you are more liable to cross-linking, like A-types, and for this, vitamin B_1 and the mineral selenium are effective, as are the extra A and E (see Chapter 14 for a complete discussion of these aging effects).

Calcium is of concern to many women in avoiding osteoporosis, or brittle bones. I have given you 500 mg., but if you are postmenopausal, I recommend you increase your supplementary calcium to 1000 mg.

Prolon and Lipocal are special formulations I've developed for Skinny School. They are an extremely effective combination for the mobilization and burning of fat. In your case they are balancing for your upper-body–lower-body disproportion. The combination of the amino acid L-glutamine with the B vitamins choline and inositol produces nourishment for your brain.

The G-type Chinese Herbal Formula is a formula derived from Chinese medicine that I have found to be helpful in stabilizing the balancing effects of the supplement program.

Ovarian substance is useful to give a mild nourishment and stimulation to the ovaries, and to "tweak" their hormone production in a gentle and helpful way.

SUPPLEMENTS FOR GONADAL TYPES

NUTRIENT	AMOUNT	RDA*
Vitamin A	15,000 I.U.	5000 I.U.
Vitamin B$_1$ (Thiamine)	75 mg.	1.5 mg.
Vitamin B$_2$ (Riboflavin)	100 mg.	1.7 mg.
Vitamin B$_3$ (Nicotinic acid)	200 mg.	20 mg.
Vitamin B$_5$ (Pantothenic acid)	75 mg.	10 mg.
Vitamin B$_6$ (Pyridoxine)	250 mg.	2 mg.
Vitamin B$_{12}$	250 mcg.	3 mcg.
Beta carotene	50 mg.	***
Vitamin C	5000 mg.	60 mg.
Vitamin D	400 I.U.	400 I.U.

Vitamin E	1000 I.U.	30 I.U.
Vitamin K	70 mcg.	100 mcg.†
Folic acid	800 mcg.	400 mcg.
Choline	500 mg.	***
Inositol	500 mg.	***
Rutin	10 mg.	***
Hesperidin	10 mg.	***
PABA	8 mg.	***

MINERAL

Calcium	500 mg.	1200 mg.†
Chromium	1 mg.	**
Copper	2.5 mg.	2 mg.
Iodine	150 mcg.	150 mcg.
Iron	24.5 mg. two times daily	18 mg.
Magnesium	300 mg.	400 mg.†
Manganese	11 mg.	**
Molybdenum	150 mcg.	**
Phosphorus	152 mg.	1200 mg.†
Potassium	57 mg.	**
Selenium	75 mcg.	**
Silicon	4.8 mg.	**
Vanadium	50 mcg.	**
Zinc	100 mg.	15 mg.

AMINO ACID

L-Arginine	250 mg.	***
L-Cysteine	1500 mg.	***
L-Glutamine	500 mg.	***
L-Ornithine	100 mg.	***
L-Tryptophan	500 mg. at bedtime	***

SPECIAL EXTRAS

Prolon	1 tablet daily	***
Lipocal	1 tablet daily	***
Caffeine—1 cup of coffee or 200 mg.—just before your exercise		
Superoxide dismutase	2000 mcg.	***

Ovarian substance   Chew 2 tablets daily   ***
G-type Chinese Herbal Formula   ***

*   RDA means the "Recommended Daily Allowances."
**   The need for this nutrient has been established, but there is no
     RDA.
***The need for this nutrient has not been established.
†   Your food supplies most of these.

THE ADRENAL TYPE SUPPLEMENT PROGRAM

Your supplements work with your A-type diet and exercise plans to reduce your tendency to congestion and stiffness. By stiffness, of course, I don't just mean not being able to touch your toes: I mean internal lockup as well—hardening of the arteries, stiffness in the joints, wrinkling, hard fat, coarsening of the skin. None of these are inevitable, but you do have the tendency—so you must be prepared to offset it with every aspect of your health and longevity program.

I've given you extra vitamin E and vitamin B_3, both of which increase blood flow and reduce cholesterol. Extra B_6 acts as a diuretic, B_{12} is for nervous and mental fatigue. Extra quantities of vitamin E, vitamin C, vitamin A and Thiamine (vitamin B_1) also increase internal flexibility by decreasing cross-linkage (see Chapter 14 for an explanation of cross-linkage and aging).

The amino acid L-glutamine and the B vitamins choline and inositol feed your brain, increasing mental alertness and flexibility. They are available together in Brain Food.

Calcium is of concern to women in avoiding osteoporosis, or brittle bones. I have given you 500 mg., but if you are postmenopausal, I recommend you increase your supplementary calcium to 1000 mg.

The use of supplementary glandular substances—in your case adrenal substance—can be very helpful in supporting your dominant gland. The substance gently "tweaks" the gland and rounds out the effects of the other supplements.

The A-type Chinese Herbal Formula is a formula derived from Chinese medicine that I have found to be helpful in stabilizing the balancing effects of the supplement program.

Finally, caffeine—which can mean a cup of tea or coffee, or a Skinny School preparation called Go-55 ("fast enough, and safe")—taken before exercise enables you to obtain better cardiovascular conditioning and muscle tone than exercise alone.

SUPPLEMENTS FOR ADRENAL TYPES

NUTRIENT	AMOUNT	RDA*
Vitamin A	20,000 I.U.	5000 I.U.
Vitamin B$_1$ (Thiamine)	100 mg.	1.5 mg.
Vitamin B$_2$ (Riboflavin)	75 mg.	1.7 mg.
Vitamin B$_3$ (Nicotinic acid)	300 mg.	20 mg.
Vitamin B$_5$ (Pantothenic acid)	75 mg.	10 mg.
Vitamin B$_6$ (Pyridoxine)	300 mg.	2 mg.
Vitamin B$_{12}$	250 mcg.	3 mcg.
Beta carotene	50 mg.	***
Vitamin C	3000 mg. (7000 mg. if you smoke)	60 mg.
Vitamin D	400 I.U.	400 I.U.
Vitamin E	1600 I.U.	30 I.U.
Vitamin K	70 mcg.	100 mcg.†
Folic acid	800 mcg.	400 mcg.
Choline	500 mg.	***
Inositol	500 mg.	***
Rutin	10 mg.	***

| Hesperidin | 10 mg. | *** |
| PABA | 8 mg. | *** |

MINERAL

Calcium	500 mg.	1200 mg.†
Chromium	1 mg.	**
Copper	2.5 mg.	2 mg.
Iodine	150 mcg.	150 mcg.
Iron	24.5 mg.	18 mg.
Magnesium	300 mg.	400 mg.†
Manganese	11 mg.	**
Molybdenum	150 mcg.	**
Phosphorus	152 mg.	1200 mg.†
Potassium	57 mg.	**
Selenium	75 mcg. (250 mg. if you smoke)	**
Silicon	4.8 mg.	**
Vanadium	50 mcg.	**
Zinc	75 mg.	15 mg.

AMINO ACID

L-Cysteine	1000 mg.	***
L-Glutamine	500 mg.	***
L-Tryptophan	500 mg. at bedtime	***

SPECIAL EXTRAS

| Superoxide dismutase | 3000 mcg. | *** |

Caffeine—one cup of coffee or 200 mg.—just before your exercise

Go-55 (a special herbal tonic available
from Skinny School)   ***
Adrenal substance   Chew 2 tablets daily   ***
A-type Chinese Herbal Formula   ***

---

*   RDA means the "Recommended Daily Allowances."
** The need for this nutrient has been established, but there is no RDA.
***The need for this nutrient has not been established.
†   Your food supplies most of these.

THE THYROID-TYPE SUPPLEMENT PROGRAM

The T-type supplement program works with the Nutrition and Exercise Programs against your greatest weakness: your energy swings. Physical steadiness and the freedom from mental and emotional swings that goes with it are the main objects here.

The supplements I've selected to stabilize your energy concentrate first on the brain. Choline, inositol, and L-glutamine (combined in Brain Food) give you, literally, very usable food for your brain. Your system, you see, will protect the brain—its most important organ—by giving it what it needs first of all. This means that your body may be fatigued because the brain is getting all the available nutrients. If you feed your brain itself, brain and body both will benefit.

Another amino acid, L-tryptophan, works to help your system recover from vitamin and mineral depletion. It is also calming, which is an effect T-types can definitely use! The extra calcium is calming as well.

Speaking of depletion, T-types are very likely to become deficient in the water-soluble B vitamins. You have efficient kidneys and excrete the water-soluble vitamins rapidly. The caffeine you've drunk (in the past, hopefully) also contributes to this effect. B vitamins are crucial if your body is to make use of any of the vitamins you take—I've given you extra of all of them for this reason.

You also take extra quantities of the minerals magnesium, manganese, chromium, and zinc. These are extremely important for you in two ways. First, they stabilize by reducing irritability; then, they act on your sweet and starch cravings. This mineral combination is amazingly effective in the reduction of cravings.

Calcium is of concern to women in avoiding osteoporosis, or brittle bones. I have given you 500 mg., but if you are postmenopausal, I recommend you increase your supplementary calcium to 1000 mg.

Your program is also designed to reduce the tremendous stress and wear-and-tear that comes from the energy swings of your metabolism. Cross-linkage and superoxidation are the results, but supplementation can reduce this damage (see Chapter 14 for a fuller explanation). Stabilizing your energy helps reduce both, and additional supplements are also helpful: the extra vitamin C, vitamin B_{12}, vitamin A, and vitamin E, the extra zinc, the amino acid cysteine, and the superoxide dismutase.

The use of thyroid glandular extract, or thyroid substance, is helpful for supporting your thyroid. It "tweaks" the gland in a mild way and rounds out the effect of the other supplements. Note that it is not the same as thyroid hormone, about which you should consult your physician.

The T-type Chinese Herbal Formula is a formula derived from Chinese medicine that I have found to be helpful in stabilizing the balancing effects of the supplement program.

Finally, I've used supplementation to improve body strength, which is also highly stabilizing for you. The L-arginine and L-ornithine are growth hormone releasers. Taken in conjunction with the T-type Exercise Program, you'll notice an amazing increase in body strength in a very short time.

SUPPLEMENTS FOR THYROID TYPES

NUTRIENT	AMOUNT	RDA*
Vitamin A	15,000 I.U.	5000 I.U.
Vitamin B_1 (Thiamine)	50 mg.	1.5 mg.
Vitamin B_2 (Riboflavin)	100 mg.	1.7 mg.
Vitamin B_3 (Nicotinic acid)	125 mg.	20 mg.
Vitamin B_5 (Pantothenic acid)	75 mg.	10 mg.

Vitamin B$_6$ (Pyridoxine)	150 mg.	2 mg.
Vitamin B$_{12}$	500 mcg.	3 mcg.
Beta carotene	25 mg.	***
Vitamin C	5000 mg.	60 mg.
Vitamin D	400 I.U.	400 I.U.
Vitamin E	800 I.U.	30 I.U.
Vitamin K	70 mcg.	100 mcg.†
Folic acid	600 mcg.	400 mcg.
Choline	1000 mg.	***
Inositol	1000 mg.	***
Rutin	10 mg.	***
Hesperidin	10 mg.	***
PABA	8 mg.	***

MINERAL

Calcium	500 mg.	1200 mg.†
Chromium	1 mg. three times daily	**
Copper	2.5 mg.	2 mg.
Iodine	150 mcg.	150 mcg.
Iron	24.5 mg.	18 mg.
Magnesium	300 mg. two or three times daily	400 mg.†
Manganese	15 mg. two or three times daily	**
Molybdenum	150 mcg.	**
Phosphorus	152 mg.	1200 mg.
Potassium	57 mg.	**
Selenium	75 mcg.	**
Silicon	4.8 mg.	**
Vanadium	50 mcg.	**
Zinc	150 mg.	15 mg.

AMINO ACID

L-Arginine	500 mg.	***
L-Cysteine	1500 mg.	***
L-Glutamine	1000 mg.	***
L-Ornithine	250 mg.	***
L-Tryptophan	1000 mg. at bedtime	***

SPECIAL EXTRAS

Superoxide dismutase	1000 mcg.	***
Brain Food	1 tablet daily	***
T-type Chinese Herbal Formula		
Thyroid substance	Chew two tablets daily	***

* RDA means "Recommended Daily Dietary Allowances."
** The need for this in human nutrition has been established, but there is no RDA.
***The need for this in human nutrition has not been established.
† Your food supplies most of these.

THE PITUITARY-TYPE SUPPLEMENT PROGRAM

Every aspect of the P-Type Perfect Health Program is designed to stimulate your lower body—to nourish your adrenals and sex glands and to increase your sense of integration with everything below the neck (where you instinctively feel that life stops). Your supplements work to help this process along. I have used vitamins, extra minerals, amino acids, and glandular extracts to improve the relationship of the brain and the pituitary gland to the rest of the body. You'll find some remarkable changes in about four weeks—improved body tone, muscle size, and strength—especially if you are also doing the P-type Exercise Program.

The amino acids L-arginine and L-ornithine are called "growth hormone releasers." They work by directly stimulating the pituitary gland to release body-stimulating hormones—thus putting your dominant gland in a more direct relationship with your body. The doses I recommend are basically just enough to "tickle" the pituitary back to functioning in a balanced way. Using these amino acids helps the two parts of the pituitary—anterior and posterior—work together.

One patient of mine questioned why, if he's a P-type and his pituitary gland is overstimulated, he should take something that stimulates it even more. The answer is that in fact P-types tend to overstimulate only half of the pituitary gland, the posterior, which is related to brain and higher functions. The other half of the gland, the anterior, which controls the body's development, tends to be understimulated.

Balancing the metabolism also means reducing cravings. The supplement program helps out in a couple of ways. First, extra quantities of the minerals magnesium, manganese, zinc, and chromium reduce sweets cravings (many P-types do in fact crave sweets as well as dairy foods, or more commonly sweet dairy foods like ice cream). It works by affecting the brain, the pancreas, and the organs connected with sweets craving and sugar metabolism.

I've given you extra Vitamin C—100–200 times the RDA. I've found you really need it to increase your energy and reduce stress. C also reduces membrane weakness, the specific weakness in your body that inclines you so often toward allergies.

Calcium is of concern to women in avoiding osteoporosis, or brittle bones. Because you need largely to avoid dairy products, I have given you 1000 mg. daily.

Two special formulas work together to reduce your craving for dairy products. Prolon is a milk derivative that will give you the satiety effect of milk without its prolonged stimulation to the pituitary. With Prolon, you'll definitely crave milk less. Lipocal, which is always taken with Prolon, is a vitamin and amino acid combination that nourishes the brain and reduces your craving for pituitary stimulants. Lipocal also mobilizes fat and increases the amount of energy used by your muscles.

The P-type Chinese Herbal Formula is a formula derived from Chinese medicine that I have found to be helpful in stabilizing the balancing effects of the supplement program.

Finally, the use of the glandular substances—adrenal and pituitary—is useful for "tweaking" the gland in question in a mild way that tends to round out the effect of the other supplements.

SUPPLEMENTS FOR PITUITARY TYPES

NUTRIENT	AMOUNT	RDA*
Vitamin A	15,000 I.U.	5000 I.U.
Vitamin B₁ (Thiamine)	50 mg.	1.5 mg.
Vitamin B₂ (Riboflavin)	100 mg.	1.7 mg.
Vitamin B₃ (Nicotinic acid)	100 mg.	20 mg.
Vitamin B₅ (Pantothenic acid)	100 mg.	10 mg.
Vitamin B₆ (Pyridoxine)	100 mg.	2 mg.
Vitamin B₁₂	500 mcg.	3 mcg.
Beta carotene	25 mg.	***
Vitamin C	6000–10,000 mg.	60 mg.
Vitamin D	800 I.U.	400 I.U.
Vitamin E	800 I.U.	30 I.U.
Vitamin K	70 mcg.	100 mcg.†
Folic acid	600 mcg.	400 mcg.
Choline	1000 mg.	***
Inositol	1000 mg.	***
Rutin	10 mg.	***
Hesperidin	10 mg.	***
PABA	8 mg.	***

MINERAL		
Calcium	1000 mg.	1200 mg.†
Chromium	1 mg. two times daily	**
Copper	2.5 mg.	2 mg.
Iodine	150 mcg.	150 mcg.
Iron	24.5 mg.	18 mg.
Magnesium	300 mg. two times daily	400 mg.†
Manganese	15 mg. two times daily	**
Molybdenum	150 mcg.	**

Phosphorus	152 mg.	1200 mg.
Potassium	57 mg.	**
Selenium	75 mcg.	**
Silicon	4.8 mg.	**
Vanadium	50 mcg.	**
Zinc	100 mg.	15 mg.

AMINO ACID

L-Arginine	500 mg.	***
L-Cysteine	2000 mg.	***
L-Glutamine	1000 mg.	***
L-Ornithine	250 mg.	***
L-Tryptophan	1000 mg. at bedtime	***

SPECIAL EXTRAS

Prolon	1 tablet daily	***
Lipocal	1 tablet daily	***
P-type Chinese Herbal Formula		
Adrenal substance	Chew 2 tablets daily	***
Anterior pituitary substance	Chew 2 tablets daily	***
Superoxide dismutase	1000 mcg.	***

* RDA means the "Recommended Daily Allowances."
** The need for this nutrient has been established, but there is no RDA.
***The need for this nutrient has not been established.
† Your food supplies most of these.

10

THE BODY TYPE EXERCISE PROGRAM

You're now on your way to a fully balanced and integrated metabolic system and to full implementation of the Body Type Health Program. You've started eating right for your body type, and you're on your way to organizing what you need for nutritional supplementation. But what about exercise? If you're like most of my patients, either you're exercising now, or thinking you should be—but you're not as unquestioningly enthusiastic about the whole thing as you once were. You have some questions about the value of exercise and maybe some small injuries or nagging discomforts that you relate to the exercise you do. You're ready to examine whether what you're doing is really right for you.

It's been some time now since the exercise craze first swept the country. Today, people everywhere are exercising, but sometimes *they* seem crazed: they've bought the idea that exercise is a fountain of youth and vitality, but they face a reality of injury and exhaustion.

"I exercise five times a week!" my patients tell me. "Why am I still getting sick? Why don't I feel the way the books said I would? Doctor, I can run six miles and bench press two hundred fifty pounds. Why do I still have cellulite on my behind, and heavy arms?"

The truth is that exercise is one more panacea that is ripe for reexamination. Washed up on the beach by a tidal wave of new information are cute sneakers, baggy clothes with designer patches, and a fortune in leotards. The people you know who are still exercising compulsively are caught in a trap, driving around desperately looking for a road sign, instead of stopping and looking at the map.

If you still want to believe that exercise is an unmixed blessing, consider the fact that Sports Medicine has become a major growth industry. The very term should tell you there's something not quite right. "Sports" implies vibrant, youthful health; "medicine" deals with sickness and injury. Are we talking about Ponce de Leon with shin splints? What are the words sports and medicine even *doing* together?

In fact, the contradictions implied in the term are very real. Exercise *is* potentially both valuable and injurious; it *can* lead to either vitality or exhaustion. It has both good and bad effects, and the secret of an effective exercise program is to balance the gains against the cost. That's why in this chapter I want you to take a good hard look at what you want your exercise to do. You can't automatically conclude that just because you're exercising, you're going to be getting the good effects. Unless you have a clear idea of what you're doing, you may well be getting the bad effects.

EXERCISE AND YOUR BODY TYPE

Exercise is intense activity. Because of its intensity, its effect is never neutral—if it's not extra positive for you, it's extra negative. If you choose the right exercise, you can produce genuine and profound improvements in your total metabolic system. But to avoid the downside, you need an entirely new understanding of what exercise does and a clear conception of the effects of various types of exercise on *your particular body type*.

Exercise, like diet, has to be considered in the context of the needs of the exerciser. You now know that you can't figure out the best diet for yourself without considering your own metabolism. No food is good or bad in itself—it can only be judged by the effects it produces, for good or ill, on your own individual system. Exercise must be judged in exactly the same way.

Exercise, by its character, stimulates different organs and different parts of the spinal cord. These varying stimulations change the chemical balance of the body. Similarly, the fact that exercise does affect the spinal cord on different levels also affects the character of arousal of the brain. We're all familiar with beta-endorphins and the "runner's high," but that's only one well-advertised aspect of the complex chemical changes that exercise produces. These include the glandular balance, the balance of the sympathetic and parasympathetic nervous systems ("fight or flight" vs. "stay and play"), and the balance of mental functioning. With all these complex variables, it's essential to take into account your body type in deciding which exercise to do.

Far too many people today are pinning all their hopes for perfect health on an exercise program that might be good for someone else, but completely wrong for them. It's vital for them to stop and look at the map—the one that indicates the direction they need to go for perfect health. If an exercise program is moving you in that direction, it's the right one for you. If not, it isn't—no matter what Jane Fonda, Richard Simmons, or anyone else has to say. While we're on the subject, take a look at Jane Fonda's feet. They definitely show the effects of all that exercise—they're worn and knobby. This is just a little of the downside of exercise peeking out from under the chic legwarmers.

The kinds of exercise that will work for you are those that specifically develop the abilities your body needs, and that specifically offset weaknesses that your body type tends to have. Like food, exercise does have very definite effects on the whole system, and this fact throws a completely different light on most of the exercises that are so popular today. Taking the time now to understand which forms of exercise will work for you, and *why,* will pay off by giving you the benefits you really want from exercise, now and for a lifetime.

"THOU SHALT EXERCISE"

"Muscular development of the body does not necessarily mean a healthy body, as is commonly assumed, for health is a state where all organs function perfectly under the intelligent control of the mind." So wrote Swami Vivikananda, an expert on the yoga system of integration of mind and body, and I agree. Certainly muscular development is the least of what an exercise program should provide. A common mistake is to consider exercise only in terms of its superficial effects—like the way your pectoral muscles show off the logo on your shirt—and to ignore what it does to the functioning of the organs, the organ systems, and the body as a whole.

We need to use a better yardstick than just looks in judging the success of an exercise program. But even judging by looks, the wrong exercise program won't give you what you want. On the contrary, most of the heavy exercisers I see in my practice have a strained, out-of-balance look that is a direct result of the wrong kind of exercise for their body type. The thyroid types on the wrong program look stringy and gaunt. The adrenal types tend to be heavy and musclebound. The pituitary types look overintense and fanatical, and the gonadal-type women often look toxic and have exaggeratedly large (though muscled) rear ends. The results of the wrong exercise program, rigidly adhered to, are all too apparent to the practiced eye.

The fact is that left to ourselves, most of us will choose a type of exercise that uses abilities we already have, and neglects to develop the abilities we *need.* Like the wrong diet, the wrong exercise program results in strain, fatigue, and cravings. Doing a form of exercise not suited to your body type will actually increase your cravings for your downfall foods. If you are a T-type and crave sweets after a workout, or a G-type who needs a creamy lunch after exercise class, you're almost certainly doing the wrong exercise and stimulating your nervous system and body chemistry in the wrong way. The wrong program can also produce a craving *for the exercise itself*. If you are, for example, an adrenal type and find that you actually crave a session with your weights, you are doing the wrong kind of exercise. Exercise should not have the features of an addiction.

This, along with the desire to keep wear-and-tear to a minimum, are the main reasons I do not recommend exercising more than four times a week once you are in condition. You must keep in mind the importance of rest and remember that there is an *optimal* amount of exercise for you—more is not necessarily better.

THE MIXED BLESSING OF EXERCISE

Of course, exercise is also a handy excuse to forget your body-type nutrition guidelines and indulge yourself in your downfall foods. A patient of mine once came back from a hiking trip around the High Sierra camps in Yosemite having gained five pounds in ten days. "But I walked ten miles every day!" she said lamely. "If I couldn't eat whatever I wanted then, when can I?" The answer, of course, is that you *never* can, if what you're talking about is allowing yourself to wallow in your cravings. My patient had used the hard hiking as an excuse to return to her old eating habits, and her cravings had multiplied day by day.

The fact is that *any* exercise, even one that's perfect for your body type, is still something of a mixed blessing. By raising your metabolism it does, in fact, increase wear and tear—aging—of your system. In a car, we talk about "wearing in" an engine so that the parts mate more perfectly and, ultimately, function more efficiently. But a body isn't quite like a car, and we can accept wear and tear only up to the point where it results in truly better overall functioning. Besides, in a car we can change the oil and get out the gunk that wear and tear put there. Doing the same thing for the body would also be desirable, but exercise isn't the way. (What does work is the Long Weekend of Rejuvenation—see Chapter 12.)

Very high levels of physical fitness cause a correspondingly high degree of stress on the system. Athletes accept this stress in return for the feelings of accomplishment and the moments of glory, but the price is very high. But since the rewards of athleticism are reaped in youth, and the price usually paid in later life, the connections aren't always clear.

All of which means that today's trendy commandment—"Thou shalt exercise"—must be taken very carefully indeed. The chances are that if you choose an exercise without knowing what it's doing to your body type, you're going to choose one that increases, rather than decreases, your typical imbalance. Considering the aging effect that *any* exercise is going to have, this is simply not a worthwhile trade-off for anyone to make. You're giving up something when you exercise: you must be sure that what you're getting in return is worth the price, or it's no bargain.

IMBALANCE AND EXERCISE: A CASE HISTORY

To give you an idea of what imbalance in exercise means, let me tell you about a young computer designer named Carlos E. Originally from Argentina, Carlos became a patient of mine when he took a job with a prominent computer company in Los Angeles. He's a classic adrenal type: strong, solid-looking, perhaps just a little too red in the face, but by the usual outward signs, a healthy man.

When he came in for his annual physical I found that his cholesterol was too high, and we talked about diet and exercise. I recommended that he cut down on the steaks and other rich, adrenal-stimulating meats that, like many South Americans, he was accustomed to eating, and increase fresh vegetables, fruit, and whole grains. Like most of us, Carlos ate what his mother had taught him to eat, which meant that the trail of his eating habits could probably be traced back through the dark ages and into prehistory. I mean no criticism of anyone's tradition; I'm sure every mother in every culture does her best to feed her kids correctly, but there comes a time when change is truly necessary. At this point, changing to the Adrenal Type Diet was, for Carlos, of vital and urgent importance.

However, he was dubious. He didn't see why he needed to make changes, even with his cholesterol as high as it was—because, he said, "I'm taking care of that problem with exercise." What he had chosen to do was to keep up his muscles by lifting weights six or seven days a week. This, he felt, was giving him the cardiovascular insurance he needed.

I explained to him that this form of exercise—one aimed primarily at building a solid musculature—was the very opposite of what he should be doing for himself. Its overall effect on his system was very similar to that produced by his steak-and-buttery-potatoes diet: it acted to *stimulate his dominant adrenal glands*. I wanted him to change to a diet that would nourish his thyroid and pituitary glands, and I also wanted him to do a kind of exercise that would reduce adrenal stimulation and give a workout to his other glands, so as to create balance in his metabolism through activity.

WHAT CARLOS
NEEDED

The exercise that would provide this effect needed to be one that worked on precise eye-hand coordination and physical flexibility. Squash, handball, or basketball, or a martial art like tai chi, would give flexibility and integration to his system, and push his body strongly toward a more balanced style of functioning.

Carlos just wouldn't see it. "Exercise is exercise, Doctor," he argued. "Sure I could play a little handball, but I *like* lifting weights. Why should I stop?" (I think that he was a bit vain and worried about his wardrobe.) I couldn't persuade him that the weights were acting like a drug on his system, just as the steaks were. However, I didn't worry too much about his skepticism. For someone like Carlos, diet is first in importance and exercise, only second; I assumed I would have time to repeat my advice at his next visit. I didn't. The next week I had a call from the hospital, where Carlos had just been admitted to intensive care with a heart attack. He was thirty-one years old.

In the end, despite this catastrophe, Carlos emerged more or less okay. His attack turned out to be fairly mild, and since it happened when he was young and otherwise robust, his recovery was rapid. He should not have had to endure a heart attack, but at least he was now motivated (to put it mildly!) to get serious about a plan for his own health. I connected with his cardiologist, and we put him on the A-type Exercise Program as soon as we agreed he was ready for it. (I also recommended EDTA chelation therapy, one of the preventive medicine programs I discuss in Chapter 14.)

By the time a year had elapsed, he was in far better shape—in terms of cardiovascular condition *and* overall health—than he had ever been. There is no doubt that his condition was serious, entailing as it did loss of heart tissue that he will never get back. But his motivation is still strong, and his prognosis for the future is excellent.

THE GARDEN PATH: IMBALANCE IN EACH BODY TYPE

Luckily, Carlos's case was unusual. Few people, even strong, A-type men living on steak and stress, are going to experience the catastrophe of a coronary occlusion at so early an age. But Carlos was typical in one respect, at least: his tendency to choose a form of exercise that contributes to imbalance, rather than balance, in his metabolism.

Each body type, in its own characteristic way, does precisely this. "I love horseback riding," says Sarah H., a G-type woman I know. Certainly she does—but it's hard to tell whose haunch is more prominent, Sarah's or her horse's. Sarah's is tight and muscled, but it's entirely out of proportion to her body, and the rest of her reflects the same imbalance as her rear end. But riding makes her feel good, and she misses it intensely when she doesn't spend every weekend on her horse. It works out her body mainly below the waist, giving plenty of blood flow and stimulation to her sex glands. Other G-type women ride bicycles, do intense lower-body calisthenics, or high-kicking jazz dancing.

Sarah's husband Gerald is a pituitary type, and he's into compulsive, long-distance running. Never mind that he's exhausted and fanatical—he's got an elaborate theory on the philosophy of running and doesn't really care what he's doing to his body. For him, as for most P-types, exercise is primarily a *mental* stimulant. What he really needs is to feel more connected to his body and more coordinated, but what he does is put his legs on automatic pilot and go for the "runner's high."

Louanne B. is a thyroid type, and her sport is tennis. Tennis fits in with the way Louanne always does everything: in short, intense bursts of energy that leave her totally wiped out. Every Saturday morning Louanne drinks four cups of coffee, goes out on the courts, and runs around like a mad person for a couple of sets. Then she falls into a chair, where she drinks cokes and talks nonstop until she's ready for her afternoon nap. She can never figure out why her game doesn't seem to improve from one weekend to the next. She needs to realize that she's making her T-type instability worse with exercise that is intermittent and unsustained.

Like Carlos, the weight-lifting adrenal type, each of these people has chosen a form of exercise that fits into his or her typical body-type energy pattern. All of them have chosen what I call the garden path of exercise: the form of exercise that confirms imbalance rather than corrects it. Exercise like this lets you think that you're healthy ("I exercise, don't I?"), but really leaves you as badly off, or worse, than if you did no exercise at all.

What each of these people needs to do is just what we all must do: change from a form of exercise that increases imbalance to one that increases balance. The Body Type Exercise Program is one that gets you off the garden path and onto a new path: the path of invigoration. In the next section I'm going to show you how to analyze any exercise in terms of its effects on your total system. When you put this together with what you know about the needs of your body type, you'll be able to find the path of invigoration that is right for you.

EXERCISE FOR INVIGORATION

I remember clearly the session in which Carlos, my A-type patient, and I worked out his new exercise program. I explained that he could easily analyze any exercise he was considering in the light of his needs as an adrenal type and then decide for himself whether it would work for him.

What Carlos needed to do, and in fact what anyone regardless of body type must do, is to *invigorate* those physical abilities that his or her body lacks and to use exercise to *offset* tendencies toward stress and disease. For Carlos, as an A-type, the needs were for cardiovascular conditioning, increased flexibility, and better eye-hand coordination. Development of muscular strength wasn't necessary, as A-types derive sufficient musculature from their abundance of the many and varied adrenal and sex hormones.

To decide on a program, Carlos needed only to analyze an exercise to see whether or not it would give him these results. As I told him, any exercise produces one or more of these effects: strength, endurance, coordination, and flexibility, but there is often a tradeoff. For example, weight lifting tends to reduce flexibility in exchange for increased strength. Other exercises produce more than one main effect—basketball develops coordination *and* endurance; backpacking, endurance plus strength; jazz dancing, flexibility and coordination, and so on through the list. If you think about it, you will find that there is always a predominant and a secondary effect from any exercise you might want to do.

Using this analysis, Carlos understood why weight lifting wasn't particularly helpful for him and decided that he would do best with a program alternating an easy handball game twice a week for coordination, with swimming three times a week for cardiovascular conditioning. "But what about flexibility?" he asked. He knew that he needed it, but he wasn't sure which exercises were best to develop flexibility.

I told him that flexibility is developed not through vigorous exercise per se, but by gently stretching the body in various ways. The most effective way he could get the flexibility his body needed was through a daily, five-minute routine of yoga-like positions. As a matter of fact, the value of yoga goes beyond flexibility and into the area of profound effects on the internal organs.

Yoga and other ancient and modern systems of health development through body positioning have definite medical effects on many bodily organs. I have selected, from the literature on such postures and their effects, a brief routine for each body type that will provide flexibility and exactly the form of internal invigoration that each needs. I recommend these postures to the patients who come to my office, and I do them myself every day and have for many years. The fact is that you'll be amazed at what a pretzel you'll become in just a short time, and what a soothing and balancing effect the postures have on you when you do them regularly.

Carlos left our session with a complete exercise program for himself: a routine of body-type postures to do each day and a five-day-a-week program of exercise designed around the needs of his body type. (He would cut down to four times a week once he was in condition.) The particular exercises he chose—handball and swimming—were not his only possibilities, and he may in fact change, for variety or convenience, to other exercises at some point. He may decide to jog instead of swim, or play squash instead of handball; but if he makes changes, he will base them on the principles of the Body Type Exercise Program. He is, of course, in regular consultation with his cardiologist. Understanding gave him the ability to make the right choices, and it will do the same for you.

PRINCIPLES OF EXERCISE: WHAT *EACH* BODY TYPE NEEDS

In the following pages, you'll find a description of the principles that apply to each of the four body types. The program for pituitary types is on page 194; for thyroid types, on page 192; for adrenal types, on page 191; and for gonadal types, on page 190. Each type has its own routine of body positions, for flexibility and internal invigoration; each type has a description of the *type* of exercise it needs and a choice of specific exercises that provide these effects. Not every type needs the same quantity of exercise, so you'll also find guidelines on how much time to spend on each of your suggested exercises. The exercises are illustrated on pages 200–209.

I don't even try to teach you each exercise in this book. Handball, running, tai chi—these are the province of other books or of exercise teachers. My purpose here is to give you direction and understanding of the effects of various types of exercise—not to duplicate what is already being done well elsewhere.

Whether you are already exercising or not, it is wise to check with your doctor and get his or her approval for what you want to do. If you are on a program of exercise already, you need only shift your current exercise over to the exercises for your type. In many cases you will find that your Body Type Exercise Program takes *less* time than you are spending now. If you aren't currently doing any exercise, it's important that you start easily and work into your full body-type program. You don't want to overdo, especially at the beginning.

You must start your program by doing no more than ten minutes of your exercise three times a week. After a week at that level, you can work up gradually to your specified times, adding time as you feel comfortable. Don't forget—especially if you're over thirty or have any doubts at all about your ability to exercise—you should definitely check with your physician before beginning the program.

Also, keep in mind that it's just as important to begin gradually with the body positions as it is with the other exercises. The positions seem very simple, but their effect is cumulative and extremely profound. They actually direct the energy of your body, and the effect is felt on your internal organs even more than it is on your outer flexibility and tone.

To begin doing the positions, assume each one only to the extent that is comfortable for you and hold it for no more than ten to fifteen seconds. Each day you will be able to get a bit closer to the ideal, but this will never be accomplished by forcing or strain. Be very careful about this—if you strain, your body will just backlash, and you'll get stiff.

Now you're ready to begin. Good luck and enjoy yourself!

THE GONADAL TYPE EXERCISE PROGRAM

WHAT YOUR BODY NEEDS: Your G-type body requires better coordination between its upper and lower halves. You also need to work on hand-eye coordination and to develop strength in your arms. Another need is to improve circulation, to help move out the toxins that accumulate below the waist in your body type. You have reached your ideal development when you see that your upper body is in proportion with your hips, thighs, and rear (and not by developing fat arms to match!).

EXERCISES THAT WORK: Jogging with "heavy hands," aerobic dancing, and gymnastics are good for providing needed stimulation to the sluggish areas below the waist. For upper-body strength, tai chi, and Nautilus-type workouts concentrating on arms are good. You should jog, dance, or do gymnastics twice a week, and your upper-body workout twice a week.

   You must drink at least two full glasses of water after each exercise session to help eliminate the toxins you'll be releasing from your system. Also, spend a few minutes after each session massaging your legs, thighs, and buttocks working from the feet toward the head, then rest for a moment or two with legs elevated. Again this will help the toxins move on out. For flexibility, do the G-type Positions every day.

EXERCISES THAT DON'T WORK: Horseback riding, bicycling, skating, or repetitive calisthenics that focus mainly on your lower body.

G-TYPE POSITIONS

THE ADRENAL TYPE EXERCISE PROGRAM

WHAT YOUR BODY NEEDS: Your greatest needs are development of eye-hand coordination, cardiovascular conditioning, and improved flexibility. Strength is not a need—you are naturally well provided with muscular strength and do not need to focus on it greatly. You should have no bulging muscles—you need to be a lean machine.

EXERCISES THAT WORK: Handball, squash, tennis, basketball, pingpong—exercises that require quickness and sharp focus—are your best bet. Tai chi, Akido, or other less aggressive martial arts are also possible choices. For cardiovascular conditioning, you need to jog or swim regularly as well. Nordic track is also good. You are quite susceptible to the deleterious consequences of a sedentary life, so you alone of the body types should exercise five, rather than four, times a week and only until you get into condition. Then, when you are conditioned, you should reduce your workouts to four times a week. (Do five times a week for a maximum of eight weeks.) You should alternate a "focusing" workout one day with a jogging or swimming workout the next. For flexibility, do the A-type Positions each day.

EXERCISES THAT DON'T WORK: Avoid rowing—it tends to overstimulate your adrenal glands. No lifting weights— you don't need to, and it overstimulates your system. Avoid Nautilus for the same reason.

A-TYPE POSITIONS

1. Body Toning (page 196)
2. Back Stretch (page 197)
3. Plough Position (page 197)
4. Fish Position (page 197)
5. Cobra Position (page 198)
6. Shoulder Stand (page 198)
7. Locust Position (page 199)
8. Bow Position (page 199)
9. Twist (page 198)
10. Relaxation Position (page 200)

THE THYROID TYPE EXERCISE PROGRAM

WHAT YOUR BODY NEEDS: Most important for you is to develop endurance and stamina, and the most valuable effect you can get from an exercise program is that you can make yourself less vulnerable to cycles of fatigue and depression. Increasing your muscular strength is also valuable. You are typically well coordinated and fairly flexible, so these areas need less attention than strength and endurance.

EXERCISES THAT WORK: Nautilus-type workouts will give you the strength you need, and the aerobic workouts provided by sustained swimming or rowing will give you endurance. You should swim or row for twenty to thirty minutes at each session (no more), and do a session three times a week. Do a Nautilus or other muscular development session twice a week at first and then cut back to once a week when you are conditioned. Backpacking is good for both strength and endurance, and makes a good vacation sport. The same goes for rowing a boat, rather than a machine. For flexibility, do the T-type Positions every day.

EXERCISES THAT DON'T WORK: Avoid bicycling with under-slung handlebars—the angle of your head with your neck is too acute and puts strain on your thyroid gland. You can, however, ride or use an exercise bike if it allows you to sit up straight.

T-TYPE POSITIONS

1. Body Toning (page 196)
2. Back Stretch (page 197)
3. Plough Position (page 197)
4. Fish Position (page 197)
5. Cobra Position (page 198)
6. Twist (page 198)
7. Modified Shoulder Stand (page 199)
8. Relaxation Position (page 200)

THE PITUITARY TYPE EXERCISE PROGRAM

WHAT YOUR BODY NEEDS: Your greatest need is mind-body integration. This means that you must consider your body carefully: exercise must never be done compulsively or to the point of exhaustion. *Do not* do highly repetitive exercise—you need your mind *involved* in what you're doing. You also need to develop moderate endurance. As far as strength is concerned, you require slender but not bulging muscles. The right look for you is a moderately muscled one. You will know you're at your best in muscular development when you can see that your head no longer seems a bit big for your body, but looks more in proportion instead.

EXERCISES THAT WORK: For endurance and integration, your best exercise is aerobic dancing, especially fairly complicated routines that make you think about what you're doing. Karate, tai chi, or other martial arts also have this value of close mind-body involvement. Do an aerobic session or a session of martial arts three times a week. For strength, a balanced Nautilus-type workout once a week is *plenty*. Get instruction for a full-body routine; don't get tripped out on the big muscle syndrome—it has no place in your life. For flexibility, do P-type Positions every day.

EXERCISES THAT DON'T WORK: Anything repetitive or highly mechanical, such as long-distance running or repetitive calisthenics. If you feel you must run, you will do better with Swedish-style running, in which you vary your pace every few steps. Avoid rowing—it's too mechanical and gives the wrong kind of muscular development. A handy rule of thumb for you: if you can get spaced out and start obsessive rumination during your exercise, it's the wrong one for you.

P-TYPE POSITIONS

1. Body Toning (page 196)
2. Back Stretch (page 197)
3. Plough Position (page 197)
4. Fish Position (page 197)
5. Cobra Position (page 198)
6. Twist (page 198)
7. Relaxation Position (page 200)

THE POSITIONS

The way to do each position is to move into it gently and hold it for about twenty seconds; then move, gently again, out of the position. When you begin, hold each position no more than ten seconds, and *gradually* increase your time to twenty seconds.

Never strain, even the least bit, as this is absolutely against the idea of the body-type positions. Go only as far as you comfortably can in assuming a position. Without forcing, your body will *gradually* increase in flexibility, and you will be able to get closer to the ideal of each position. It's all right to feel stretch, but not strain. If you strain, you will have muscle spasms and become less flexible, rather than more.

You should do your Body Type positions every day. The best time to do your routine is in the morning before breakfast. If you wish to do it in the evening, the best time is at least forty-five minutes before your evening meal. If you need to do the positions after breakfast, wait an hour—they should be done with a mostly empty stomach.

Spread a light blanket or rug on the floor, and begin your routine by sitting quietly for a moment. Then start the positions in the sequence given and do them one after another. Except on the Long Weekend of Rejuvenation, they are to be done only once each day.

1. BODY TONING (P,T,A, and G): This is a two-minute toning-up procedure in which you press the blood gently toward the heart. When you press and release, do it in such a way that your palm and fingers, while releasing the grip, don't lose contact with the body.

First, sit comfortably cross-legged on the floor. Press the top of the head with the palms and fingers of both hands. *Gradually* begin to press and release, moving the hand pressure forward over the face, reaching the neck and the chest (see illustration 10-1, page 200).

Press the top of the head with the palms and fingers of both hands together. Again, *gradually* press and release, moving the hand pressure down over the back of the neck and coming around to the chest.

Grasp the fingertips of the right hand with the palm and fingers of the left hand so that the palm of the left hand is down. Gradually move the pressure upward along the arm reaching up to the shoulder and chest (see illustration 10-2, p. 201).

Grasp the fingertips of the right hand with the palm and fingers of the left hand so that the palm of the left hand is up. Press and *gradually* move the pressure along the arm reaching up to the shoulder and chest. Repeat the two previous procedures, but this time grasp the left hand with the right hand.

With the tips of the middle fingers meeting horizontally at the navel and both hands on the abdomen, begin to press and release the abdomen. *Gradually* move the pressure up toward the heart, reaching the lower edge of the ribs.

Using both hands, begin to press and release the middle of the back and ribs up toward the heart as far as you can reach.

Start now with the right foot. Grasp the top of the toes with the right hand and the sole of the foot with the left hand. Together, press and release, *gradually* moving the hand pressure to the calf, thigh, and up to the waist. Repeat this movement on the left foot (see illustration 10-3, page 201).

Lie on your back, draw your knees up toward your chest, and clasp your hands over your knees. Raise your head slightly. Roll to the extreme right until the right wrist touches the floor; then roll to the extreme left by pushing up with the right elbow and moving your head to the left. Repeat several times in each direction. Finally, assume a full-supine position and relax for a moment (see illustration 10-4, page 202).

2. BACK STRETCH (P,T,A, and G): Lie on your back and raise your hands above your head. Slowly and gradually come up to a sitting position and then bend forward, still with arms extended, and reach toward your toes. Go only as far as is comfortable. Remain in this position for ten seconds at first, *gradually* increasing to twenty (see illustration 10-5, page 202).

3. THE "PLOUGH" POSITION (P,T,A, and G): Lie on your back, arms at your sides. Slowly raise your legs to a half-vertical position. When your hips come off the floor, support them with your hands. Continue raising your legs over your head, and then lower them towards the floor *behind* your head. You need not touch the floor with your feet—go only as far as is comfortable (see illustration 10-6, page 203). Hold the position for a maximum of five seconds. When you are in the position, put your hands behind your head to stabilize yourself (see illustration 10-7, page 203). Then lower your legs gradually until you are once again lying flat on the floor.

4. THE "FISH" POSITION (P,T,A and G): An exercise for the shoulder muscles, the cervical vertebrae and the pelvic organs. Lie on your back. Stretch the legs and tuck your hands, palms down, under the buttocks. Raise your chest with the help of your elbows and, bending the neck as much as possible backwards, rest lightly on the top of your head (see illustration 10-8, page 204). Begin by assuming the position in this way and holding it for ten seconds. After a few weeks,

when you're used to the position, do it with your legs crossed in front of you instead. The technique is the same—tuck your hands beneath your buttocks and raise your chest with the help of your elbows (see illustration 10-9, page 204).

5. THE "COBRA" POSITION (P,T, and A): A backward-bending position which strengthens the pelvic muscles and the lower back. Lie face down on your blanket and relax all your muscles. Place your palms on the blanket next to your shoulders. Gradually raise your head and upper portion of the body, like a cobra raising its hood. Roll back your spine slowly, feeling each vertebra in turn. Your body from the waist down to the toes should still be touching the blanket. Go only as far as is comfortable and do not strain. Do not press hard with your palms on the floor (see illustration 10-10, page 205). Hold the position for ten seconds at first, gradually increasing to twenty seconds; then, reversing the process, slowly return your head until you are face down on the blanket.

6. THE TWIST (P,T,A and G): A position increasing lateral flexibility of your back and improving circulation to the liver, spleen, neck, and shoulders. Sit on your blanket with the right leg stretched out in front of you. Raise your left leg and place your left foot next to your right knee. Then, in this position, turn the trunk to the left and reach with your right arm around your left leg to hold your right leg below the knee. Turn your trunk and head to the left so that you look over your left shoulder. At the same time, reach behind you with your left hand and, if you can, touch your right thigh from behind (see illustration 10-11, page 205). Hold the position for ten seconds or less. You may hear your spine pop or crackle. Slowly return to your original position. Repeat with the other leg.

7. SHOULDER STAND (A and G): The effects of this position are to strengthen and cleanse the thyroid gland and improve circulation to the head—thus improving eyes and hair, and relieving mental fatigue. Lie on your back. Slowly raise the legs. Lift the trunk, hips, and legs to a vertical position. Rest your elbows firmly on the floor and support the pelvis

with both hands. Raise your legs until they become vertical. Your chin will press against your chest (see illustration 10-12, page 206). Hold this position for ten seconds at first, gradually increasing to twenty seconds. If you have any difficulty with this position, begin by doing the Modified Shoulder Stand (see illustration 10-13, page 207) for a week or two until you feel ready for the full shoulder stand.

8. MODIFIED SHOULDER STAND (T): Lie on your back. Slowly raise your feet to a half-vertical position. When your waist begins to rise, support your hips with your hands and let the palms help you raise your waist into position. (You don't have to straighten out your waist totally, but just let your legs—with the feet tilted more toward your head— go as far up as your arms can support them from underneath.) (See illustration 10-13, page 207.) When you have reached the position, hold it for ten seconds, gradually increasing to twenty seconds. Slowly return to your original position by bending the knees to balance the trunk until your buttocks touch the floor. Then straighten the legs and lower them slowly.

9. THE "LOCUST" POSITION (A and G): This is a position that strengthens the back in the lumbar region and is also very strengthening to the female sex glands. Lie on your stomach with your arms at your sides, palms up. Let your chin rest gently on the floor. Raise your legs, *one at a time*, keeping them as straight as possible (see illustration 10-14, page 208). Hold the position with each leg for a few seconds, then lower it to the blanket again. If you find it difficult to raise both legs together, raise one leg at a time. Hold for a few seconds, then lower and repeat with other leg. Work up to raising both legs together. Repeat two or three times.

10. THE "BOW" POSITION (A): This is a position that greatly increases flexibility of the whole spine. Lie prone on the blanket, relaxing your muscles. Bend your legs at the knees and raise your feet backward over your thighs. Catch hold of the right ankle with the right hand and the left ankle with the left hand. Hold firmly. Raise your head, body, and knees by tugging gently at your legs with your hands. Your

back will be bent backward, like a bow (see illustration 10-15, page 200). Hold the position for ten seconds or less, but gradually increase your time to twenty seconds. Do not strain or use your legs to force your body backward. If you are very stiff, you will find that you can't lift your body very much. Never mind—be happy just to hold your ankles with your hands for a few seconds. Your flexibility will increase gradually.

11. RELAXATION POSITION: (P,T,A, and G): Lie flat on your back with your arms at your sides. Let your mind and body be free and loose for a minute or two. For this minute, you have as much purpose in life as a puddle of water. Always end your positions in this way (see illustration 10-16, page 209).

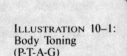

ILLUSTRATION 10–1:
Body Toning
(P-T-A-G)

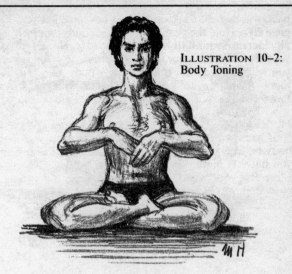

ILLUSTRATION 10–2:
Body Toning

ILLUSTRATION 10–3:
Body Toning

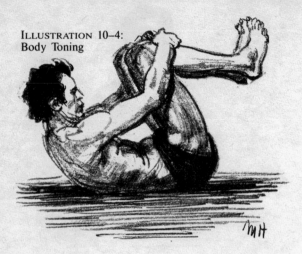

ILLUSTRATION 10–4:
Body Toning

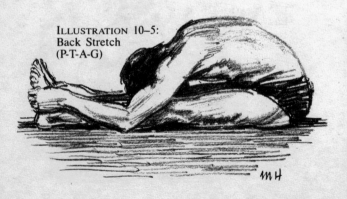

ILLUSTRATION 10–5:
Back Stretch
(P-T-A-G)

ILLUSTRATION 10–6:
Plough Position
(P-T-A-G)

ILLUSTRATION 10–7:
Plough Position

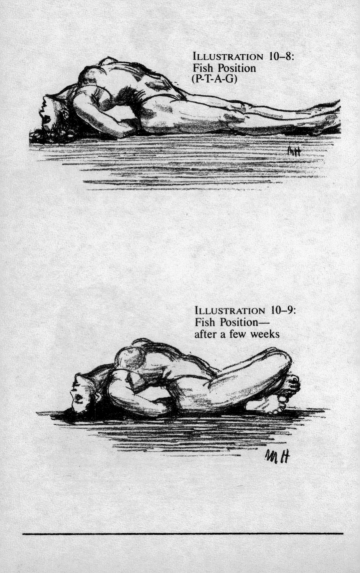

ILLUSTRATION 10–8:
Fish Position
(P-T-A-G)

ILLUSTRATION 10–9:
Fish Position—
after a few weeks

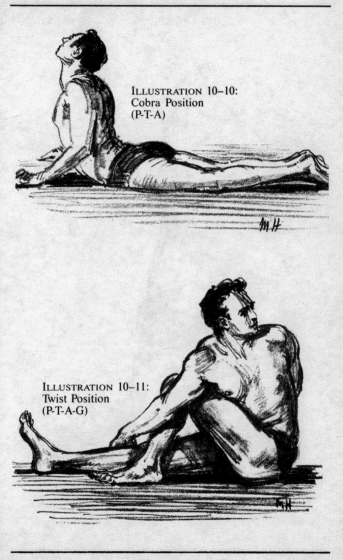

ILLUSTRATION 10–10:
Cobra Position
(P-T-A)

ILLUSTRATION 10–11:
Twist Position
(P-T-A-G)

ILLUSTRATION 10–12:
Shoulder Stand
(A-G)

ILLUSTRATION 10–13:
Modified Shoulder
Stand (T)

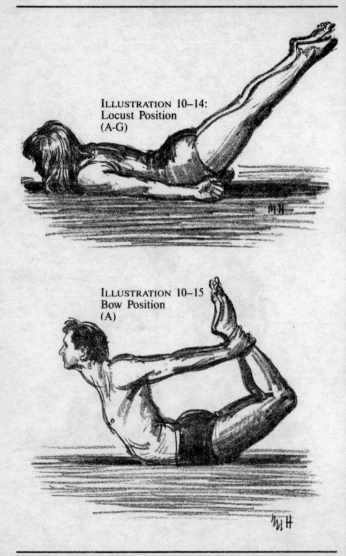

ILLUSTRATION 10–14:
Locust Position
(A-G)

ILLUSTRATION 10–15
Bow Position
(A)

ILLUSTRATION 10–16:
Relaxation Position
(P-T-A-G)

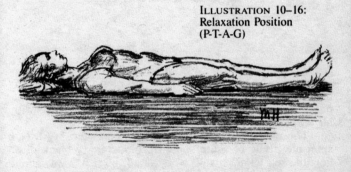

11

STRESS REDUCTION FOR YOUR BODY TYPE

A few years ago a friend of mine decided to fulfill a long-standing desire to take a fishing trip to Florida. A busy man, he went through a lot of trouble to arrange the vacation: he put his professional life on hold, made many small deals with his wife, and took off.

The way I heard it, the trip was a disaster. My friend spun me a tale of acute sunburn, bloodthirsty black flies, horrible seasickness, and, worst of all, no fish. I was about to sympathize when I caught the rapt, contented expression on his face. "You know," he concluded, "I'd have to say it was just about the best week of my entire life." And he went on to urge, with great sincerity, that I too go and fish the Florida Keys.

I think I would die first. To me, his trip sounded incredibly stressful. I'd rather row back to California through the Panama Canal than sit in a rocking boat under the broiling sun, chewed up alive by bugs and waiting in vain for something, anything, to happen. But I'm a thyroid type, while he's an adrenal; for him the trip was complete and utter bliss. What it required from him, he had. Therefore, it simply wasn't stressful.

Stress, you see, is a highly relative thing. One man's

restful vacation is another man's nightmare. One woman's challenging business day is another woman's pressure-filled burnout. A day taking the kids to the beach, which Dad handles easily, makes Grandmother want to bury her head in the sand—forever. No experience is stressful in and of itself— stress lies in the *relationship* between what's happening out there and the response we can or can't give. The same goes for disease. No virus or other agent is a disease by itself. If you're susceptible and you catch it, then it's a disease for you. But not necessarily for someone else.

And if stress is relative to the individual, so is stress reduction. To reduce the wear and tear of stress on your system, it's important to be aware of what sorts of experiences are stressful to you, and then to find ways of dealing with them and turning stressfulness into challenge and even enjoyment. Sound impossible? It isn't. It requires real understanding of your own range of responses, and for that you need the insights that come from an understanding of your body type.

"I LOVE MY STRESS: IT MAKES ME STRONG"

Do you really believe you love your stress? Don't be embarrassed if you do, it's certainly not an uncommon belief, but it's based on a profound misunderstanding of what stress really is. Men, particularly, tend to have this idea—I guess men are supposed to be able to "handle anything"— but many women also believe that stress is a terrific stimulant to life.

"I wouldn't want to live without stress," I remember one of my patients telling me. He was an overburdened, T-type executive with terrible bags under his eyes, twenty extra pounds, and an ulcer. "Yes, you would," I responded. "You just don't know how. If you think you love your stress, you won't believe how much you're going to love your un-stressful life."

What my patient was really worried about, in all fair-ness, was the idea that without stress his life would be bor-ing. He pictured something like a child's idea of heaven—you know, sitting around in a robe, playing the harp. We can only hope it won't really be like that—for who wouldn't be wild with boredom within a day?

The thing is, though, that boredom—or lack of stimula-tion—is also a stress. If you think you love stress, what you really love is experience, activity, life. Yet you *can* have lively experiences without the stress—in fact, that's one big secret of an interesting and fulfilling life.

Stress comes in many packages; too much input can be stressful, and so can too little. As a matter of fact, there are psychological studies showing that students taking examina-tions (a stressful situation to most of us) do best when there is *just the right amount* of pressure. If there's too much anx-iety, the students "clutch" and forget what they know. If there's not enough, they don't do well either, perhaps be-cause they aren't challenged enough.

What we all need, in fact, is enough challenge to make what we're doing feel exciting, but not so much that we get anxious and overwhelmed. Stress occurs at precisely the point when the pressure we need for motivation goes critical and becomes, simply, too much. The point varies for dif-ferent people and for the same person at different times. But we all have such a point, and it's important to be aware of it, because it is at precisely that point that stress begins to oc-cur.

Depending on your body type, it can also happen that certain stresses are perceived as direct stimulants and give a kind of illusory "lift" to your system, in the same way that a food stimulates your dominant gland. For example, thyroid types are stimulated by extremely frantic and pressure-filled situations, which call on an extra effort from the thyroid gland. Adrenal types sometimes get this kind of stressful stimulation from watching violent movies—the "fight or flight" syndrome aroused by scenes of violence gives stim-ulation to the adrenal glands. A boxing match will do it, too. According to your type, you can actually come to crave certain stresses, just as you can crave certain stimulating foods. But these cravings tend to disappear as you improve the balance of your system.

STRESSABILITY: WHERE ARE YOUR RESERVES?

Stress, for most people, is overload of the system. It occurs at the point when any experience overtaxes our reserves and becomes too much to handle. But precisely how much is too much? At what point does excitement turn into stress? This depends upon you and upon the extent and nature of your reserves.

If you take a moment to think about yourself, you'll find that there are reserves you can rely on—responses of yours that you can count on to be there when you need them—and areas in which your reserves are small or nonexistent. Where you have low reserves, you have what I call "stressability." But to determine your stress and nonstress areas, you must really think hard about yourself, because most people take their strengths for granted and don't focus on them as they do their weaknesses.

I once complimented a patient of mine, a woman named Mary L., who had been waiting for some time to see me (sometimes, unfortunately, this happens in a medical practice) with her two young boys. As I checked the waiting room periodically, I noticed that she was handling her children beautifully. She allowed them to express their frustration at waiting, but helped them keep their dignity and self-respect—and I told her so.

"Oh, well," she replied. I could tell she really didn't realize she was extraordinary. A situation that for most people would have been very stressful, that would have resulted in bad temper and hurt feelings, and in general would have been a real downer, she'd taken totally in stride. She'd even used it to help her sons grow in maturity. But if I'd asked this woman to describe her strengths, she probably wouldn't have even thought of it!

We all have reserves of strength like this. They are our, shall we say, proven reserves, like the wealth of oil that we *know* lies in the oilfields of Texas just waiting to be tapped. But we also have areas where our reserves are painfully thin. This same woman, to whom real mothering came so naturally, told me how difficult she found dealing with any kind of tension in social situations. Parties where she didn't know the people well were agony for her. In this area she lacked reserves—overload was her reality.

WHEN GOOD THINGS FEEL BAD

Interestingly, stress isn't confined by any means to "negative" occurrences. It's true that negative situations are more apt to overload our capacities, but intensely positive situations can also tax our reserves.

Thomas H. Holmes, M.D., has compiled a list of stressful events called the "Social Readjustment Rating Scale" that assigns relative values to various life events. The higher the number, the more stressful the event. The most stressful occurrence, "death of spouse," is given 100 points; "divorce," 73; "foreclosure on a mortgage," 30; "minor violations of the law," 11. But on the same scale Dr. Holmes assigns 45 stress points to "marital reconciliation"; "outstanding personal achievement" is given 28; "vacation," 13; and "Christmas," 12. Evidently, according to Dr. Holmes's research, reconciling with your spouse, while not as stressful as getting a divorce, also carries a considerable toll of stress.

This is important to keep in mind, because the consequences of stress are very real. Every physician is aware of this fact; those of us in family practice are especially alert to clues revealing the stress behind the disease. Whenever I hear that a patient is undergoing more stress than usual, I introduce the stress reduction techniques for his or her body type because I've learned that stress and sickness go hand in hand.

Dr. Holmes's research verifies this. He found that people who had more than 300 "stress points" on the Holmes Stress Scale in a single year had an 80 percent chance of getting a serious illness within two years. Now, getting 300 stress points in one year means going through a *lot* of changes, more than most of us experience all at once, but the point applies to us all. Stress produces increased vulnerability; it reduces our ability to repair our bodies, to "bounce back" after exertion; it makes us slower, less agile and flexible in all our responses. It shortens life. Reducing stress isn't just something we should do to become more "mellow"; it's a vital part of getting and keeping perfect health.

BODY TYPE STRESSABILITY

Dr. Holmes's scale rates various stresses and relates them to our chances of getting sick; but as with all scales designed to measure everybody on a single yardstick, it's apt to leave out some vital information. That information is *you*. All stresses are not the same, and according to your body type, they will have a greater or lesser impact on you, and greater or lesser consequences for your health.

Your body type, as you know, is a description of the *response pattern* of your entire system. Whichever your type, you will tend to respond to stress with a burst of energy from your dominant gland. As long as your dominant gland remains strong and active, it provides you with your main area of proven reserves—the response patterns you can count on to bring you successfully through a crisis. A challenge to your dominant gland will be far less stressful than one that challenges your less-active glands.

For example, say you're a pituitary type. The pituitary gland gives mental energy, a coordinated response of the entire metabolism, but one without a strong physical component. When faced with a stressful situation, your response is to use your pituitary and *think of something*. Your proven reserves are mental, and you have confidence that you'll be able to come up with an idea that will get you through the crisis. But when faced with a physical or emotional challenge, where your less-active glands are needed. You will feel far more stressed and less confident.

For each body type, the dominant gland gives an area of confidence and competence, where stress is at a minimum and challenges are welcomed, not feared. On the other hand, each type has its less-developed areas—the response areas associated with the less-active glands. These are the areas of body type stressability.

So Holmes's stress scale is only valid up to a point. According to your body type, you'll find that some events are more stressful for you, and some less than they are for other people. The first five events on Holmes's list are "death of a spouse" (100 points), "divorce" (73), "marital separation" (65), "jail term" (63), and "death of a close family member" (also 63). These traumatic events are terribly stressful for all body types—but after that the variation begins.

The next most stressful item is "personal illness or injury" (53 points). But if you're a pituitary type, and your stress comes in through the body, this item deserves a much higher rating on *your* scale. An extremely unbalanced P-type patient of mine was in a minor car accident—a rear-ender on the freeway under stop-and-go conditions. It wasn't much of an accident; but it was *totally stressful* for this woman, and she nearly fell apart. Even the cure was stressful. Coming in for the physical therapy she needed was very difficult for her—so much focus on her body.

It just so happened that her husband, an adrenal type, was in the car with her when the accident happened. Like most A-types, his robust physique and level of comfort with his body allowed him to take the event in stride. For him, the stress quotient of the accident was probably down in the 20s, while for his wife it was at least in the 60s. If this A-type man were fired from his job, on the other hand, it would be much more serious for him. "Fired at work" rates a 47 from Dr. Holmes, but it's a major A-type stressor and would give him at least 60 stress points, if not more.

CHINKS IN THE ARMOR: HOW EACH TYPE GETS STRESSED

Before I go on to provide specific, practical techniques for your body type to reduce your stressable areas, I want to be sure you're clear about the stress areas for each type.

Pituitary types, as I mentioned, can usually cope confidently with mental challenges. If a coworker throws out a statement such as "Where on earth did you get these figures?" or "I don't follow your thinking on this report *at all*," it couldn't bother you less. Not only isn't it stressful, you're secretly rather pleased to have an excuse to go through the report, justify the figures, make your thinking clear. You go home from work thinking that you had a good day, more interesting than usual.

At home, maybe your spouse tells you that you've got a complicated mixup on your credit card billing. No problem! Your pituitary is still working, you rise to the challenge and sort out the difficulty. A good, stress-free day all around.

Your P-type stress arrives in situations when mental energy won't help. All physical problems are stressful to a pituitary type—and that means almost anything to do with the body. Cooking and eating are stressful—you rarely cook, and mealtimes make you anxious, so you snack instead. Doctor's visit? Panic time—you'll put it off and put it off, even if you're really sick. The doctor, you know, might want to do a blood test—a big pituitary-type fear.

Sex is another P-type panic-button pusher. It's not that you don't enjoy sex—you can, with the right partner—but any sexual difficulty at all is very anxiety-producing. What you doubt is your ability to deal with the difficulty, whatever it may be. Probably your least-favorite thing to hear from your loved one is, "Honey, I feel like we should do something about our sex life." And your response—"Hey, let me go think about that"—isn't really very helpful.

Animals are another big problem—you either hate animals or (in a sort of backfield switch) love them *too much*. Either way, animals are stressful to you. They are *physical*—you can't reason with them, so your proven reserves don't help you much. And right up there with dogs and cats as stress-producers are strong feelings and heavy emotional confrontations of any kind. These cause physical sensations you're uncomfortable with—your heart pounds, you get butterflies in your stomach. You'd rather avoid such sensations altogether. Your idea of dealing with feelings is to read a book about them. Which, let's face it, means they are going to continue to be stressful for you because you'll never resolve them in your head.

ADRENAL TYPE STRESSES: THE STRESS OF CHANGE

Adrenal types are a contrast to pituitary types in all their stressful areas. If you're an A-type, your reserves—which are considerable—are in the body, not the head. Anything that can be handled by sheer power, force of will, persistence, or pure head-down, shoulder-to-the-wheel pushing is basically all right with you.

You can even withstand rejection—the most stressful of all events for other types—and manage not to take it personally. You're a good salesperson, and I mean that with the greatest admiration: sales is, in essence, the art of making things happen, and in some ways it's the most difficult, un-appreciated, and necessary work in the marketplace. You do what you must do to make things happen—and you do it *well*.

Stress comes in, for you, on the heels of change. Unpredictability is what makes an event go critical: that and the suggestion that your force of will may not be sufficient to make things go your way. Art makes you profoundly nervous, because it brings to your attention those forces in the world that you'll never be able to control. How many A-types have frustrated their spouses by refusing to go to any movie they think is even remotely "arty"?

Often you have difficult relationships with your children, unpredictable little beings that they are. As an A-type patient of mine remarked, "At work, when I tell my secretary to do something, she does it. My son wants to know *why*. I like it better at work." It wasn't a joke—home life was often very stressful for him, and the only solution he could come up with was to work late and send his son to a military school in the hope that he'd become more like his secretary. His son, it just so happened, was a T-type; he came back from military school more balanced than before—but he still wanted to know why!

So many A-types become workaholics for exactly this reason. Life at work is predictable (relatively, anyway), non-emotional, and responsive to the kind of pressure you're good at applying. It requires unflappability, endurance, and the ability to deal with repetition and detail—all of which you have. I don't want to say that your approach to work is uncreative, because there *is* a kind of creativity involved in your single-minded application of power to problems; but in general you tend to believe that creativity is the province of women and underlings.

"Call in the creative people," says a typical A-type executive I know. He gets their input and moves on—and in this way pretends that a stressful area for him is under control. He believes that the creative work can be done by the people who eat quiche. I didn't want to tell him that if the T-types eat enough quiche, they may take over his job!

The same sense of vulnerability is behind A-type alcoholism. Alcohol dulls the edges of unpredictability in social life. You're more comfortable telling jokes and stories than exchanging ideas and views—and the convivial A-types in the bar, who seem to be having such a good time, are often just waiting for their turn to tell a story that no one will really hear.

The good news is that none of this is cast in cement. Whether you're a pituitary type who feels uncomfortable outside of your head, or an adrenal type who feels threatened by change, you're that way because of imbalance in your body type. You're relying too much on the energy of your dominant gland, on your proven reserves—yet you could be using all the potential of your three less-active glands to reduce your stressability.

When you activate your balancing glands with the Body Type Health Program, experiences you used to find extremely stressful become manageable, and ones that were merely trying are not stressful at all.

THYROID TYPE STRESS: POWERLESSNESS

For a thyroid type, as you might expect, the experiences that are stressful are not the same as those that are stressful for adrenal and pituitary types. For T-types, situations that require steadiness, power, and endurance are the ones that are most likely to make you run for cover. At the same time, the sort of highly challenging experiences that are difficult for A's and P's, you take in stride because your dominant thyroid gland provides you with such different sorts of reserves.

Unpredictability, far from being stressful, is in fact the very breath of life to you. Change in general you perceive as a stimulant—and you know how much you love stimulants! The T-types I know love the rush and excitement of starting new projects, but can become very stressed with the detail and repetition involved in finishing them.

I know a thyroid-type man who is a very successful surgeon. This man thrives on challenge and the unexpected. When he does surgery that challenges him with three or four unusual and unpredictable outcomes, he emerges from the operating room looking relaxed and exhilarated, and not particularly stressed. Another surgeon I know, an adrenal type, comes out of this kind of operation with a tense, unhappy expression, but not my T-type friend—it's his great strength, and he is justly valued for this ability.

I know that if I ever needed the kind of surgery that requires flexible thinking and the ability to change course in mid-operation, he's the one I'd want to perform it. But if it was a routine, repetitious procedure involving minimal challenge and lots of tiny, painstaking stitches, I'd just as soon someone else did it. I wouldn't tell him this, but it's true. I'd be afraid he'd get bored doing it, and the stress could affect my outcome. Boredom, routine, repetition, waiting—these are the stresses that get to T-types every time.

MORE T-TYPE STRESSABILITY: PHYSICAL CHALLENGES

T-types are also, like pituitary types, easily stressed by physical problems, but with a difference. P-types feel any intrusion of the body as a sort of affront to their pure, mental being. T-types, on the other hand, experience stress from physical demands that require endurance and steadiness on their part.

For T-types, the difficulty is that the dominant thyroid gland is so unsteady, so cyclic, that they can't count on their physical reserves being there when they need them. Pain, even minor pain—a cut, a tiny bruise, an injection—might be tolerable at any moment *or it might not*—and they never know in advance. From this they get a nervousness about pain that in fact makes their fears materialize more often than not. Hypochondria—a typical T-type stress response— has its roots in this same nervousness.

The typically thyroidal nervousness also extends into personal relationships. If you're a T-type, you know that you fear rejection terribly—you doubt that your physical reserves can handle it, and you suspect (rightly) that it might make you actually ill. When a T-type sits in my office complaining of nervous stomach, insomnia, headaches, or other such stress symptoms, I ask about his or her personal life; you'd be amazed how often T-types are reacting to some real or perceived rejection.

"My daughter hasn't called me in three weeks," a patient will tell me—and that's how long she's had the gnawing sensation in her gut. Yet she rarely has alleviated her feelings of rejection by making a call herself. Without confidence in her physical reserves, this T-type has been unwilling to face the challenge of verbalizing her feelings, or of taking the risk of asking for something better. Where an adrenal type might have dealt with this situation by attempting to *force* her daughter to call, a T-type will either resort to elaborate stratagems, or more often withdraw and take the stress in the pit of her stomach.

Anorexia nervosa is an example of this T-type response taken to an extreme. I've practiced medical weight control for many years and have seen large numbers of anorexics, and almost every one has been a thyroid type. The disease is truly a syndrome involving every aspect of thyroidal stressability. Feelings of rejection, unwillingness to confront problems, lack of a secure sense of personal power, and a profound feeling of *boredom* coming out of an unchallenging, unchanging environment—these are the ingredients I've found in the T-type anorexics I've treated.

Getting through to an anorexic T-type involves understanding that this person is struggling for feelings of self-control and self-worth. Confrontation and intense involvement are the keys to breaking up this pattern—in most cases professional help is needed to make it happen. Then, once you've broken through the ice, the T-type Health and Weight Maintenance Program is vital so that the ice won't form again.

If you know a lot of T-types or are one yourself, you might think that they are the most easily stressed of all body types. It's a mistaken impression, but it seems true because T-types are so irritable under stress and complain so much more than any other type. But the other side of it is that T-types can reduce their stressability more dramatically than any other type by improving the balance in their metabolism. I've provided a list of specific options for T-types on page 231, but they're all designed to add a feeling of personal strength and power to your repertoire of responses. I'm not saying you'll ever be able to wait more than fifteen minutes without losing all hope, or miraculously gain the ability to do the same thing more than twice without existential despair— but they will help more than you'd think anything ever could.

GONADAL TYPE STRESS: WHY SOME WOMEN WOULD RATHER STAY HOME

Statistics indicate that the number of women with outside jobs and those who work inside the home is now about equal. It would be interesting to know whether in fact there are more gonadal-type women in the second group, because the G-types of this world have an impressive way of making a success out of working in their homes. If you possess a G-type metabolism, your unique set of reserves helps you to withstand the very real stresses of homemaking better than any other type, while your stressability is usually higher in a marketplace situation.

I hope this doesn't appear sexist; it's difficult to make

this sort of statement, which recognizes a distinct characteristic, without giving that impression. The G-type metabolism exists, and it's important to be aware of its strengths and stressability. It doesn't mean that a G-type "must" stay home; stressability is no binding limitation. But if you're a G-type woman and want an outside career, you need to take positive steps to minimize your stressability and get what you need to function at your best.

The proven reserves of the gonadal type are found in responsiveness, patience, persistence, and warmth unequalled by any other body type. This gives you the ability to withstand the stress of child-raising and turn it into a joyful challenge. Like Mary L., my patient I told you about at the beginning of this chapter who handled her sons so well, your metabolism gives you the physical, mental, and emotional reserves to do all the never-ending educational and psychological work that is the backbone of mothering.

You also have tremendous reserves against the stress of tedium and nonstimulation: G-types are rarely bored, even in situations that would drive other types wild with boredom. Routines that would exasperate thyroid types beyond bearing, which pituitary types would simply not do, and which adrenal types would try to change into something else, G-types use in their own way.

As Mary L. told me on another occasion, when I asked her whether she didn't get tired of the routines of being with young children, "It's not that I like doing things over and over—it's more that I never feel that I'm repeating *anything*. I'm aware of the small changes, the development, in my kids and in me." These are reserves of a high order, and while raising children isn't the only task that uses them, it's perhaps the most important one we have.

Where G-types are stressed, by contrast, is in situations where these reserves feel exploited, or where they don't seem to produce any worthwhile results. The exploitation aspect is a highly stressful one. Many G-types with jobs end up in helping professions—education, medicine, social work—but don't have the assertive qualities they need to resist doing too much and burning out. Many a boss has treasured the devotion of a G-type secretary, and, frankly, used it to his or her own gain.

Competition, also, is stressful for most G-type women. It feels wrong, as if by competing you are doing something bad. The essence of competitiveness is to be strongly pro-yourself—it's at odds with the caring a G-type wants to give to others. Superficial business-type relationships are also stressful—you like to form intimate, emotional bonds that are, actually, inappropriate in most business situations.

WINNING BY ADAPTATION

By now you may be wondering if this means that the old slander that a woman's place is in the home implies G-type women only. Not necessarily—and the case of Phyllis Schlafly (the famous-infamous G-type woman who almost singlehandedly blocked the passage of the ERA) is an interesting case in point.

In a recent article by Jean Libman Block in *Good Housekeeping,* Mrs. Schlafly was asked to describe herself. She ticked off "industrious, cheerful, and dedicated"—all G-type virtues. She is clearly a homemaker and mother par excellence. When each of her six children was born, she spent "at least" six weeks on the second floor of her home, and devoted herself entirely to nursing and taking care of the new infant and herself. (Her husband took charge of the other kids and brought up all her meals.)

Schlafly feels that this would be the ideal of every woman—but would it be? I asked several T-type mothers, who replied that their main thought would be, "When do I get out of here?" P-types would never think of doing such a thing, and A-types wouldn't need to; but for a G-type, it's a dream come true.

Yet when her children were launched, Mrs. Schlafly went on to have a spectacular career. All those G-type reserves were mobilized toward outside achievement—with undeniable effect. She's a lawyer, has written nine books (one of which sold three million copies), and she out-maneuvered some pretty powerful opponents to defeat the ERA. Obviously, her reserves were more than equal to the requirements.

Politics aside, Mrs. Schlafly is, in many ways, an extremely striking example of her body type. It's worth considering whether the fact that she is a G-type hasn't influenced her intense advocacy of the G-type style of functioning—even though it may not be what other women want for themselves. Is it appropriate for a woman of one body type to insist on the same thing for women whose bodies suggest a totally different life-style? I would say no, but what would you say?

STRESS: IT REALLY COMES FROM WITHIN

The point, really, is that stress is not the same for everyone. For some people, physical discomfort is intensely stressful; for others, mental strain is far harder to cope with. For some women, stress is found in typical work situations; for others, Mrs. Schlafly notwithstanding, stress begins at home. For some men, change and unpredictability are stressful; for others, the exercise of power is what hurts. But for each person, stressability is an internal affair and comes from some lack of ability to respond to a challenge from the environment. How many points your life stresses are worth really does depend on you.

A practical approach to stress reduction must take this fact into account and must open up new ways of responding for each individual, according to the individual's needs.

Now let's go on to the specifics. You should now begin to apply what I've said to yourself. You know your body type, and you know what situations have been most stressful *in your own life*. You're ready to begin selecting, from the following sections, those techniques that will extend your proven reserves into a fuller range of strong, nonstressful responses.

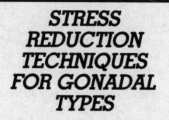

STRESS REDUCTION TECHNIQUES FOR GONADAL TYPES

YOUR STRESS AREAS

Competition
Interruptions
Disorderliness
Changes in routine
Asserting yourself
Risks (physical, mental, or emotional)

STRESS REDUCTION TECHNIQUES

FOLLOW THE G-TYPE DIET—to increase your ability to handle risky, challenging, nonroutine demands. At first the diet will make you feel comparatively "spacy"—that is, not as solid and rooted as before. That, for you, is the best kind of change. Once you get used to it, you'll find you can handle all kinds of situations that previously seemed intimidating because they were unfamiliar. In fact, you'll find they're actually fun.

FOLLOW THE G-TYPE EXERCISE PROGRAM—not only for physical conditioning, but also for safe practice in competition and self-assertion. Competition at play also makes competition in real life easier to handle. Your exercise routine is also planned to make you more adept at handling change and surprise. Not every exercise program will do this, so be sure to check page 190 for specific instructions.

WORK ON CHANGING YOUR ENVIRONMENT OFTEN—even if it's just rearranging the furniture. The more you can make little changes in the world around you, the more you'll feel in charge of your life, and the less you'll feel stressed by change that comes from the outside.

AVOID TOO MUCH ROUTINE: You can reduce your tendency to get stressed by life changes by keeping yourself feeling lively and stimulated. Start with baby steps, but keep on making changes and taking risks *on your own*. You'll be amazed—it feels great.

ASK FOR WHAT YOU NEED FROM OTHER PEOPLE: You're good at nurturing, but you usually find it stressful when you don't receive the kind of care you give. You must realize that not everyone in this world is a G-type. You can get the love and attention you need—and if you have to ask your T-type, P-type, or A-type friends for it, what's wrong with that? You're just sharing with them the enjoyment of nurturing you already have. So go ahead, ask, enjoy.

STRESS REDUCTION TECHNIQUES FOR ADRENAL TYPES

YOUR STRESS AREAS

Unpredictability
Creativity ("the arts")
Situations you can't control with willpower
Your children
Emotional complexity
Vacations

STRESS REDUCTION TECHNIQUES

FOLLOW THE A-TYPE DIET—to improve the flexibility and creativity of your responses to all stressful situations. You know in your heart that there's more to life than business, more to relationships than "Me Tarzan, you Jane" or "Me Wonder Woman, you Jim." But what, exactly, is this "more"? It lies waiting somewhere in the parts of life you now find stressful: emotional involvement, creativity, play. Your diet will help you move into these areas by stimulating the creative parts of you, and you'll be amazed to find how enjoyable they really are.

FOLLOW THE A-TYPE EXERCISE PROGRAM—which has been designed to complement the diet in increasing your ability to handle change. Most A-types do exercise—but in the wrong way. You do some sort of mindless physical pushing—and you come in more stressed than you went out. You need to spend less time on exercise than you think, but what you do should involve bending, stretching, and coordination (see page 191).

SET ASIDE TIME TO "WASTE": Every minute of the day doesn't have to be Productive with a capital P. Give yourself some free minutes—not even for exercise or "self-improvement." Go for a walk, or just sit there (really!). You probably think this is a huge waste of time, but what's really going on is that you're afraid of what will happen. Do it anyway. Those "monsters from the ad" are probably just sexual fantasies.

STOP DRINKING: If you don't drink alcohol, that's great—but many A-types do, and it's an influence that makes any attempt at stress reduction more difficult. I'd like you to experiment with not drinking for a week and see how you feel. If this seems very difficult, try an AA meeting. I'm not saying you're an alcoholic, but the people at AA can help you deal with even moderate alcohol use.

MAKE YOURSELF LISTEN to the people in your life. This means your spouse, your children, your subordinates at work—all the ones whom you tend to disregard because they aren't powerful enough to be interesting. Besides there are more kinds of power than the ones you're used to. Don't try to change them in any way. Just listen. Try to learn. There's a whole world you could be enjoying, and it's not as hard as you think.

STRESS REDUCTION TECHNIQUES FOR THYROID TYPES

YOUR STRESS AREAS

Repetition
Continuing demands (from other people or your environment)
Details
Rejection
Pain (even minor)
Lack of change or stimulation

STRESS REDUCTION TECHNIQUES

FOLLOW THE T-TYPE DIET—to improve endurance, steadiness, and personal power. For most T-types, the diet is a major change—one that you often want to resist. All right, you know that all change is somewhat stressful, but as a T-type you're basically adaptable and will get into this change quickly. The T-type diet is designed to give you the ability to cope with the demands of real life—and you'll soon find how much less stressful it can be. And deep down you know you *need* a steadying influence.

FOLLOW THE T-TYPE EXERCISE PROGRAM—for a whole range of benefits, both psychological and physical. Regular aerobic exercise gives you relief from your wound-up emotional nervousness, greater endurance to deal with long-range demands, a sense of your own physical reserves, and greater confidence in your ability to keep going when you want to.

GET ENOUGH REST—a vital stress reduction technique for any thyroid type. Your tendency always is to ignore your need to rest, and to choose stimulation instead. Take breaks. Accept your limits, even as they are expanding. Do I need to tell you again how much of your stress comes from this?

MAKE YOUR HOME AND WORKPLACE AS SOOTHING AS YOU CAN: Your inner life is so active that you need less outside stimulation than other types. Ringing phones, bustle, pressure—you like these, but they're basically stimulants, like coffee and a pastry, and your creativity will be less dissipated and easily used up in a calmer, more relaxed environment.

TAKE LIFE ONE DAY AT A TIME: It's important for you to keep the perspective that your life is your own, and that you do whatever you want to with it, provided you keep your head and make changes one at a time. A major source of T-type stress comes from the fact that you want to do everything all at once. The better way is for you to learn to pace yourself, alternate activity with rest, and come back to a stressful situation with your T-type freshness and creativity revived. If you learn to do this, you'll find that there is truly nothing you can't accomplish in a satisfying and stress-free way.

STRESS REDUCTION TECHNIQUES FOR PITUITARY TYPES

YOUR STRESS AREAS

Your body
Emotions (yours or others)
Sex
Food (cooking, eating, thinking about it)
Being sick (even having a checkup)
Animals
Any conflicts that can't be reasoned away

STRESS REDUCTION TECHNIQUES

FOLLOW THE P-TYPE DIET—to stimulate body awareness. P-types often find the diet itself stressful at first. It is designed to pull your attention down to your body—which is the key to *all* your stress-reduction techniques. Stay with it.

FOLLOW YOUR BODY TYPE EXERCISE PROGRAM—regularly, vigorously, in a totally physical way. You won't enjoy it at first—but it will do wonders for expanding your reserves against stress. See Chapter 10 for specific exercise programs designed to enliven your physical resources. Exercise will make sex less scary.

CREATE REAL MEALTIMES—as relaxed and sensual as you can make them. Don't just snack. Think about what you want to eat (not what you crave), and either prepare it or go to a restaurant and order it. Then sit down, look at, smell, and taste your food. In fact, do this to each bite.

You'll have reactions: many P-types have told me that food actually looks unappealing, gross. Keep going with this anyway. No matter what you think, food is good stuff. Once you understand the physical pleasure of food, you'll have taken a big step toward making friends with your body.

FIND A GOOD DOCTOR—one you feel comfortable talking to, and tell him or her your worst fears. Find out as much as you can about your physical self. Again, this is part of recognizing your body, making friends with it, and letting it also take care of you.

ACKNOWLEDGE CONFLICTS—taking this one step at a time. Realize that conflict situations are stressful for you, but don't run away from them. When reality is at odds with your preconceived ideas, compromise. This will get easier—and when you find you can handle conflicts without too much stress, your whole life will be less stressful in a very significant way.

A STRESS REDUCTION TECHNIQUE THAT WORKS FOR ALL BODY TYPES

Throughout this chapter I've written about expanding your areas of reserve and reducing your stressability. The basic principle I've utilized has been that the body's four glands give us resistance to stress in different ways. Since each body type has a different strong, dominant gland, each one can withstand some sorts of stressful influences while remaining vulnerable to others. Whichever body type you have, you use various parts of the Body Type Health Program to balance your system and stimulate your less-active glands, and this turns out to make your more vulnerable areas far less easily stressed.

There is, however, something else that you can do to reduce your stressability, and this is the practice of Transcendental Meditation. I recommend this strongly to all my patients, whichever body type they are, and I practice it regularly myself because I have come to believe that it is the most effective form of stress reduction available in the world today.

What Transcendental Meditation, or TM, does is to provide your mind and body with a state of *deep rest,* which many studies have shown to be deeper and more restful even than deep sleep. Rest is the potent antidote to stress of all kinds; if sleep knits up the raveled sleeve of care, the deep rest of meditation creates a new and better garment altogether.

However you are dealing with stress at present, whether well or badly, you still have been through stressful events in your life, events that inevitably leave their mark on your mind and body. TM gives you a way of actually recovering from the stresses of the past and renews your strength to cope with the stresses still to come.

TM enjoyed a vogue in the U.S. in the mid-seventies, and since then seems to have fallen out of general popularity. I think this is a pity because the technique is a valuable one and has helped, and is still helping, many individuals. It is still very popular worldwide, but in the U.S. was unfortunately treated like a fad. A great deal of scientific research now exists, clearly showing the relation between the practice of TM and many improvements in physical, mental, and emotional health.

Many people believe that it doesn't matter whether you do TM or some other technique of relaxation (such as the Relaxation Response), as long as you do *something.* I disagree. As a matter of fact, much of the research that is *attributed* to the Relaxation Response was actually done on people who practice TM. It doesn't make good scientific sense to conclude that if TM works, *any* relaxation technique works. I believe strongly that TM is uniquely beneficial.

TM, like the Body Type Health Program, takes into account the fact that people are different, and certain aspects of the technique are taught according to the characteristics of the individual. Unfortunately, unlike finding your body type, determining your meditation procedure can't be done with a questionnaire, and actual instruction in TM has to be done in person.

You learn TM through a four-day course that takes about an hour and a half each day. You might wonder if it's worth it. That is really a personal question. There are many forms of meditation around, but when you are looking for hard-edged, real-world results, not just a trip, the field narrows considerably. When you also add the requirement that the effects should last and become a permanent part of your functioning, you start seeing how important it is to decide on the right technique.

As I said, I recommend TM over any other form of meditation. It is not a flash in the pan. But if, for personal, family, or other reasons, you want to use another meditation technique, here are the guidelines you *must* use to see if the technique is good enough for you. It should provide:

1. Deep relaxation
2. Increased energy
3. Increased clarity of mind
4. A better feeling about yourself
5. Better functioning at work
6. Better relations with others
7. An easier and more enjoyable life
8. Increased resistance to disease.

Benefits like this are hard to come by. If someone can teach you how to get them, or if you can learn something from a book, I have no complaint. If not, try TM. It's the choice way to get these effects, which is why I do it.

TM is taught in centers located throughout the country. To take the course, look in the phone book under "transcendental meditation" for the location nearest you. If you follow only one recommendation from this chapter, follow this one; there is no single thing you can do that will help you more.

12

THE LONG
WEEKEND OF
REJUVENATION

You now know most of the elements of the Body Type Health Program. Nutrition, supplements, exercise, stress—all are under control, or at least you know what you *should* be doing. But maybe you want more. Wouldn't you like to get started on your health program with a real push, give yourself some tremendous momentum in the direction of balance and integration? That's what the Long Weekend of Rejuvenation is all about.

Let's say it's the Thursday before Memorial Day weekend. You're exhausted, not surprisingly, since you haven't had a day off since Presidents' Day. You're thinking about the stress of the busy season or the stress of the slow season, whichever, with the kids out of school and their need to be organized. This long weekend will be your last break for three months. What are you going to do? You want to make the best possible use of your brief respite, but so far all you can think of is to take the kids on a long, exhausting outing to the lake where half the world is also going, and then watch a ball game on Monday afternoon. It's what you've always done, and it's never quite worked as a vacation. You always feel more tired than if you hadn't gone—but you've never found a satisfactory alternative.

It just doesn't seem to be enough—and it isn't, because

237
---

it starts from the wrong premises. Perhaps in the past, when life was simpler and less stressful, it would have been enough; but now we all need more respite, more rejuvenation, more rest out of whatever breaks we get in our incredible routines.

The thing is, to sustain our pressured, intense lifestyles, we need terrifically intense periods of *rest*. The deeper the rest we are able to gain, the more resources we have to draw upon in our active life. Rest is absolutely basic—to effectiveness, to enjoyment, to our very survival.

ACTIVITY AND REST

Rest is terribly underrated in the modern world. None of us rest enough, or deeply enough. In today's emotional climate, where success is measured by achievement no matter what the cost, "kicking back" seems a weakness.

Most of our heroes are workaholics. They enter the fray in three-piece suits and football cleats. They're high-energy all the time, and if the fray seems to fray *them*, well, those are the breaks. When work's over, they change into running shoes and work out, instead of in. But the cost is *tremendous*, to them and to society. The life of constant activity is grinding and wearing down our best people. Burnout is a major problem.

In my own profession of medicine, the ideal of constant work prevails. Doctors are supposed to want to work thirty-six-hour shifts. It's hip, it's macho, it proves dedication—and it guarantees mistakes. A recent study showed that physicians in emergency rooms who have been up all night make 70 percent more mistakes in reading EKGs. I don't know about you, but the doctor I want reading *my* EKG is one who's gotten some rest lately.

How many fights have you had with your spouse late at night that seem absurd in the morning? What makes the difference is rest. Exhaustion degrades the quality of life and health at the same time. Fatigue reduces metabolic efficiency, and rest improves it. Here personal experience and medical knowledge dovetail: both indicate that *something must be done to reverse this trend and give rest its rightful place in our lives*. This chapter is about rest—the technology of rest, and how to use it for health and life.

THE REST OF YOUR LIFE

The Body Type Long Weekend of Rejuvenation is a model of effective rest. It's a detailed, specific schedule for you to follow whenever you have a chance to spend some time purely upon yourself. *This is not a luxury—this is a necessity*. The Long Weekend has the effects of a totally restful vacation, and the feeling of an exciting holiday. It's a refreshment for yourself and your idea of yourself. It will send you back to your active life with a flexibility and freshness you may not have known since childhood.

If you're like many people, the idea of resting seems almost sinful. A friend told me that as a child, she was actually forbidden to just sit, *ever*. She always had to be reading, or doing something, or else be up and about. These admonitions are still there in the back of the mind, but let me give you a new one to answer that inner voice with: You *need* to rest if you want to do anything worthwhile in activity.

The Long Weekend is a schedule to follow whenever you have a Saturday through Monday available—Memorial Day, Labor Day, Presidents' Day, in the middle of the week between Christmas and New Year's Day, or whenever else you can arrange for a day off beside the weekend. What you do on the Long Weekend is give yourself an intense exposure to the Body Type Health Program. The Weekend puts together all the elements of the program—the diet and the nutritional supplements, the special body-type soups and herb teas, the exercises, the positions, the stress reduction techniques. It then adds a special program of Body Type Acupressure Massage (explained fully in Chapter 13), and some special extras especially for this luxury time. All this happens in the context of a focused and carefully scheduled time period—and the result is that the elements reinforce each other to produce wonderful results. You go for the maximum in a short time.

The Long Weekend is a serious proposition, and should not be undertaken lightly. It's an intense experience that will actually *change* you. You must really have the time; don't think that you can just do the Saturday schedule, and jump back into your usual routines on Sunday. *It doesn't work that way*. The Long Weekend has its own rhythms. You must be able to do the entire schedule, or don't do it at all.

If your doctor told you to take a course of medication for a week, it would be absurd to take the pills he or she prescribed for three days and then stop, correct? If you change the oil in your car, you don't put back only half as much as your car requires. You wouldn't have half an operation. And so, you shouldn't do half of the Rejuvenation program, either.

Most of us dig ourselves a well-intentioned rut and think we've found a groove. Getting out of the groove is what you'll be doing on the Long Weekend. I have done the Long Weekend of Rejuvenation at least twenty times over the years since I developed the schedule, and it has always worked. Frankly, I wouldn't want to function without it. Over the years I have improved it as new knowledge has come along, but the basic idea of structured rest has remained the same. I know that life is heavy at times, but the Long Weekend lightens the load, reduces the stress, and gets me attuned to myself again—to my own needs and to what I really want.

You should be sure to check with your physician before starting the Long Weekend of Rejuvenation. Get his or her approval and make sure that he or she is aware of what you are up to.

CHANGES NEED COMPANY

I do not want you to do a Long Weekend of Rejuvenation alone. As I said, the Weekend is all about change, and when you're making rapid changes it's good to have another person around as a sort of reference point, or stable contact. You use a "buddy system" on the Long Weekend, because change is more comfortable in company.

Ideally, your buddy will be someone who is doing a Long Weekend too. Choose someone compatible whom you find pleasant to be around—not necessarily your best friend (you may just talk all weekend, and you need to follow the schedule closely). Spouses are fine, but don't choose to do a Long Weekend with your spouse if you're feuding—in the process of purification, when you feel unsettled, you may decide that the feeling is somehow your spouse's fault. Anyway, your problems will seem easier after you've gained the increased clarity and flexibility that comes from a Long Weekend.

Whomever you choose for your companion, it's best to have separate rooms, and to meet briefly for Acupressure Massage (the back points), and at meals. (You can eat alone at lunchtime if you wish—but do join your buddy for dinner.) You can also take your walks or exercise together, or take them alone if you prefer. If separate rooms are impossible to arrange, designate separate areas for yourselves and agree to ignore each other except at these times. You can sleep in the same room with your spouse if you wish, but sex should wait until the Weekend is over.

Though preferable, it's not necessary that your buddy be on a Long Weekend. If you want to do a Long Weekend and your spouse can't join you, or you can't arrange to do one with a friend, interest a buddy in just taking a weekend of golf, shopping, or walks in the country. Again, join your buddy at meals, and ask him or her to help you with your Acupressure. Having someone with you who is aware of what you are doing is very important for you to get the results you want from your Long Weekend. And by the way, nine times out of ten your nonparticipating friend will want to join you on your next Long Weekend of Rejuvenation. The process—and the results—are too exciting to resist.

THE ELEMENTS OF REJUVENATION

Rejuvenation is an extremely exciting concept. Just the thought of turning back the clock (not as far back as acne and adolescent angst, but back) is thrilling. The reality, you'll find, is even better than the thought. Rejuvenation has many elements, and by putting as many of these elements as possible together, we can make them work synergistically and increase the effectiveness of them all. Synergistically means, simply, making the whole *greater* than the sum of its parts.

Rejuvenation means becoming younger. Since aging can be defined in terms of fatigue, loss of flexibility, increasing imbalance, and the gradual deterioration of the entire physical mechanism, it is fair to say that rejuvenation must involve rest, purification, rebalancing, and repair. This seems so logical, but nobody else seems to follow this idea consistently. In the Long Weekend of Rejuvenation, the schedule enables you to work on all these factors, separately and together, in a controlled, simple, but remarkably profound manner.

Rebalancing, of course, is the goal of all your Body Type Health techniques. Offsetting the fixed tendencies of your type, increasing the flexibility of your responses, and broadening the base of support for your energy and vitality are what perfect health is all about. The Rejuvenation Program draws its rebalancing elements from the Body Type Health Program, using special features of the diet, positions and exercise, and nutritional supplement programs for each body type. In addition, the Rejuvenation programs have unique features to give you deeper rest, purification, and mental and physical repair.

Deep rest is provided by periods of meditation and by the schedule of the Long Weekend itself, which as you will see is incredibly tranquil and soothing. *Purification* comes with special breathing exercises, with meditation, and with other techniques I'll explain as we go through the schedule. *Repair,* too, is a function of rest. Meditation is the most efficient method of bodily repair that we know of today, and you'll find that the entire Rejuvenation period gives you a sense of ongoing repair that will be unprecedented in your experience. Life can be very punishing; you need repair.

The final element is a special program of *Self-Acupressure Massage*. I've designed a series of simple but extremely effective Acupressure treatments that you give to yourself (only one or two require some assistance). Depending on your body type, you'll be learning how to stimulate your less-active glands and to soothe and rest your dominant glands. The Self-Acupressure program gives a major boost to the processes of rebalancing, purification, and repair.

Forget what you've already learned about rejuvenation—the Long Weekend is very different. It's innovative, exciting, logical, and time-tested. As my patients tell me, the Rejuvenation program makes them feel as if they've been suddenly lifted from one level of functioning to another, much higher level. "When I come off a Long Weekend," one patient said, "it's like I've had a glimpse of the feeling of perfect health you're always talking about." This was after her second Long Weekend; I told her that by the time she'd done four or five, the glimpse of perfect health would be turning into a more complete impression. The Long Weekend creates new patterns in your body's responses that carry over into daily life to give you balance, poise, energy, and perspective. The Long Weekend really does set your body in the direction you want it to go, and it provides tremendous momentum toward your goal.

GETTING READY FOR YOUR LONG WEEKEND OF REJUVENATION

A Long Weekend of Rejuvenation is a luxury in the truest sense of the word. It's a gift to yourself of time, the rarest and most valuable commodity that is yours or anyone's to command. So to make the most of it, you need to organize your time in advance, before starting your Weekend. That way all the time of the Weekend will be totally yours, to use for your own luxurious benefit.

This means, first of all, that you must familiarize yourself with every element of the Weekend. You must understand and be comfortable with the diet, exercise, nutritional supplements, and body positions. The diet you'll be following is the Purification Diet for your body type, as given in Chapter 7. The exercise and positions for your type are found in Chapter 10, and the nutritional supplements for your type, in Chapter 9. There are some special additions to the supplements, but they are added to the *regular* Body Type Supplement Program, which you should follow precisely during the Long Weekend. The Acupressure is described in the next chapter, Chapter 13.

It's important that you become comfortable with the Self-Acupressure Massage before the Weekend. The techniques are fairly detailed, but not difficult to do. The most effective way to learn them is to read through the material with a friend and try out the methods on one another. Mastering the techniques on another person will make you much better at it than if you just learn the points and do them on yourself. So get together one Saturday morning and just go through the instructions for your type until you understand what to do and can do it.

FINDING THE TIME
AND PLACE

Once you've mastered all the elements of the Weekend, you need to organize the place and time to do it. Finding the time is usually the hard part. You need a full, long weekend or equivalent—a Saturday, Sunday, and Monday. Of course, if you can choose your own schedule, a Tuesday, Wednesday, and Thursday schedule is fine. You may need to take off a bit early on Friday, as well. Another way to do it is to take three days out of the middle of a more active vacation—say, the Tuesday, Wednesday, and Thursday of a week at the beach.

But what is most important is that you really have the whole time *free*. You won't be able to combine the Rejuvenation Weekend with taking care of your kids, catching up on paperwork from the office, paying your bills, seeing a few shows, or indeed with *anything*. So don't even try to do it if you know you're going to have to deal with anything else beside your own rejuvenation process.

When you've chosen your time, you need to decide on a place. My recommendation, if it's possible, is to go to some place that combines beauty, tranquillity, and moderate seclusion. You needn't go to Nepal or Machu Picchu, but a friend's condo out on the lake, or a nearby out-of-season resort, is ideal. You and your companion for the Long Weekend will probably do best if you have separate rooms so you can rest undisturbed. (Also, this is a very restful weekend, and you should conserve all energy, including sexual energy.)

Look for a place close to nature, with peace and quiet, and a place to walk or exercise. Avoid the kind of place where the eighteen-wheelers downshift outside your cabin window to make the grade. Family-type resorts that have facilities for cooking and storing food are most convenient. You can use the cooking facilities for making your Body Type Broth (see below, p. 248) and preparing your herb tea. The broth *can* be made on a portable stove, and the herb tea can be made with a little immersion heater; but a stove and refrigerator will make your Long Weekend easier.

If you're at a place without cooking facilities and plan to take all your meals at a restaurant, you will have to use a little creativity when ordering to stay on your Purification Diet. However, my patients have found it's not really difficult. Virtually every restaurant today offers green salads. You can request that chicken and fish be broiled without sauce, and you can make any substitutions you like for the vegetables: use reason and common sense, and you'll be fine.

When you've found the time and place for your Long Weekend and have familiarized yourself with all the elements, all that remains to do on the Thursday before the Weekend is to go over the schedule and make sure you have everything you need. Check the menus and buy the food for any meals you plan to cook yourself. Don't forget the herb tea and the vegetables for your broth. Get any of the extra things that you don't have (NaPCA, a loofah sponge, mineral salts for your bath, an enema bag, extra vitamins as specified for your type). Review your Self-Acupressure Massage. Once Friday night arrives, your Long Weekend begins.

THE LONG WEEKEND OF REJUVENATION: SCHEDULE

THE DAY BEFORE (USUALLY FRIDAY):

1. Plan to arrive at your Long Weekend location by about 5 P.M. Unpack, arrange your belongings, sniff out and settle your territory.

2. Take a gentle, cleansing tap-water enema (see instructions, page 260.)

3. Take a warm shower and use your loofah to gently rub your whole body.

4. Take a twenty-minute tub bath, adding mineral salts to the water. (You may use any mineral salts you buy in a pharmacy or health-food store.)

5. Dry yourself off gently and apply NaPCA to your entire body. (NaPCA* is a chemical your skin produces to keep moisture in and keep itself supple. It tends to decrease with age. NaPCA in spray form replaces the skin's own element, is nonoily, and leaves open the path of elimination through the skin. It is available at most health-food stores.)

6. Do your Body Type Positions all the way through, twice.

7. Lie down on your back for half an hour (no radio or TV).

8. Have your Body Type Purification Diet dinner (see Chapter 7), with an extra serving of Body Type Vegetable Soup.

9. After dinner, take a slow, 15- to 20-minute walk.

10. Take the following supplements after your walk:
1000 mg. L-Tryptophan

A stress vitamin (choose a high-potency B complex from a health-food store, or order the Long Weekend Stress Formula from Skinny School, see page 164)

1000 mg. L-Cysteine (an amino acid—available in a health-food store)

2000 mg. Vitamin C

11. Be in bed by 9:30, and rest even if you can't sleep. You may feel restless at this point, as your body shifts from sympathetic to parasympathetic mode. Don't worry if you do—just rest and take it easy. Whatever you're feeling at this point is a sign that your body is getting ready for the deep repair it will be undergoing when the Long Weekend proper gets under way.

---

*NaPCA. 2-pyrrolidone-5-carboxylic acid.

THE TWO FULL DAYS (USUALLY SATURDAY AND SUNDAY)

Follow this same schedule for both of the two full days of your Long Weekend. *Do not* get out of bed before 8:00 A.M., even if you awaken very early. Lie there and rest. Lying awake is not easy for most people, and it may not be easy for you. A-types, particularly, will be longing to get up and get *busy rejuvenating;* you seem to hear an inner whistle and a shout that says, "Okay, campers, hit the rejuvenation trail." Wrong: the way to rejuvenation is through rest, so *stay in bed*. Tossing and turning is okay and actually part of it. If the bed's a tangled mess when you get up, it's *working*!

THE MORNING PROGRAM

8:00   Shower.

8:15   Body positions all the way through once.

8:30   Breathing exercise (see p. 259)

8:35   Twenty minutes of Transcendental Meditation, your own meditation, or lie down and rest.

8:55   Body positions again.

9:10   Two cups of Body Type Broth. The Body Type Broth is made by taking the same vegetables as in your Body Type Soup, cutting them up fairly fine, and boiling them in three cups water for about eight minutes. Strain and discard the vegetables, and drink the liquid. During this time you can read or listen to music if you wish. But read something inspirational, or listen to some soothing music—no wild rock, no bloodcurdling book.

9:45   Lie down and rest for fifteen minutes. This may not be easy to do—by this point you will probably feel either restless or very energetic, or totally exhausted. But what you are doing is breaking a cycle here, and it's vitally important to do so. You may find that your body is full of unexplained tensions as you rest. If so, this is okay—don't think there's any particular way you "should" feel. Just lie there and feel the way you do. You will find it's an interesting sensation to lie down, experience many sensations and feelings, and not feel you have to *do* anything about it!

10:00	Body Type Self-Acupressure Massage.
10:15	Rest for another fifteen minutes.
10:30	Breakfast from the Purification Diet for your body type.
11:30	Pituitary and thyroid types: half an hour of the aerobic exercise for your body type. Adrenal and gonadal types: half-hour walk. Do this even if it's raining.
12:00	Breathing exercise.
12:05	Twenty minutes of Transcendental Meditation, your own meditation, or lie down and rest.
12:55	Body positions.
1:10	Self-Acupressure Massage.
1:25	One cup Body Type Broth.
1:45	Lunch from the Purification Diet for your body type. Take your Body Type Nutritional Supplements now.

HOW YOU'LL FEEL BY LUNCHTIME

By the time you've finished your lunch, the chances are you're going to feel very unusual. The effects of the Rejuvenation Program are really starting to take hold now, and your body and mind are going through intense purification. Until you have taken enough Long Weekends to get some definite perspective, *you won't be fully aware that purification is what's happening right now*. You'll just feel weird.

Purification, which in this instance means rebalancing and restructuring of your system, is a sort of housecleaning process. It produces all kinds of temporary dust in your atmosphere, which tend to settle on this or that piece of your mental furniture. What does this mean? It means you might think you're mad at your mother, or delighted with your son, or have any of an infinite variety of feelings. You feel emotional: perhaps upset, or out of sorts, or euphoric. This is totally normal for this stage of the rejuvenation process.

DON'T WORRY ABOUT ANYTHING NOW

None of what you're feeling right now has any real meaning in terms of your true inner state. Whatever you feel will pass soon, you can take my word for it. If you feel angry at me and decide that the Rejuvenation Program, and in fact the whole Body Type Health Program, is nonsense, don't worry too much about that either (this has happened occasionally on Weekends I've run for my patients, so I know the feeling's temporary). *All that's going on is purification;* by Tuesday you're going to feel different. So let it go and just carry on with the schedule, no matter how you happen to feel.

Some people find, at this point, that they feel extremely restless and want more than anything to go out after lunch and shop, play golf, or do a little work at the office. *Don't.* You can't fully realize how relaxed and spaced-out you are: how nonpredatory, how open, how vulnerable to sensory input. Even a trip to the grocery store right now will be too much. *Stay where you are,* and go on with the program.

THE AFTERNOON AND EVENING PROGRAM

2:45 Take an easy walk.
3:15 Back to your room. Rest, read, listen to music (no rock).
5:00 Shower (use loofah).
5:15 Body positions.
5:30 Breathing exercise.
5:35 Twenty minutes of transcendental meditation, other meditation, or lie down and rest.
5:55 Body positions again.
6:15 Rest.
6:30 Self-Acupressure Massage.
6:45 Rest.
7:00 Dinner from the Purification Diet for your body type.
8:30 Take another nice, easy walk.
9:00 Back to your room. Cup of Body Type Broth.
Take the following supplements:
   1000 mg. L-Tryptophan
   Stress vitamin
   1000 mg. L-Cysteine
   2000 mg. Vitamin C
9:45 Lights out. If you cannot fall asleep, just lie there awake, eyes closed. No television.

THE EFFECTS OF REST (AFTER THE FIRST DAY)

You will discover, by the end of your first day, how un-used you are to resting. Most people feel very tired, much more so than at the beginning of the day. If you're one of these, you may be thinking that resting makes you tired, or that the Rejuvenation Program isn't restful. These thoughts are signs that your rejuvenation is under way. They're dust flying, nothing more. You have, in essence, *released* deep, stored fatigue from your body, in the form of toxins and other unwanted chemicals. They are now in circulation, and will be eliminated in the course of the weekend. It's working.

It's also possible that you may feel extremely restless or stir-crazy. I remember one patient telling me, "At noon on Saturday I was overwhelmed with fatigue. By Saturday night I was raring to go; I wanted to go dancing. Fortunately, I didn't. Sunday morning I was exhausted again—after an early night and eleven hours' sleep. It wasn't until Monday afternoon that I realized that what I thought was energy on Saturday night was just nervous restlessness, sort of like summer lightning." The point to note here is that on the Long Weekend it's *extremely hard to evaluate what you're feeling*. These waves of fatigue or restlessness can be quite overwhelming, and it's usually not till the weekend is over that you get back your perspective on them.

Some people at this point feel wonderful. To be honest with you, much as I would like to take credit for a great result, euphoric feelings should be passed over just as much as tired or restless ones. *All* feelings at this point are the result of purification.

YOU MIGHT FEEL SOMETHING NEGATIVE—BUT IT'S REALLY POSITIVE

Occasionally it happens that your body responds to the rejuvenation process with some slight physical or emotional side effects. The kind of things I'm talking about here are quite mild and not long-lasting. You may experience a passing headache or some slight nausea, for instance—you won't get a migraine or a severely upset stomach. If you have any physical symptom that makes you very uncomfortable, or if you're alarmed for any reason, be sure to consult your physician.

The physical effects, like the emotionally stirred-up feelings, come from the toxins and other unhelpful chemicals temporarily in circulation in your system. You may not get any of them, but if you do it is important to be aware of what's happening to you. When you read the list, don't you feel amazed at how much badness is just waiting for an opportunity to be eliminated from your system? And aren't you impressed at how flexible and creative your body can be in getting it out, once you give it a chance?

Often a cup of your Body Type Herbal Tea will help relieve the feelings.

1. WEAKNESS. A feeling of weakness is not uncommon during the Long Weekend. There are three possible reasons: (a) you are releasing hidden fatigue; (b) you are releasing toxins; or (c) you are in a state of chemical imbalance occurring as part of the rebalancing process. The weakness comes from the body's way of turning its energies toward repair rather than activity.

2. STIFF MUSCLES. The reason here is usually that you have strained while doing your body positions. Never force *any* position past the point of comfort. Go just as far as you

comfortably can, feeling *stretch but no strain*, and hold for the time specified. Never try to match yourself against your friend, who may be more limber than you are.

3. MILD HEADACHE. This, or feeling head pressure, can come from the same causes as weakness. You can also get a headache if you have been used to drinking a lot of coffee. This can feel like a migraine, but is rarely so intense and usually lasts only a day, at most a day and a half, and does not come back. Occasionally, the Self-Acupressure Massage can give you a headache due to the great rebalancing of your body that it produces. Be sure to observe scrupulously the fifteen-minute rest after the Acupressure—this will usually take care of a headache caused in this way.

4. FUZZY THINKING. The best way to deal with this— which, frankly, almost everyone has on the Long Weekend—is to resolve in advance not to make any major decisions—any decisions at all, in fact—while you are doing the program. Just follow the schedule and take it easy. Afterward, your thinking will be much clearer, so wait until then to decide anything.

5. BAD MOOD. A-type anger, G-type frustration, P- and T-type depression are the most usual. If these occur, it's important to remember that they are far more closely related to the rebalancing in your system than to any circumstances in your life. This is not to say you may not have good reasons to be angry or depressed, but they aren't the main causes right now. It's a good idea not to do a Long Weekend with your spouse if you're in the middle of a feud—why take a chance of increasing your problems? Later, when your mind is clearer, you can better deal with it all. Meanwhile, on the Weekend, take 500 mg. of L-tryptophan to cool you out.

6. WORRY. The rest you're getting is letting pent-up tensions come out; again, let them take their course. Take 500 mg. of L-tryptophan if you wish.

7. FUNNY SMELLS. The release of toxins can give you various funny smells: bad breath, body odor, urine and feces

that are smellier than usual. All these are caused by the body using whatever channels of elimination it can to get rid of those same old toxins. A coated tongue is the same thing; so are hives (though this is extremely rare). It will all pass. For any symptoms that you feel are of real concern, consult your physician. It is unlikely that you will have any.

THE LAST DAY (USUALLY MONDAY)

Follow the morning program of the two full days (see p. 248) up to 11:30. End with the exercise or walk. Then, at noon, lie down and rest for fifteen minutes. Then begin to pack up to go home.

At 1:00 (or so) have the Maintenance Diet lunch for your body type, either at home or on the road. After lunch, take a thirty-minute walk. Talk. Go somewhere where there are some people, but not a lot of noise—a shopping center, for instance. What you're trying to achieve is a sense of contact with life, in a pretty nondemanding setting. A well-used park is another good place to walk. By letting your mind move around from one stimulus to another, you're regaining a sense of your usual reality.

Around 3:00, continue to your home. At home, you must take it *very easy*. There should be no business calls (tempting though it may be to go through the messages on your answering machine and deal with all the "crises"). Don't go to a loud party, either, or go dancing, and don't decide to take a long jog or do anything very strenuous at all. Have the dinner from your Health and Weight Maintenance Program, then watch TV or read a book. You can go out to a movie if you have an overwhelming desire to *do* something, but pick a reasonable (PG) one. Go to bed at your usual time.

THE DAY AFTER (USUALLY TUESDAY)

As you get up in the morning of the day following your Long Weekend of Rejuvenation, you should notice how you feel. I believe you'll be very surprised; most of my patients are. Nothing in the Weekend itself, which is often full of feelings of restlessness, stir-craziness, and funny bodily sensations, quite prepares you for the freshness you feel when the Weekend is over.

What most people report (and what I certainly find myself) is that the greatest gain is in mental and emotional expansion. My mind feels more capable and my heart more loving. Problems—personal, work, all kinds—seem not less challenging, exactly, but more soluble. Tension seems less necessary. I always have a sense that I'd been worrying more about my problems than was ever necessary.

Occasionally patients report that they thought at first that they were having a hard time getting back into their work, but then realized that what was actually happening was that they were working more efficiently and with less stress. This may well happen to you—it has happened to me after several Long Weekends. Other times it seems that the people you work with are trying to get you frantic again. Just realize that you don't need a mask of frenzy to feel as though you are functioning.

DO IT RIGHT, AND ENJOY THE MARVELOUS RESULTS

As long as you go through your Long Weekend with care and attention, you're going to enjoy the most marvelous, delicious feeling of restfulness and freshness for weeks afterward. Problems that come up after the Long Weekend—which mean feelings that are not pure freshness and vitality—usually mean that you weren't careful about the schedule. If you feel any sort of strain, for example, in picking up the threads of your routine, it usually turns out that you changed the schedule in some important way. For instance, you may have done the Acupressure Massage more times than was scheduled, or meditated more times, or skipped a meal, or didn't do your body positions or your exercises.

Meditation and acupressure are powerful tools that produce many changes in your system. Too much of either one can be, well, just too much. Exercise and body positions, by contrast, are stabilizing influences that you should never skip. Even if you feel as though you can't do the positions at all, it's better to approximate them without strain than to skip them one day.

You could also feel not quite perfectly fresh if you spent the evening following your Long Weekend at a disco or a loud, violent movie. You *must* take it easy on this evening for best results. You're still going through the purification process, and there's a lot going on in your system that demands rest to complete.

The Long Weekend of Rejuvenation is going to teach your body a better way to function. By taking the time to do it, you switch your approach from fight-or-flight to stay-and-play. And you'll find that when you get back to the dog-eats-dog world, your stay-and-play will remain with you. This is actually an expanded state of consciousness that you're experiencing, and bringing it back into the fight-or-flight world must be done carefully and correctly. So please follow all the directions accurately. The schedule of the Long Weekend is tried and true: it works. If you let it, it will work for you, too.

IF YOU HAVE MORE TIME

Sometimes patients who have done two or three Long Weekends ask me if it's possible to follow the schedule for a little longer time. Yes, you can, but only if you've *already* done at least two Long Weekends and are thoroughly familiar with the entire schedule and the results.

To extend the Long Weekend, you repeat the schedule for the *two full days*. You always end with the schedule for the final day, and begin with the schedule for the day before. For example, suppose you have five days free, beginning on a Monday. Monday would be like the Friday of the Long Weekend. Tuesday, Wednesday, and Thursday would be like the Saturday and Sunday of the Long Weekend; Friday, like the Monday of the Weekend.

Two important points. *Never* do the Rejuvenation Program for more than a week at a time, and be sure to have someone with you on the Program whenever you extend your schedule. Finally, be doubly, triply sure to take it easy on the day, or even for two days, after your Rejuvenation period. You will be deeply involved in the rebalancing process, and it is very important that you give your system ample opportunity to get all the benefits through deep rest.

HOW TO MEDITATE

The schedule for the Long Weekend of Rejuvenation calls for three twenty-minute periods of meditation on each of the two full days. In order to get the most out of these meditation times, I strongly recommend that you take a course in Transcendental Meditation before your first Long Weekend. The course in TM takes just a few days to complete, at the end of which time you will know how to meditate without further instruction being required. If you started TM in the seventies, as many people did, but haven't kept it up, it's a good idea to have a "checking" (a brief refresher on the technique, offered without charge by TM centers) before your Long Weekend.

More about some of the benefits of TM, along with how to locate a center for instruction, appears in Chapter 11.

HOW TO DO THE BREATHING EXERCISE

This simple breathing exercise comes from the tradition of yoga. The yogis say it strengthens the heart and lungs, improves digestion, purifies the nervous system, and conserves energy. You are using it for all these reasons, and above all for its ability to balance your entire system. Though simple, it is amazingly effective.

It's a good idea to practice the breathing exercise a few times before beginning the Long Weekend. To begin, sit in any position that is comfortable for you in which your back is fairly straight. You could be cross-legged on the bed, in a comfortable chair, or wherever. You can even sit in the "lotus position" on the floor, if this happens to be comfortable for you.

Take your right thumb and press gently on the side of your right nostril, closing the nostril. Breathe out slowly and completely through the left nostril. Noiselessly breathe in through the same nostril. Then press gently with your ring and middle fingers of your right hand on the left nostril, closing it, while opening your right nostril to breathe out. Breathe out noiselessly, slowly, and completely through the right nostril. Breathe in again through your right nostril in the same way.

Continue in this way, alternately breathing out and in, then changing nostrils, for five minutes. Take it easy. There is no rush. Go slowly and don't hyperventilate, or you'll get dizzy or upset. The purpose of this breathing exercise is to settle and calm you, not to make you tense! You don't need to breathe in and out so slowly that you don't feel you're getting enough air—breathe *comfortably*. Once you get used to it, it's very pleasant.

HOW TO TAKE AN ENEMA

For many, the idea of an enema is kind of repulsive. They don't like to have anything to do with what goes on "down there" and especially don't want to think about it. But we're going to think about it now just for a minute.

The intestines are the avenue for the absorption of nutrients and the elimination of waste. This elimination can be more or less efficient. Bad or toxic food, stress, fatigue, lack of exercise, and other bad habits all contribute to a disturbance in the efficiency of elimination.

On the Long Weekend of Rejuvenation we want all the routes of elimination to be working as well as possible to get the most out of the program. Meditation, acupressure, the Purification Diet, the positions, and all the rest contribute to improved cleansing and balancing of the body. This means that the routes of cleansing and elimination must work well.

The enema at the beginning of the Weekend is designed to cleanse one route that carries toxins from the blood, liver, and fat to the outside. The skin is another route of elimination, and this is the reason we also cleanse it carefully (the shower, loofah, and bath on the first day). The lungs eliminate as well, which is why your breath may become foul.

So an enema is just really another form of cleansing that facilitates rejuvenation. It is not simply "icky"—it has a purpose.

Many people have never taken an enema. Others do take them, but for constipation rather than cleansing. The enema I want you to take is to cleanse your colon, stimulate the lining to allow toxins to be eliminated, and to remove toxins and feces that are currently accumulated.

Here is precisely how to go about it:

1. Buy any standard enema bag in a drug store. Buy some petroleum or lubricating (K-Y) jelly.
2. Use the enema nozzle, which is the smaller of the two nozzles that comes with the bag.
3. In the bathroom, put a towel down. You will be

lying on it. Find a place where you can hang the bag so the bottom is about three feet above the floor.

4. Fill the bag with tepid water and run it out so the tube is filled. Clamp the tube shut. Hang the bag and apply a small amount of petroleum or lubricating (K-Y) jelly to the tube tip.

5. Lie down on your *left* side and insert the nozzle as far as it will go. Be gentle. Don't hurt yourself. If you've never done this before, it will definitely feel weird. Don't let it pop out.

6. With one hand slowly undo the clamp so that water runs out of the bag. Let about half the water in the bag go in slowly. You may get an instant cramp and have to "run for it." Go ahead. If not, wait about two minutes and then expel the water into the toilet.

7. Refill the bag. This time, lie on your back. Slowly allow three-fourths of the water in the bag to flow in. With the clamp shut but still lying on your back, massage your abdomen gently from the lower left up to the bottom of your ribs, then right across the abdomen just below the ribs, then down the right side of the abdomen. You will hear the water gurgling around. You may have to stop or go to the toilet because of cramps. If you don't, massage back up the right side, across, and down the left side. Expel the water and toxins. It will look and smell very strange—these are the toxins.

8. Repeat the procedure using a whole bag of water if it's comfortable to do so. Do not at any time lie on your right side, only your left side and then your back.

9. Shower.

Some people find they are oddly invigorated after an enema, others feel tired. You are starting to get your elimination system going. Some people (men and women both) feel sexy, because toxin congestion affects sexuality (the ovaries and prostate are in this area too). You may feel "airy" because of the cleansing effect. Whatever you feel, take it easy. Don't have sex. Follow the program—bath, NaPCA, body positions, rest. You are going to be using all your energy for rejuvenation, so remain focused. There's plenty of time for *everything* else—later, after the Long Weekend of Rejuvenation.

ENTRAINMENT: WHY YOU'RE DOING ALL THIS

I want you to keep in mind, as you wonder on reading through this section, how it will work to do all these things, some weird and some familiar, on the Long Weekend, that you're doing all this for a reason. I've spoken in terms of rebalancing, refreshment, and rejuvenation; another important feature of the Long Weekend is what is called *entrainment* of your total system.

Entrainment is a term that means bringing your various systems into step with one another, so that they work together in an integrated manner. Entraining your system means creating a synergistic effect—the whole becomes greater than the sum of its parts.

All the features of the Long Weekend contribute to entrainment. The Purification Diet entrains the glandular system. The meditation entrains the brain (there are fascinating studies that have been done on people practicing TM showing that the various parts of the brain begin to work more coherently together). The breathing exercise works to entrain the spinal cord and the brain. The body positions entrain the nervous system and the internal organs. Nutritional supplements entrain the entire system at the biochemical level. Exercise helps entrain organs, glands, and the brain. Acupressure entrains the energy of the various organs, especially of the dominant gland. Finally, the total rest of the Long Weekend allows all these entrainment effects to be coordinated for greatly increased harmony of functioning.

This is the technology of rest. Rest alone can enable these effects to occur, rest gives the quietness in which positive change can happen. The technology of rest explains how such profound changes can happen in such a short time. The improvements of the parts come together—and the improvement of the whole is assured.

13

BODY TYPE SELF-ACUPRESSURE MASSAGE

The Self-Acupressure Massage I am going to teach you in this chapter is derived from the ancient Chinese medical art of acupuncture. Acupuncture is a method of treatment that involves inserting tiny needles (much smaller than hypodermic syringes) at various points of the body, usually for about twenty to thirty minutes. Acupressure works on the same principle, but involves massage of the points rather than needles. You can do it to yourself, and it is comfortable and very effective.

What both acupuncture and acupressure do for you is affect not just the place where you massage or insert the needle, but the various organs and glands throughout your body. Chinese medicine has located certain points and related them to the various organs and organ systems—for example, a point on the arm can stimulate the thyroid, another point on the head works to calm down the pituitary, and so on.

Each organ or system of the body has a channel of energy that governs it, called a *meridian*, and points along that channel alter the character of the energy that supports the organ or system. These are the points used in both acupuncture and acupressure. By using the right points or combination of points, physicians or trained acupuncturists balance the organs and systems and can effectively treat many diseases and conditions. Indeed, the Chinese feel that when they use acupuncture or acupressure they are plugging into the Cosmic Force in each person. After using it on yourself, you may feel the same way!

Finding and using the points in Self-Acupressure Massage, and experiencing their effects, is truly exciting. It gives you a unique insight into how truly *organized* your body is. That there should exist a point on your leg that affects your liver, that this point should be well known to many people, that you can either stimulate or calm your liver by simple pressure on this point—well, it's simply fascinating that this should be so. It reveals to you a body full of electrical impulses, hidden connections, marvelous relationships—as if your body were a vast computer, but you were missing the instruction book and didn't know all the things it could do.

And there is a great deal that you can, in fact, accomplish. Recent research has proven that acupuncture can help, among other things, chronic duodenal ulcer, arthritis, and sciatica. As more research is done, many more areas of effectiveness will be scientifically established. It sometimes takes science decades to prove what has been generally known for thousands of years.

Since acupuncture works through balance—stimulating organs or glands that are weak and calming those that are overactive—it has interesting applications to the Body Type Health Program. I use acupuncture when it's useful in my practice, and I wanted to find a way to bring the benefits to you, whether you had an acupuncturist available to you or not. For this purpose Self-Acupressure Massage is ideal.

ACUPRESSURE FOR STIMULATING OR CALMING THE GLANDS

For each of the four body types, there are points on the body that relate to the dominant gland and the less-active glands. What you'll be doing with your Self-Acupressure Massage treatments is to use the points that quiet down the dominant gland, and gently stimulate the balancing glands. If you're a pituitary type, for example, you'll be using the massage technique to calm down the points that relate to your exhausted and overworked pituitary gland, and to stimulate your underactive adrenals and sex glands.

I have been asked why we don't stimulate the dominant gland with acupressure, since it's the dominant gland that is exhausted. The answer is that even though your dominant gland may be very tired and underactive, it's still your dominant gland, and it's still trying too hard to dominate your metabolism. It needs to be calmed down with acupressure so it doesn't try so hard—persuaded to quiet down and rest. At the same time, the less-active glands need to be stimulated to become more active and take some of the burden from the dominant gland. Balance, remember, is the key—through balance comes harmony.

Each Self-Acupressure Massage treatment takes about fifteen minutes and is always followed by a fifteen-minute period of rest. *Following acupressure with rest is just as important as doing it*. You need the rest to allow the effects to take place.

On the Long Weekend of Rejuvenation you give yourself three acupressure treatments per day. It is very important that you don't do it more often than that. It's a powerful treatment, and three times a day has very profound effects. You may also do the treatments on yourself once a week at home. It's best to do it on the weekend; Saturday or Sunday morning is best, and again, you *must* follow each treatment with fifteen minutes of actual rest, lying down.

Each Self-Acupressure Massage you do speeds up the rebalancing that comes from your diet, exercise, supplements, and stress-reduction techniques. This is part of the synergistic and entraining effects I discussed in the last chapter. Acupressure will relax you, tone up your energy, and give you a great feeling of well-being. It seems so simple, and it is—just a little finger pressure in the right place—but you're going to be amazed at the results.

HOW TO DO BODY TYPE SELF-ACUPRESSURE

Body Type Self-Acupressure is not difficult to do, but it takes a certain amount of concentration to locate the points the first time through. Since it is *self*-acupressure, you will be doing most of the points on yourself. But there are a few points on the back which require a partner to give you a helping hand.

The first step in the massage is to find the point. For this, look carefully at the appropriate illustration. Using it as a guide, *feel* for the point using either your index or ring finger. You will be attempting to feel the acupressure point with the "pad" of your finger. This is the slightly flattened area just in front of the "bulb" of the finger. The bulb is the most sensitive part to touch, but the pad is most sensitive to pressure.

When you're over an acupressure point, you sense something that feels either a little grainy or slightly mushy and hollow. The spot will usually also be slightly sensitive. It will feel either "funny" or will be slightly tender. Occasionally, pressure on the spot will make you slightly nauseous, if the organ to which it is linked is heavily overworked or stressed.

Once you've located the spot, there are two ways to massage it: the *stimulation technique* and the *quieting technique*. The difference between a stimulating and a quieting acupressure massage touch is one of degree of pressure and time of pressure. Stimulation requires a very light pressure of short duration. Quieting requires longer, harder pressure and is repeated more times.

HOW TO STIMULATE AN ACUPRESSURE POINT

Stimulation of an acupressure point is done as follows. Use your fingertip, the part of your finger just forward of the part you used to find the acupressure point. (This part of the finger is slightly harder than the sensitive pad you used to find the point.) Feel the point. Then press lightly with a *counterclockwise* massaging motion for three or four seconds. Release quickly.

Often you will be stimulating a pair of points—for instance, one on each hand. To stimulate, alternate between sides, then wait fifteen seconds. Repeat, again doing both points for another three to four seconds. Continue alternating between sides, waiting fifteen seconds between massages, until there is a slight tingling or heat in the area of the point during the fifteen-second interval.

Once you feel the heat or tingling, *stop* stimulating the point. The acupressure massage for stimulation of that point is complete. *Do not go on,* or you can reverse the effect. If you're not sure whether or not you felt the heat or tingling, stop after a total of four stimulations on each side. You will find this is a matter of experience. After a few sessions you will be more attuned to the experience and will be able to recognize the heat or tingling when it appears.

Keep an eye on the point while you are doing the massage. Occasionally you can see a local reaction—the spot becomes motley red with a distinct center, not just a fingerprint, and it seems to spread out. Other times the tissues around the point seem to flutter slightly. Either of these reactions means the stimulation is complete, and you should stop.

If, after your third massage session, you're still not sure whether or not you feel heat or tingling, do a total of five stimulations, rather than four, on each side.

HOW TO QUIET AN ACUPRESSURE POINT

Quieting an acupressure point is done with a technique exactly opposite the stimulation technique. Use the same part of the finger, but instead of a light pressure you should press *quite firmly*—enough to feel slightly uncomfortable or tender, though not enough to cause actual pain.

Massage the point by maintaining firm pressure and moving your finger in a circular, *clockwise* direction. Continue for thirty seconds, and release *slowly*. Do the other side. Repeat one more time, then stop.

If at any time during an acupressure session you feel nauseous or dizzy, you should stop, lie down, and do no more acupressure for that session. Some people, due to the imbalances in their system, are extremely sensitive to the balancing effect of the massage. But don't give up on your acupressure if this happens. Try it again the next day, but don't go on with any session if you feel nauseous or dizzy.

In the following pages are descriptions of the points to be used for stimulation and quieting for each of the body types. The illustrations will give you the locations as accurately as any illustration can, but finding the points is really a matter of feeling carefully for them. Those of you who are familiar with acupuncture will see from the illustrations that these are classical Chinese acupuncture points relating to the glands and glandular systems mentioned.

SELF-ACUPRESSURE MASSAGE POINTS FOR GONADAL TYPES

STIMULATION OF THE THYROID GLAND:

To stimulate your thyroid you will be using a total of ten points: two on your feet, two on your hands, four on your chest, and two on your back.

1. The first point to stimulate is located on the side of the foot (Illustration 13-1, point 1). The best way to find it is to slide your finger up the valley that begins between your littlest and next-to-littlest toe. Go up the valley until it stops: the point is right there. Stimulate this point on both your right and your left foot.

2. Next, stimulate the point on your hands. The point is located between your pinkie and ring fingers, just over the ridge of your knuckles (Illustration 13-10, point 2). You will easily be able to feel the hollow of this point.

3. Next, do the chest points. The first chest point is located by finding the notch on the top of the breastbone (Illustration 13-8, point 1). The point is just above the notch. *Simply hold* this point firmly, but not so hard that you cough, for thirty seconds.

4. Next, do the remaining three chest points (Illustration 13-8, points 2 and 3). To find the upper two points, count ribs. The points are along the breastbone between the second and third ribs from the top. The last point is located by finding the spot where your ribs meet the bottom of the breastbone. Move your fingers slightly up the breastbone from this spot; the first indentation you feel that is slightly tender is the spot you want.

5. Finally, do the points on your back. Most people find they can reach these points themselves, but you may need your partner. They are located by finding the prominent knob at the base of your neck. From there, feel down the spaces between your vertebrae. The points are in the second space below the knob (Illustration 13-9).

STIMULATION OF THE PITUITARY GLAND:

You will be using two points to stimulate your pituitary gland.

1. The first point is on your head, directly in the center and at the top of your forehead (Illustration 13-6, point 1). To find the point, locate the center of your forehead between your eyes. Run your finger up the center line. There's an indentation in the middle (the "third eye"). Keep going; there's another indentation at the top of your forehead, at the level of your original (i.e., youthful) hairline. This is the point you want. Note that with this point, it's possible to become confused whether you're going clockwise or counterclockwise, because you have to imagine you're outside your head looking in. This is stimulating, so you want to go counterclockwise. The way to do it is to move your finger first to the right.

2. The second point is on your lower lip, just where the red part meets the skin, in the center (Illustration 6, point 2).

STIMULATION OF CIRCULATION:

This stimulation point is used to reduce congestion in the female organs. The point is located near your knee (Illustration 13-13). To locate the point, extend your leg straight out in front of you and raise the foot toward you. A muscle on your calf will raise up somewhat; you can feel it even if you can't see it, so hold your leg at this point. Follow the line of this muscle down from the hollow on the outside of your lower knee about two inches. The point is on the very middle of the muscle and will definitely be tender to the touch. Once you find the point you can relax your leg.

STIMULATION OF CIRCULATION AND IMMUNE SYSTEM:

This is another major female-organ spot; in addition to reducing congestion, it also helps your immune system. The point is on the inside of your leg (Illustration 13-14). To locate the point, follow the line of the bone up from your ankle about three inches, just to the point where the muscle of the calf flattens out. The point is just off the bone. It feels deep.

QUIETING OF THE ADRENAL GLANDS:

You will be using six points to calm your adrenal glands: two on your stomach and four on your back.

1. Begin with the stomach points. They are located on either side of center about an inch or so above your navel (Illustration 13-12). To find the points, draw an imaginary line up from your navel at a 45-degree angle to the left and to the right. The points are about an inch to an inch and a half up from your navel along this line. They will feel slightly tender, or possibly slightly numb. Some people do not feel very much at these points, so don't worry if they're not extremely evident on you.

2. Next, do the points on the back—which will require your partner. You locate the points by counting ribs: they are between the first and second, and the second and third ribs from the bottom, in the depression on either side of your backbone (Illustration 13-2).

CALMING OF THE SEX GLANDS:

To calm your sex glands you use two sets of points: one on the foot and one on the inside of the elbow. Sedation of these points is soothing to the sex glands and is also useful for the immune system.

1. First, do the point on your foot (Illustration 13-15). This point is especially easy to locate if you have bunions; in any case it's behind the "knuckle" of your big toe just at the point where the skin changes from bottom-of-the-foot skin to top-of-the-foot skin.

2. Then, do the points on the inside of your elbow (Illustration 13-16). To locate this point, rest your hand on your knee. Feel the inside of your elbow: there is a depression in the very middle, about a half inch below the crease—actually on your lower arm, but just below the elbow.

Summary: G-Type Self-Acupressure Points

Stimulation
1. Illustration 13-1, point 1
2. Illustration 13-10, points 1 and 2
3. Illustration 13-8, point 1
4. Illustration 13-8, points 2 and 3
5. Illustration 13-9
6. Illustration 13-6, point 1
7. Illustration 13-6, point 2
8. Illustration 13-13
9. Illustration 13-14

Quieting
10. Illustration 13-12

11. Illustration 13-2
12. Illustration 13-15

13. Illustration 13-16

SELF-ACUPRESSURE MASSAGE POINTS FOR ADRENAL TYPES

STIMULATION OF THE THYROID GLAND:

To stimulate your thyroid you will be using a total of ten points: two on your feet, two on your hands, four on your chest, and two on your back.

   1. The first point to stimulate is located on the side of the foot (see Illustration 13-1, point 1). The best way to find it is to slide your finger up the valley that begins between your littlest and next-to-littlest toe. Go up the valley until it stops: the point is right there. Stimulate this point on both your right and your left foot.
   2. Next, stimulate the point on your hands. The point is located between your pinkie and ring fingers, just over the ridge of your knuckles (see Illustration 13-10, point 2). You will easily be able to feel the hollow of this point.
   3. Next, do the chest points. The first chest point is located by finding the notch on the top of the breastbone (Illustration 13-8, point 1). The point is just above the notch. *Simply hold* this point firmly, but not so hard that you cough, for thirty seconds.
   4. Next, do the remaining three chest points (Illustration 13-8, points 2 and 3). To find the upper two points, count ribs. The points are along the breastbone between the second and third ribs from the top. The last point is located by finding the spot where your ribs meet the bottom of the breastbone. Move your fingers slightly up the breastbone from this spot; the first indentation you feel that is slightly tender is the spot you want.

5. Finally, do the points on your back. Most people find they can reach these points themselves, but you may need your partner. They are located by finding the prominent knob at the base of your neck. From there, feel down the spaces between your vertebrae. The points are in the second space below the knob (Illustration 13-9).

STIMULATION OF THE PITUITARY GLAND:

You will be using two points to stimulate your pituitary gland.

1. The first point is on your head, directly in the center and at the top of your forehead (Illustration 13-6, point 1). To find the point, locate the center of your forehead between your eyes. Run your finger up the center line. There's an indentation in the middle (the "third eye"). Keep going; there's another indentation at the top of your forehead, at the level of your original (i.e., youthful) hairline. This is the point you want. Note that with this point, it's possible to become confused whether you're going clockwise or counterclockwise, because you have to imagine you're outside your head looking in. This is stimulating, so you want to go counterclockwise. The way to do it is to move your finger first to the right.

2. The second point is on your lower lip, just below where the red part meets the skin, in the center (Illustration 13-6, point 2).

STIMULATION OF THE HEART:

There are two sets of points you use that give gentle stimulation to your heart: one on your hand and one on your arm.

1. Begin with the hand points. The point is located at the inner corner of the nail of your little finger. You can

easily feel the depression at this point (Illustration 13-10, point 1).

2. Next, do the points on your arm (Illustration 13-11). This point is located as follows: put your hand palm down on your knee. Trace an imaginary line from the inside knob of the elbow (the funny bone) down to the knob on the outside (thumb side) of your wrist. Run your finger down this line from your elbow about an inch to an inch and a half to two inches in the valley between the muscle. You'll feel an indentation spot that will feel numb, very heavy or tender. This is an effective spot for you; it stimulates your heart energy without draining it.

QUIETING OF THE ADRENAL GLANDS:

You will be using six points to calm your adrenal glands: two on your stomach and four on your back.

1. Begin with the stomach points. They are located on either side of center about an inch or so above your navel (Illustration 13-12). To find the points, draw an imaginary line up from your navel at a 45-degree angle to the left and to the right. The points are about an inch to an inch and a half up from your navel along this line. They will feel slightly tender, or possibly slightly numb. Some people do not feel very much at these points, so don't worry if they're not extremely evident on you.

2. Next, do the points on the back—which will require your partner. You locate the points by counting ribs: they are between the first and second, and between the second and third ribs from the bottom, in the depression on either side of your backbone (Illustration 13-2).

Summary: A-Type Self-Acupressure Points

Stimulation
1. Illustration 13-1, point 1
2. Illustration 13-10
3. Illustration 13-8, point 1
4. Illustration 13-8, points 2 and 3
5. Illustration 13-9
6. Illustration 13-6, point 1
7. Illustration 13-6, point 2
8. Illustration 13-10, points 1 and 2
9. Illustration 13-11

Quieting
10. Illustration 13-12
11. Illustration 13-2

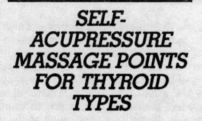

SELF-ACUPRESSURE MASSAGE POINTS FOR THYROID TYPES

STIMULATION OF THE ADRENAL GLANDS:

To stimulate your adrenals, you will be using eight different points: two points on each foot and four points on your back.

1. The first point to stimulate is located on the side of the foot (see Illustration 13-1, point 1). The best way to find it is to slide your finger up the valley that begins between your littlest and next-to-littlest toe. Go up the valley until it stops: the point is right there. Stimulate this point on both your right and your left foot.

2. Next, do the second foot point, which is on the

outside of your littlest toe (Illustration 13-1, point 2). The point is on the side of the toe just behind the first joint, and you will be able to feel a little hollow right there.

3. When you have done both foot points, do the two adrenal points on your back (see Illustration 13-2). These are points that need a partner; you can't reach them yourself. To find the points on your partner, locate the ribs by looking or feeling on the side. Feel along the bottom rib to the spine. The points are located parallel to the spine between the first and second, and the second and third ribs from the bottom. They are not on the backbone itself, but in the hollow depression just parallel to the spine. They can be stimulated together, using your right and left hands.

STIMULATION OF THE SEX GLANDS:

For the sex glands (ovaries and testes) you use six points: one on each of your middle fingers, one on each of your big toes, and one on each side of your groin.

1. Begin with the fingers. The point is on the end joint of your middle finger *on the thumb side*, and is in the hollow you can feel next to the bottom corner of your nail (see Illustration 13-3).

2. Next, stimulate the toe point. This point is in the depression beside the inside corner of the big toenail (see Illustration 13-4).

3. Last, stimulate the points on your groin (Illustration 13-5). To find these points, draw an imaginary line between your hipbone and the edge of your pubic bone, at the crease where your legs join your body. Run your finger along this imaginary line and find a sort of "dip" about the middle. Massage this point. This is a fairly large point, so if you are in the vicinity at all you will probably hit it. You can do both sides at once.

QUIETING OF THE THYROID GLAND:

You will be using a total of five points to calm your thyroid gland: three on your chest and two on your back.

1. Begin with the chest points. The first point is located by finding the notch on the top of the breastbone (Illustration 13-8, point 1). The point is just above the notch. *Simply hold* this point firmly, but not so hard that you cough, for thirty seconds.

2. Next, do the remaining two chest points (Illustration 13-8, point 2). To find the points, count ribs. The points are along the breastbone between the second and third ribs from the top.

3. Finally, do the points on your back. Most people find they can reach these points themselves, but you may need your partner. They are located by finding the prominent knob at the base of your neck. From there, feel down the spaces between your vertebrae. The points are in the second space below the knob (Illustration 13-9).

Summary: T-Type Self-Acupressure Points

Stimulation
1. Illustration 13-1, point 1
2. Illustration 13-1, point 2
3. Illustration 13-2
4. Illustration 13-3
5. Illustration 13-4
6. Illustration 13-5

Quieting
7. Illustration 13-8, point 1
8. Illustration 13-8, point 2
9. Illustration 13-9

SELF-ACUPRESSURE MASSAGE POINTS FOR PITUITARY TYPES

STIMULATION OF THE ADRENAL GLANDS:

To stimulate your adrenals, you will be using eight different points: two points on each foot and four points on your back.

1. The first point to stimulate is located on the side of the foot (see Illustration 13-1, point 1). The best way to find it is to slide your finger up the valley that begins between your littlest and next-to-littlest toe. Go up the valley until it stops: the point is right there. Stimulate this point on both your right and your left foot.

2. Next, do the second foot point, which is on the outside of your littlest toe (Illustration 13-1, point 2). The point is on the side of the toe just behind the first joint, and you will be able to feel a little hollow right there.

3. When you have done both foot points, do the two adrenal points on your back (Illustration 13-2). These are points that need a partner; you can't reach them yourself. To find the points on your partner, locate the ribs by looking or feeling on the side. Feel along the bottom rib to the spine. The points are located parallel to the spine between the first and second, and the second and third ribs from the bottom. They are not on a backbone itself, but in the hollow depression just parallel to the spine. They can be stimulated together, using your right and left hands.

STIMULATION OF THE SEX GLANDS:

For the sex glands (ovaries in women, testes in men) you use six points: one on each of your middle fingers, one on each of your big toes, and one on each side of your groin.

1. Begin with the fingers. The point is on the end joint of your middle finger *on the thumb side,* and is in the hollow you can feel next to the bottom corner of your nail (see Illustration 13-3).

2. Next, stimulate the toe point. This point is in the depression beside the inside corner of the big toenail (see Illustration 13-4).

3. Last, stimulate the points on your groin (Illustration 13-5). To find these points, draw an imaginary line between your hipbone and the edge of your pubic bone, at the crease where your legs join your body. Run your finger along this imaginary line and find a sort of "dip" about in the middle. Massage this point. This is a fairly large point, so if you are in the vicinity at all you will probably hit it. You can do both sides at once.

QUIETING OF THE PITUITARY GLAND:

You will be using two points to quiet your pituitary gland.

1. The first point is on your head, directly in the center and at the top of your forehead (see Illustration 13-6, point 1). To find the point, locate the center of your forehead between your eyes. Run your finger up the center line. There's an indentation in the middle (the "third eye"). Keep going; there's another indentation at the top of your forehead, at the level of your original (i.e., youthful) hairline. This is the point you want. Note that with this point, it's possible to become confused whether you're going clockwise or counterclockwise, because you have to imagine you're outside your head looking in. This is quieting, so you want to go clockwise. The way to do it is to move your finger first to the *left.*

2. The second point is on your lower lip, just below where the red part meets the skin, in the center (Illustration 13-6, point 2).

QUIETING OF THE BRAIN:

These four points work to reduce your compulsive, round-and-round thinking.

1. The first points are on the back of your head (Illustration 13-7, point 1). To find them, locate the knobs on the back of your skull. The points are in the hollows just below the knobs, about halfway up the back of your head, and just *off* the center; they aren't on your neck. When you turn your head, the points should turn with it.

2. The second set of points is located on the back of your shoulders (also on Illustration 13-7, point 2). Some people find they can massage these points themselves, either using their thumbs or by crossing the arms and doing the opposite shoulder with each hand. Others need their partner to do them. To find the points, follow the line of the shoulder muscle (the trapezius) along the slope until you find a more tender spot in a small depression.

Summary: P-Type Self-Acupressure Points

Stimulation
1. Illustration 13-1, point 1
2. Illustration 13-1, point 2
3. Illustration 13-2
4. Illustration 13-3
5. Illustration 13-4
6. Illustration 13-5

Quieting
7. Illustration 13-6, point 1
8. Illustration 13-6, point 2
9. Illustration 13-7, point 1
10. Illustration 13-7, point 2

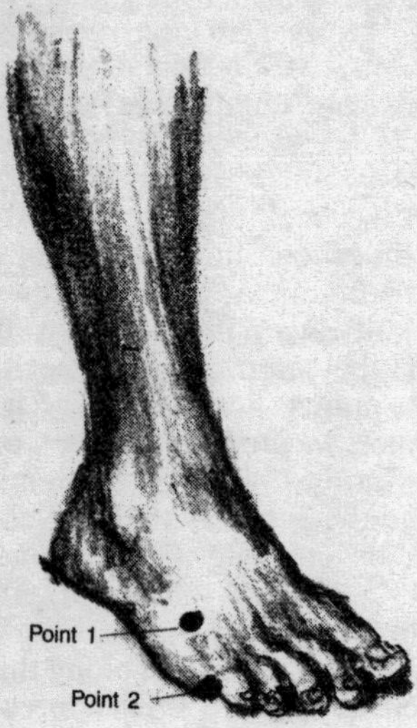

ILLUSTRATION 13–1:
Stimulation point for
G-types, A-types, P-types
and T-types. Note that in
G-types and A-types, this
point acts to stimulate the
thyroid gland; in P-types
and T-types, it has the
effect of stimulating the
adrenal glands.
To find Point 1, slide your
finger up the valley that
begins between the littlest
and next-to-littlest toe. Go
up the valley until it stops:
the point is right there.
Point 2 is on the outside of
the littlest toe, on the side
of the toe just behind the
first joint. You will be able
to feel a slight hollow at the
point.

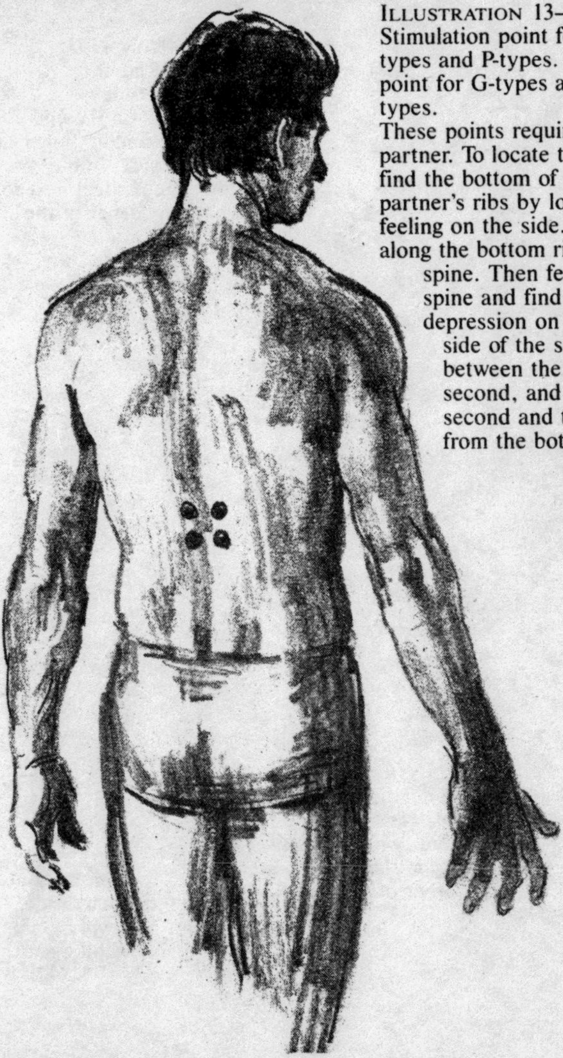

ILLUSTRATION 13–2:
Stimulation point for T-types and P-types. Quieting point for G-types and A-types.
These points require a partner. To locate them, find the bottom of your partner's ribs by looking or feeling on the side. Feel along the bottom rib on the spine. Then feel up the spine and find the depression on either side of the spine between the first and second, and the second and third ribs from the bottom.

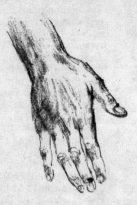

ILLUSTRATION 13–3:
Stimulation point for T-
types and P-types.
This point is on the end
joint of the middle finger on
the thumb side, in the
hollow you can feel next to
the bottom corner of the
nail.

ILLUSTRATION 13–4:
Stimulation point for T-
types and P-types. This
point is in the depression
beside the inside bottom
corner of the big toenail.

ILLUSTRATION 13–5:
Stimulation point for T-
types and P-types.
To find this point, draw an
imaginary line between the
hipbone and the edge of the
pubic bone at the crease
where your legs join your
body. Run your finger along
this imaginary line and find
a "dip" at about the middle
of it. This is a fairly large
point, so if you are in the
vicinity at all you will
probably hit it.

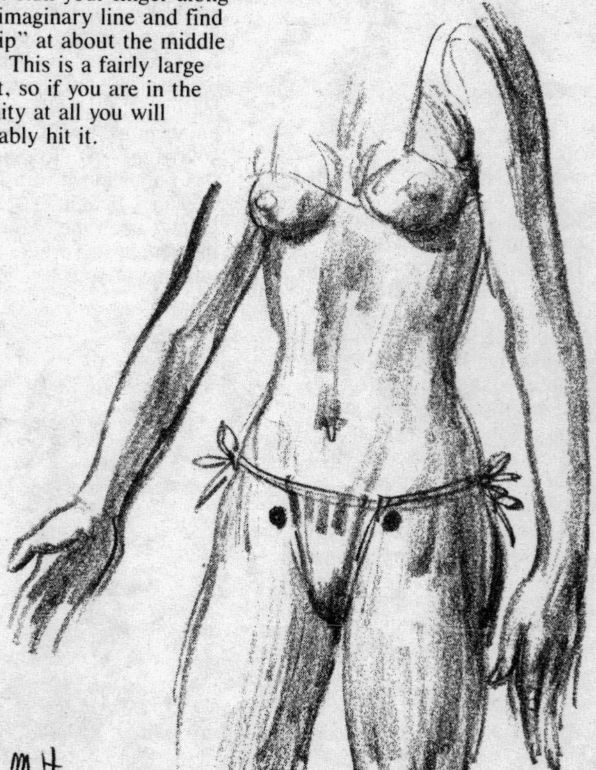

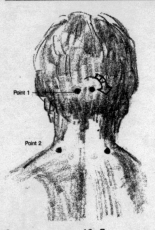

ILLUSTRATION 13–6:
Stimulation points for G-types and A-types. Quieting points for P-types. Point 1 is located by finding the center of your forehead between your eyes. Run your finger up the center line. There is an indentation in the middle (the "third eye"). Keep going until you find another indentation at the top of your forehead, at the level of your original hairline. To *stimulate* this point, move your finger to your *right* first. To *quiet* this point, move your finger to your *left* first.
Point 2 is on the lower lip in the center, just where the red part of your lip meets the skin.

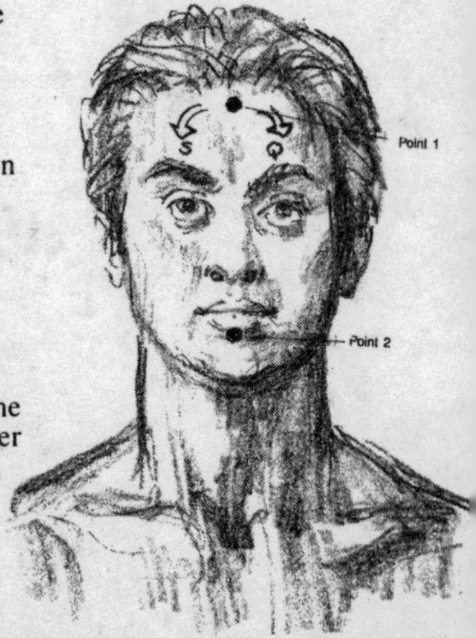

ILLUSTRATION 13–7:
Quieting points, P-types. Point 1 is on the back of the head. To locate it, find the knobs on the back of your skull. The points are in the hollow just below the knobs, about halfway up the back of your head and just off the center. They aren't on the neck, so when you turn your head, the points should turn with it. To quiet this point, move your finger to your right first.
Find Point 2 by following the line of the shoulder muscle (trapezius) along the slope until you find a tender spot in a small depression.

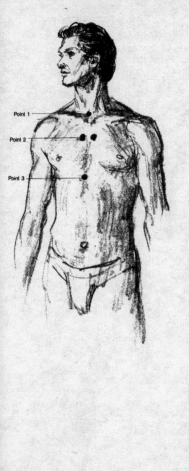

Point 1

Point 2

Point 3

ILLUSTRATION 13–8: Point 1: Holding point, G-types, A-types and T-types. Point 2: Stimulation point for G-types and A-types. Quieting point for T-types. Point 3: Stimulation point for G-types and A-types.

Point 1 is located by finding the notch at the top of the breastbone. The point is just above the notch.

Point 2 is on either side of the breastbone between the second and third ribs from the top.

Find Point 3 by locating the spot where the ribs meet the bottom of the breastbone. Then move your fingers slightly up the breastbone from this spot. The point is the first indentation you feel that is slightly tender.

ILLUSTRATION 13–9:
Stimulation point for G-
types and A-types. Quieting
point for T-types.
Locate this point by finding
the prominent knob at the
base of the neck. From
there, feel down the spaces
between the vertebrae. The
points are on either side of
the backbone in the second
space below the knob.

ILLUSTRATION 13–10: Point
1: Stimulation point for
A-types. Point 2:
Stimulation point for G-
types and
A-types.
Point 1 is located at the
inner corner of the nail of
the little finger.
Point 2 is located in the
hollow between the
knuckles of the little and
ring fingers, just over the
ridge of the knuckles.

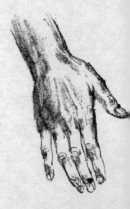

ILLUSTRATION 13–11:
Stimulation point for
A-types.
To find this point, put your
hand, palm up, on your
knee. Trace an imaginary
line from the inside knob of
the elbow (the "funny
bone") down to the center
of your wrist. Run your
finger down this line from
your elbow about an inch
and a half to two inches.
You'll feel an indentation
there that will feel numb,
very heavy, or tender.

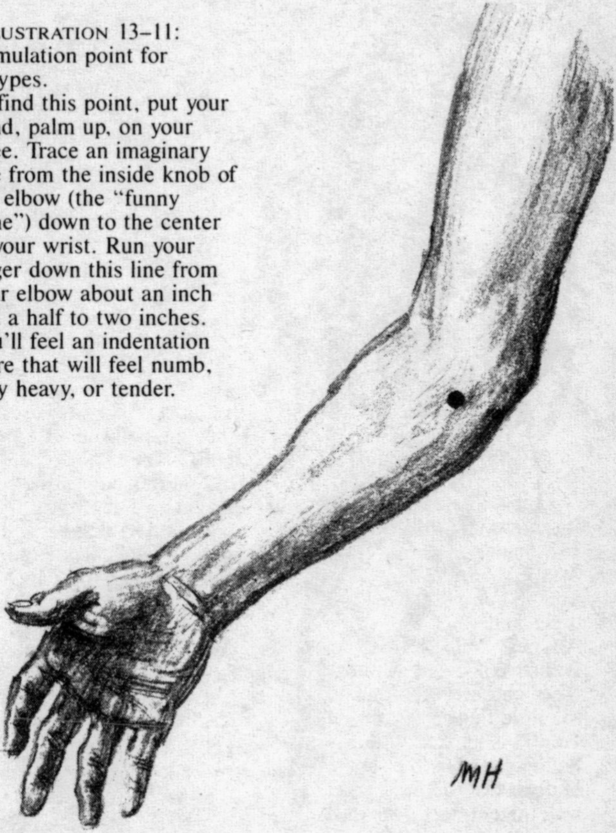

ILLUSTRATION 13–12:
Quieting point for A-types
and G-types.
To find this point, draw an
imaginary line up from your
navel at a 45 degree angle
on both sides. The point is
about an inch to an inch
and a half up along this
line. It will feel slightly
tender or slightly numb.
Don't worry if you don't
feel very much at this point.

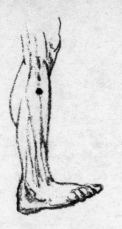

ILLUSTRATION 13–13:
Stimulation point for
G-types.
To locate this point, extend
your leg straight out in front
of you and raise the foot
towards you. A muscle on
the calf will raise
somewhat. Hold your leg at
the top and follow the line
of the muscle down from
the hollow on the outside of
the lower knee for about
two inches. The point is on
the very middle of the
muscle and will be tender.

ILLUSTRATION 13–14:
Stimulation point for
G-types.
To locate this point, follow
the line of the bone up from
the inside of the ankle
about three inches, just to
the point where the calf
muscle flattens out. The
point is just behind the
bone.

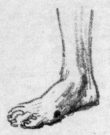

ILLUSTRATION 13–15:
Quieting point for G-types.
The point is in the hollow
just behind the "knuckle"
of the big toe on the inside
of the foot, just at the spot
where the skin changes
from bottom-of-the-foot skin
to top-of-the-foot skin.

ILLUSTRATION 13–16:
Quieting point for G-types.
To find this point, rest your
hand on your knee, palm
down. Feel down from the
inside of the elbow. The
point is a depression in the
lower arm about a half inch
below the crease of the
elbow, right in the middle.

PART III

BODY TYPES AND BEYOND

INTRODUCTION

With Part III, the Body Type Health Program turns toward the future. Part I showed you what the body types are and helped you find which of the types you are. Part II showed you how to use the knowledge of your body type to design a health program for yourself. In the remaining chapters of Part III, you'll explore what you can expect from your complete health program.

What results can you expect to achieve with body-type nutrition, with the ideal supplement regime, with custom-designed exercise and stress-reduction programs, with Self-Acupressure Massage, and regular Long Weekends of Rejuvenation? What is the goal, and how will you know when you're getting there? Will your physiology change along the way, and if so, how will it change? What are the implications for both length and quality of life? What is perfect health really like? I'll answer these questions in the following chapters.

14

BODY TYPE LIFE EXTENSION

Life extension: what is there more desirable? A longer life on this beautiful earth is the reward we hope to receive in return for all the effort we put into taking care of our bodies. For all the checkups we submit to, the weird nostrums we buy, the discipline of diet and exercise, the devotion to right living, and the hours in the doctor's waiting room—the least we should get back is a very long life.

But, actually, do we want just the longest possible life? I think we want even more. We want this long life of ours to be lived with health and vigor and with all our faculties intact. Otherwise, the prospect of great age is actually scary.

There is a story you might remember in Greek mythology about a beautiful young woman, the Sibyl of Cumae, who was loved by the god Apollo. He offered her any gift, and she chose to have as many years as there are grains of sand on the shore—but forgot to ask to keep her youth. So she lived on and on and on, growing ever older, until at last, all bent and shrunken, she passed her days hanging in a basket and conversing rather desperately with the passersby. And when anyone asked her what she wanted, she said that she wanted to die.

Life extension in this sense is not, of course, what any of us has in mind. So when I talk about long life in general, and about Body Type Life Extension in particular, I'm talking about perfecting the balance of the whole physical system from top to bottom, from the smallest part to the whole. I'm not talking about turning ourselves into shriveled creatures in a basket, but about keeping ourselves vital, strong, and aware until we reach the end—whenever it may be—of our destined life span.

LIFE EXTENSION: YOUR OWN PERSPECTIVE

The whole *point* of eating well for your body type, exercising properly, taking the correct vitamins and minerals, reducing your stress, getting deep enough rest, and fine-tuning yourself with the Long Weekend of Rejuvenation is precisely to create the most perfect balance possible. So everything in the Body Type Health Program is really part of life extension. By using the Body Type techniques, you create what is in essence a life-extension program for your individual needs.

The patients I've treated in my office, whose generous feedback has helped me utilize the latest scientific research and adapt it to the needs of each body type, have given me great hope for the longevity effects of the various body-type techniques. I've seen them grow in balance and strength and become freer from disease and the deterioration we call aging. My hope in writing this book is that you too will gain these benefits from your own body-type program.

I would also like to do something else. I'd like to use this chapter to give you a new perspective on the subject of how to go about extending your life. As I'm sure you're aware, the whole topic of life extension is very hot these days. People young and old are following the advice of various experts, loading themselves up with massive doses of over-the-counter, but not too innocuous, supplements that have major effects on the body. The question we've been asking throughout this book applies here too: Is it right for *you*? How do you know?

The question is an important one. The members of the postwar baby boom (myself included) are reaching the age of anxiety. As the saying goes, none of us is getting any younger, and even mortality seems possible. We've taken to life extension with the same zeal that some of us took to drugs and antiwar protest marches. Now, as then, we must guard against letting our zeal go to excess. We need to ask ourselves who we are and what we can expect from our bodies. Can we get our bodies to last 150 years, or just long enough to take advantage of the next new breakthrough? Are there trade-offs involved, and if so, what are they? Is there a price to pay for life extension? Is it negotiable?

So let's take a moment to think about what life extension actually is. We may find that it's not just one thing, but a complex group of decisions with results on many levels. On every level there are values to be gained and problems to be avoided. Let's take a look at the various levels of life extension and see what will work for you.

THE LEVELS OF LIFE EXTENSION

Like all doctors, I've spent some pretty heavy time in emergency rooms, and I can tell you that here we practice life extension of the most urgent kind! Often all we want is to extend the patients' lives just five more minutes, so we can get them into surgery or restart the heart.

At the other extreme, "life extension" can refer to the kind of fine-tuning you think about when you're already feeling pretty healthy. Only then do you have the time and inclination to start wondering about improving your diet, getting more out of your exercise routine, taking the right vitamins, and so on.

So life extension is not a single set of actions—it's a whole continuum of acts that you perform, alone or in cooperation with other people, to extend your life. I don't just mean "medical" actions either. Every time you fasten your seat belt or take a taxi instead of driving when you've had a drink, you're making a conscious decision to extend your life, or at least to tip the statistical scales in your favor.

On the other side, if you've abused your body, you've already accepted certain losses. You've allowed the statistical scales to tip in the other direction, and now you need to ask yourself what you have left to work with. It's like asking how many more miles you can get out of a jalopy. If you start a life extension program at age fifty, after smoking and drinking excessively for thirty-five years, you have to realize it's like taking on a car with 90,000 miles on it—there are certain limitations to what you can accomplish. It may run for many more years, but a certain amount of wear and tear will be part of the equation. This is not doom-saying; this is the reality of our current state of knowledge.

But even if we're only limping along, we want to *keep* limping along (or better yet, walking a bit more strongly), at least until the next breakthrough; at that point we'll just take it from there. That's the real goal. Maybe it will turn out to be possible to clone ourselves a new twenty-year-old body, transfer our experience into its brain, and keep the old body in cryo-sleep as a sort of parts car. Who knows? It would be a nice change from "old too soon, smart too late." But whatever lies around the next turn in the road, we'd like to be there to see and benefit from it.

Of course, the younger you are when you start working on life extension, the better your chances to have a long and healthy life. And whatever your present state, there's always *something* you can do. Life extension is as much a *mental set* toward taking action, on whatever level is appropriate and feasible, to extend our lives, as it is a medical program.

THE LIFE-EXTENSION DECISIONS

A life-extension program is really a series of decisions. Suppose you're an obese, sedentary, stress-filled smoker. You may decide to plow blindly ahead, relying for life extension on what you hope are good genes. Or you may choose to devote all your energy to the pursuit of longevity, which can also be rather ridiculous, because if you're always working on living a long time, when do you actually enjoy the life you have? Becoming a life-extension workaholic may not be much of a trade.

Finally, you can choose to take appropriate life-extension actions that you feel comfortable with and combine enjoyment of the here-and-now with an awareness of the long-term health implications. This is my recommendation; it has the advantage of moderation and suggests that you neither overlook the cream of modern knowledge, nor become so obsessed with it that you lose the joy of living. This gives us several clear directives:

1. You should decide to avoid known risk factors that will shorten life.

2. You should decide to take good care of your body, from its cells and tissues through its various organ systems, all the way up to its total integrity.

3. You should decide to take care of your consciousness, which affects both the length and quality of life.

All three decisions are important, but taking care of our consciousness is the most important of the three. If I haven't emphasized consciousness as a separate factor up to this point, it's because the Body Type Health Program has been concerned mainly with the decision to take care of the body and to affect your consciousness through general health-improvement. This is, after all, my field of expertise—it's what medicine is all about—but it's impossible to disregard the role of the direct development of consciousness. I know it to be a force for health that goes beyond any medical technique, and I believe that no discussion of life extension is complete without a look at it.

At this point you're probably wondering what, exactly, I mean by consciousness. I'm aware that in bringing up the subject I'm getting into one of the major philosophical questions of all times. But consciousness is a constant reality for all of us, and although it's abstract, it ought to be possible to talk about something we all share.

In any case, what I mean by consciousness is the most basic character of our experience. Our consciousness is seen in the fact that we are awake, aware, and participating *as ourselves* in our own unique way in any experience we have. It's the liveliness of life, the difference between someone in a coma ("unconscious") and someone awake. The stronger the consciousness, the stronger the life in us. Development of consciousness means the development of life—and more lively consciousness is an important key to life extension.

This isn't just a bald assertion on my part—there exists a great deal of new research that shows that consciousness does, indeed, play a key role in health and long life. I'll go into detail about it in the following pages and show you how consciousness is related to your other life-extension decisions. First, let's take a look at the first two decisions: your choice to avoid risk factors and to take good care of your body.

DECISION ONE:
AVOIDING KNOWN
RISK FACTORS

Risk factors are those possibilities that are known to shorten life. There are two kinds of risks: one sort you can avoid completely (for example, smoking—you can just simply not smoke); and the sort you can't eliminate, but can take steps to minimize. In this second category are risks we have from our age, sex, or heredity, or risks we take on voluntarily as part of something we otherwise want to do—for example the increased risk of a fracture that comes with skiing.

In fact, any action involves *some* risk. A glance in the rearview mirror means you take your eyes off the road ahead. Risk. A decision to eat a lower-cholesterol diet means you may choke on a fish bone. Risk. The key is to minimize those risks you must take and avoid completely those risks that can be eliminated.

The most efficient way to avoid specific medical risks is through regular checkups with a family physician. A general practitioner is in the best position to scan your general condition and keep you informed about risks you should watch out for at various times of your life. They do change, of course. By the time you're fifty, for example, you've acquired a greater risk of heart problems, but your risk of being in a car accident has greatly decreased. I advise my patients to have an exam every three years until the age of forty, and every year or two after that. You and your doctor should decide about frequency, but be sure that a discussion of your risk factors and how you can minimize them is part of the examination.

THE VALUE
OF KNOWING YOUR
RISK FACTORS

Knowing what risk factors you have is extremely valuable information. And the ability to provide this information is something new for physicians. Until fairly recently, we couldn't say with certainty which actions put our patients at risk for what. Let's say a patient comes down with a disease. The patient is a man, a construction worker, a bachelor, drinks a lot of coffee, and likes to jog. Did any of these factors contribute to his disease? How do you know? Do other construction workers get the disease? Other men, other bachelors, coffee drinkers, joggers?

From one individual's case, it's impossible to know the answer to these questions. Many doctors (and plenty of other people too) have their opinions and are ready enough to advance them (this is the "if you touch a frog you'll get warts" school of preventive medicine). But actually to *know,* first you need information about *a lot* of people who get the same disease, and second, you need the ability to look at the many factors in their lives that *might* be contributing to the disease.

We can do this now, thanks to the amazing ability of the computer to sort through vast quantities of facts and figures. With computers, researchers can take huge numbers of medical records and try out various combinations of actions that may be part of the problem. This statistical analysis is what gives us the ability to tell you that by smoking you increase your risk of *all* cancers; that women who drink alcohol during pregnancy increase their risk of having low-birth-weight babies; that chocolate *doesn't,* in fact, increase acne; that elevated blood cholesterol *is* associated with increased heart attacks, and so on.

The work of analyzing risk factors is still very much in process. Insurance companies are extremely interested in it, for obvious reasons. Look for more definite information to become available in the months and years to come. Again, keep in touch with your physician—doctors keep up with this information as part of their professional obligation to you.

And please don't think, as some of my patients do, that you'd rather not know about your risk factors. It's *far* better to know, for the knowledge gives you a chance to use preventive medicine in its crucial sense. Granted, it's scary to be aware that your chances of getting breast cancer are a bit higher if you are a woman whose mother or sister had breast cancer. But if you are aware of this, and are checked regularly, you can *greatly* improve your chances of getting well again if you should come down with the disease. If you can't avoid getting sick, you can at least be ready to get well fast. It's best to know the odds and let them work *for* you, always.

DECISION TWO: TAKE CARE OF YOUR BODY

Which brings us directly to the subject of preventive medicine. Preventive medicine is whatever you do for yourself to feel better when you're not sick. Nutrition, exercise, vitamins and minerals, stress control—these are all aspects of preventive medicine that I've organized for you by body type.

But isn't there anything else under this banner? As one of my patients once said, "Preventive medicine sounds like it should be something *fancier* than just eating right, doing aerobics, and taking it easy on the weekends. Haven't you got anything more impressive than that?" She wanted something high tech, or witch-doctory, or at the very least Chinese; the ordinary stuff of day-to-day health care just wasn't sexy enough for her.

Unfortunately, preventive medicine doesn't have a great deal more up its sleeve. If you pick up a book, even a good book with a title like *Live Longer, Feel Better, and Look Younger!*, what you'll find between the covers is usually the author's best advice on diet, exercise, and stress control. There's a reason for it—these are the areas where you can really accomplish something.

Books with titles like *Finally, the Cure for Cancer!*, or *No Heart Attacks Ever!*, on the other hand, are invariably disappointing. They tell you either to eat something strange and special (wheat grass, for instance), or else to do something *really* bizarre, like send a dollar to have the spirits cleaned out of your aura. Beware of magic cures. If there's a cure for cancer or a way not to have heart attacks, you will be notified in the usual manner.

However, despite these reservations, you should know that there *is* important work being done in preventive medicine. This work falls into three main areas:

1. Work on the body's cells, which involves finding ways to prevent aging and improve functioning in the cells themselves.

2. Work on the organs and organ systems of the body, which means the development of new techniques for improving the way the various systems of your body work together.

3. Research in the field of neural integration—ways to improve your total body's organization as a self-renewing whole.

THE LIVES OF YOUR CELLS: CELLULAR LIFE EXTENSION

To the extent that our cells are doing well, our bodies do well; when we age or get sick, it's in part because the cells in our bodies weaken or break down. Life-extension techniques concerned with our cells work from the idea that if we can keep each cell in terrific working order, loaded with all the nutrients it needs to work perfectly, we can ward off the effects of aging and maintain health throughout the body.

It is true that the body ages, in part, because the cells that make up the tissues age. The passage of time results in the accumulation of certain poisons in the cells; in mutations in basic genetic cellular material, or DNA, which occur as a result of radiation and other influences; and in irreversible damage due to the occasional lack of critical nutrients. To a large extent these effects are both unavoidable and irreversible. This means that whatever steps you *can* take to prevent them, you need to take as early as possible and to keep them up regularly. The biological clock keeps on ticking, but who determines how fast it will tick?

THEORIES OF CELLULAR AGING

At the cellular level, there are basically three theories about the way aging takes place.

The first is the *theory of cross-linkage*. Cross-linkage is the formation of links or bridges within and between important molecules, such as proteins and nucleic acids (DNA and RNA). They act like handcuffs. These links reduce the flexibility and increase the fixity, or rigidity, of the molecules in question. Much of the function of these molecules depends on their ability to maintain a certain shape, or to change shapes according to conditions.

Cross-linkage can be good—as in the cross-linking of molecules of connective tissue (tendons, ligaments, cartilage, scar tissue), or other tissue (permanent waves result from permanent cross-linking in the hair). This kind of cross-linking gives structural stability to the tissue. Hair is a tissue by virtue of its being part of the skin.

Cross-linkage can be bad—as in the cross-linking of DNA molecules, which causes mutation and loss of genetic information, or in skin, which causes wrinkling, or in arteries, which causes arteriosclerosis.

Under certain circumstances, cross-linkage can be slowed down by using nutrients and supplements such as vitamin A, various of the B vitamins, vitamins C and E, the amino acid cysteine, and the minerals zinc and selenium. Since different body types are constitutionally more or less susceptible to cross-linkage as an aging influence, you will see that the quantities of these supplements differ from one type to another (see Chapter 9).

Under other circumstances there is strong evidence that cross-linkage may actually be reversed by a new technique called EDTA* chelation therapy (see below, page 313). Reduction and reversal of cross-linkage is an important area of research at the current time, for obvious reasons (among others, the researchers themselves want to live a long time).

SUPEROXIDATION ISN'T SO SUPER

The second theory of cellular aging is the *theory of free radical formation,* or *superoxidation.* What this theory says is that under various normal and abnormal circumstances, the body forms certain molecules, called "free radicals," that are extremely chemically reactive. Your body forms a certain amount of these chemicals normally, but the number is increased when your metabolism runs faster (as in illness, fever, exercise, stress), when you are exposed to all kinds of radiation (sun rays, X-rays, cosmic rays), or when there is abnormal breakdown (peroxidation) of fats.

*EDTA ethylene diamine tetracetic acid

What it means to be chemically reactive is simply that these chemicals are very quick to oxidize, or burn, the surrounding areas of the cell. In some parts of the cell this is helpful; in most parts it wreaks havoc, like thousands of matches being struck rapidly throughout the system and burning whatever is closest, leaving little biochemical burns that accumulate throughout life.

Some of these burns the body can repair, some it can't. Some burns are to the repair mechanisms themselves—the proteins or DNA. Superoxidation, like cross-linkage, is a cumulative catastrophe.

Free radicals can cause mutations in the DNA, which can lead to cancer and loss of critical information for cell functioning. They can cause protein damage, which leads to disturbed cellular chemistry and loss of resiliency. And they can lead to cross-linkage, with the problems described above. Free radicals can also lead to the rancidity of body fat (peroxidation), which means your actual fat gets more rancid as you get older. This is a disturbing idea, but it is true, as any surgeon will attest. The old, the very ill, heavy smokers, and heavy drinkers all have this effect.

The same nutrients mentioned in cross-linkage also help to reduce free radical formation and its effects, but in different degrees. Another chemical found in the body and available as a supplement is superoxide dismutase (SOD), a free radical scavenger that appears on the Body Type Supplement lists. As before, different body-type tendencies to the formation of free radicals are reflected in the different quantities of the supplements for each type.

As for smoking, it increases both cross-linkage and free radical formation tremendously, along with all the other bad things it does. The Body Type Health Program, by improving the balance of chemistry in your new state of relaxed alertness, reduces your need to smoke.

IT TAKES A
LICKING, BUT KEEPS
ON TICKING

The *theory of cellular clocks* is the third theory of cellular aging. Basically, this theory says that each cell "knows" how long it should live—and dies on schedule. All very neat, except when the cells in question are you.

This interesting theory comes in two basic forms. The first is a *theory of cell doubling* propounded by Dr. Leonard Hayflick, a famous researcher on aging. It goes like this: All cells are able to divide a fixed number of times. The faster you live, the faster they divide. Limit, fifty doublings. The sooner you reach fifty doublings, the sooner you die—a grimly simple theory.

Do you remember earlier when we said you can only start extending your life from where you are—like a car with 40, 60, or 90,000 miles on it? We were thinking of Hayflick. If Hayflick is right, the older jalopy is getting toward the end of its doublings and must use its understanding of its body type to conserve, by a proper health program, the doublings that remain—at least until the number of doublings can be increased or made irrelevant by breakthrough research. On the other hand, Hayflick may be wrong; there is evidence to suggest that vitamin E is helpful in making increased doublings available.

The second form of the clock theory is what is usually thought of as the *theory of the metabolic clock*. This has certain parallels with the tissue-clock theory (see below), but is basically different. In its simplest form, the theory goes like this: live fast, die young; live moderately, die moderately; live slowly, die old.

The way the metabolic-clock theory measures time is in one of several ways: the total calories consumed by the cell over its lifetime; the total metabolic activity; the total oxygen consumption; and, sometimes, the total number of breaths or heartbeats. This last is where it enters the gray zone of tissue-level clocks, since breathing and heartbeats are tissue-level events. No matter. You have so much currency, and when it's spent, you're out of the game. The obvious answer is to be frugal—live slowly, live long. First of all, remove the things that increase metabolic output and speed up the clock—stress and tension, glandular imbalance, inefficiency (i.e., more work in the form of calories with less effect, hyperactivity, overwork, overexercise).

The clock theories dovetail with the free-radical and cross-linkage theories in an abstract way, but tend to rely on their own inner clock, of which free radicals and cross-links are some of the ticks.

I think from all the foregoing it is obvious why I recommend balance, "stay and play," supplementation, and moderate exercise.

THE CHEMICAL APPROACH

What can you do to avoid cell deterioration? This is controversial, and there is no general agreement in the scientific community. One recent popularization of some of the work being done in this area is by Durk Pearson and Sandy Shaw. They focus on various chemical ways of dealing with this problem—mainly by the use of extremely large quantities of vitamins, minerals, and amino acids (and also certain prescription drugs, which I'll discuss below).

The idea is that by loading up your body with huge quantities of nutrients, the cells will be protected against deterioration and become the best they can be. Presumably, the natural organizing power of the body will then take over and the whole system will work harmoniously. This step is questionable of course. Even perfectly functioning cells do not necessarily come together into perfectly functioning organs and tissues. You can use good bricks, but still build a bad house.

Pearson's and Shaw's theories are intriguing in part, but very speculative; their advice is much too untested to be taken seriously. As they themselves admit, if you take their advice, you are acting as a guinea pig for their life-extension program. They themselves are the leading guinea pigs, consuming vast quantities of some quite questionable substances. I think they have demonstrated that the substances they recommend don't necessarily produce balance.

The Body Type Nutritional Supplement Program (Chapter 9) is a much more practical and certainly far safer approach to cellular life extension. I have used my experience with tens of thousands of individuals to design a nutrient program around your actual needs. You needn't expose yourself to the experimentation of Pearson and Shaw.

THE LOW BODY-WEIGHT APPROACH

Another theory, this one based on more substantial research, but still experimental in nature, is Roy Walford's idea of Maximum Life Span. Walford, like Pearson and Shaw, is concerned about protecting the cells from deterioration and also recommends large quantities of supplementary nutrients. In addition, he recommends an *extremely low* body weight, one that most doctors would think too low.

Walford's idea of low body weight is based on some findings that rats who are fed a very restricted diet and kept at an extremely low weight live up to one-third longer than ordinary rats. Again, this is intriguing—but the concept is certainly far from proven with respect to human beings, and it would be extremely difficult and impractical to weigh what Walford says you should weigh. I recommend waiting for more definite findings and, in the meantime, staying trim, but not superskinny.

Cellular life extension is the *first, not the final,* step. Our cells do not stand alone, and we must consider not only the

workings of the cells, but the higher levels of organization as
well. It reminds one of the suppression of culture one finds
when communism replaces a feudal society of rich land-
owners and starving peasants. The peasants after a while are
able to meet their basic needs, but somehow it turns out that
the country's culture as a whole languishes. Something more
needs to be done. If you've been neglecting your cells—de-
priving them of vital nutrients—you must undertake the revolution of giving them what they need. But after the
revolution, what?

ORGANIZING YOUR ORGANS: SYSTEM LIFE EXTENSION

After the revolution, you go on to build up your new
government of the person, for the person, and by the person.
That is, you go on from an improved cellular level to build up
the next higher level of functioning—the *organization* of your
cells into tissues, organs, and organ systems. On this level
too, there is new research in preventive medicine.

This is the level on which the Body Type Health Program functions. It's a program designed around a system—
the glandular system—which integrates many of the body's
functions. The glands direct all kinds of biochemical activity—including growth, maturation, sexual function, digestion, and cell maintenance—and coordinate all these
activities to come up with a higher and more complicated
level of functioning.

In addition, because there are so many different glands
with different levels of activity, the glands give a useful in-
dicator of which systems in the body need strengthening for
greatest health and longest life. For all these reasons, the
glandular system is in my opinion the most logical choice for
a life-extension program. And my clinical results confirm
that organizing life-extension measures around the needs of

a particular glandular balance is both the most useful and the most practical method.

Other life-extension researchers choose to work with different mechanisms. The three most active areas are (1) research into the circulation system as the basis for life extension, (2) research into the brain as the principal avenue for improving the organization of your system, and (3) research on the theory of the tissue-level clock. All three have yielded some promising and interesting results.

CIRCULATION LIFE EXTENSION: THREE APPROACHES

A number of active researchers have chosen to approach life extension through the circulation system. The idea here is that circulation is basic to life. All the organs are maintained by the blood. From blood they receive oxygen and nourishment, and they give up their waste products to it. If circulation is impaired, all the functions of the cells and tissues suffer. If circulation stops completely, life stops. So there is definitely a certain logic to approaching life extension through the circulation system.

When we talk about life extension through maintaining the circulation system, we're not just talking about preventing heart attacks and strokes, although this is probably the first thing that comes to your mind. Circulation impairment is also part of diabetes, arthritis, senility, and many other diseases. This is a vital area, and all of us have a stake in the outcome of research in this area.

But what actually can be done to extend your circulatory system's life? Three approaches are currently under active investigation: diet, certain drugs, and a process called EDTA chelation therapy. (I won't discuss the surgical approaches: coronary and other bypass operations. It is generally agreed that these operations are useful more to relieve pain and improve the *quality* of life than to extend life. Also, they can only be utilized in local areas of the body and can hardly be called preventive.)

The dietary approach varies. In its less extreme form, it consists of general recommendations to reduce cholesterol-rich foods (red meat, eggs, whole-milk dairy products) in the diet and to increase fiber. These recommendations got a big boost from a huge study, sponsored by the federal government, involving ten years of research and costing $150 million.

THE
GOVERNMENT'S
STUDY

It had already been established, in earlier studies, that there is indeed a link between high blood cholesterol levels (high being defined as more than 265 mg. per deciliter of blood) and increased risk of heart disease. The government study consisted of getting men with high cholesterol either to take a drug called cholestyramine which lowers cholesterol, or to eat a lowered-cholesterol diet, and see what happened. In the cholestyramine group, the men achieved an 8.5 percent reduction in blood cholesterol, and a very encouraging 24 percent reduction in cardiac death rate. This is life extension in action!

The trouble was, the group which tried to lower its cholesterol with diet achieved only a 2–3 percent reduction, and this was not significant in lowering their heart-disease or heart-death rate. The director of the study, Basil Rifkind, went ahead and concluded that research "strongly indicates that the more you lower cholesterol and fat in your diet, the more you reduce the risk of heart disease." The study doesn't indicate this, however. It is a drug study, and it indicates that cholestyramine appears to extend life. I'm afraid the question of whether diet does the same thing is not proven.

Cholestyramine is not a pleasant drug. You must take it six times a day (in orange juice, usually), and it tastes, as one participant in the study said, like "sand." Side effects include constipation, bloating, nausea, and gas. Nevertheless, if your blood cholesterol is over 240 mg., it is worth discussing with your physician.

TWO OTHER IDEAS ON CIRCULATION

As for diet, the recommendations of the government study look innocuous enough when you compare them to the circulation-improving ideas of Nathan Pritikin. Pritikin's ideas include a drastically low-fat, high-fiber diet and an extremely strenuous exercise program. His recommendations are no more proven than the government's, and his regime is more demanding. Also, extreme exercise can have severe downsides (see Chapter 10 for more discussion of this). My recommendation: The Body Type Nutritional Program and Exercise Programs are a more reasonable approach and give you the benefits with far less potential for problems.

Finally, a third approach to circulation life extension now under extensive study is a treatment called EDTA chelation therapy. This is a procedure done in the office by a growing number of physicians. It consists of a series of intravenous infusions of an amino acid, EDTA, which appears to facilitate removal of plaque from the arteries throughout the body. As EDTA circulates in the whole body, it appears to improve circulation in all parts of the circulatory system, not just in the heart, as in a bypass operation.

Chelation therapy is a promising possibility. It may actually work to reverse certain aging changes, which is even one step better than preventive medicine! I have used it in my own practice with encouraging and sometimes quite dramatic results. Many other physicians have also had good results with this treatment, but, as I said before, this doesn't constitute absolute proof. An extensive study is now under way to determine whether chelation therapy is indeed a circulation life-extender. In the meantime, it is worth a discussion with your physician.

THE BRAIN AS A SYSTEM LIFE-EXTENDER

The third and final approach in this category of life extension is through the brain. The brain is not "life" in the same way that the circulation is; it's possible to be technically "brain dead" and still have the life of the body go on. But the brain does represent the *quality* of life. Without your brain you are a body, not a person. None of us would want life extension without consciousness or the possibility of consciousness. Calling this life is pretty much stretching the definition.

Whether or not improving brain function will actually extend life is, of course, another question completely. I can't answer this question absolutely at the present state of research, but there is considerable, strong evidence that better integration from the top down reduces the ticking of the biological clock and improves the efficiency of each tick. Besides which, even if we don't live longer, improving brain functioning is still worthwhile. If we can live better and enjoy it more, we should.

But what brain-improvement programs are available today? What researchers in this area have to offer are, basically, some experimental drugs. Pearson and Shaw suggest the daily use of Hydergine, a brain stimulant; Diapid (vasopressin), a powerful hormone produced by the brain that also acts as a memory stimulant; a combination of certain amino acids that are growth-hormone releasers and pituitary-gland stimulants; and a currently unavailable drug called Deaner, which is supposed to clean out the accumulated lipofuscin—a sort of brown gunk—from your brain cells.

These drugs are, frankly, too powerful to be recommended so freely. Recommending Diapid is, in my opinion, grossly irresponsible. Moreover, there is no distinction made among individual needs—everyone is supposed to take all the drugs without any idea of what his or her system might need or benefit from. These are extremely serious drawbacks.

In addition, the available research suggests that the *effects* these drugs are supposed to produce can actually be gained through a more integrated approach—that is, through diet and nutritional supplements. One of the most interesting results of the proper nutrition and supplement program for your body type is to enable your system to improve brain functioning without resorting to experimental prescription drugs. In "Notes for Scientists" I explain how I use particular foods for each body type to create a pathway to improved brain functioning. I believe this approach to be definitely preferable—more effective, more integrative, and far safer—to the drug approach.

It is possible that drugs or other chemicals might prove in time to have a place in a well-thought-out life-extension program. But that place has not yet been defined, and neither have the agents that will fill it. In the meantime, think twice before becoming anyone's guinea pig.

TISSUE-LEVEL CLOCK THEORIES AND LIFE EXTENSION

There are many researchers who feel that aging and death are controlled by mechanisms that exist at the level of tissue integration. These are all, basically, *tissue-level clock theories*.

The theories are all similar, they just locate the clock in different places or think that its ticks are governed or ticked off by different aspects of the metabolism. So the basic difference is how they tell time, and what room the clock is in. All these clocks are in the brain somewhere. Tissue-level clocks are felt to play a large part in the longevity of families because these clocks are genetically inherited.

Some parts of the brain tell time by ticking off the events in their own metabolism. That is, the metabolism of the brain itself, the chemical and cellular activity, is used to tell time. Some receive messages from other parts of the brain as those parts age. There are many variations, but they all monitor tissue integration in some fashion. And these clocks can only be prevented from ticking at the tissue-integration level. This is where the Body Type Health Program is so helpful: this is exactly what it is designed to do, as well as reduce the number of cellular clock ticks that feed into it. Tissue clocks tick on a foundation of the cellular mechanisms of aging, but not solely because of it. This is why attention to the cellular level of aging alone is not sufficient.

Some researchers feel that the tissue-level clock is in the pituitary gland, and that the pituitary reads and governs the gradual changes in the relationships between the glands. Certain critical glandular imbalances cause this clock to tick. I hope the idea of glandular balance and imbalance is ringing a bell here. A similar theory combines the pituitary and hypothalamus glands. They read your "inner ocean" and decide when your time has come. The Body Type Health Program is designed to keep them on page three, instead of in the last chapter.

DECISION THREE: TAKE CARE OF YOUR CONSCIOUSNESS

These ideas about life extension—balancing your glands, keeping your circulation working, nourishing your brain, slowing the biological clocks—all have value. But in the final analysis, none is truly the key to life extension.

They all have in common a spirit of good care of the body, and this is the positive side. They remind us that any knowledge about the body that becomes available should be *used*, in a practical way, to improve and extend life. Again, I agree. They all tell us to treat our bodies at least as well as an intelligent farmer treats his prized animals, not the way a derelict treats his mangy dog. But there is more to us than that. It is the quality of our consciousness, our inner life, that has the final say on how long we live and what the actual quality of life will be.

I think we all sense what a small percentage of our real inner capacity—our mental and emotional power—we actually use. Even so, taking all of us human beings together, the collective small percentages we have been able to use have resulted in advances. But while, as members of the human race, we enjoy these achievements, our personal lives are still often sadly meager. It's great that we have computers and science and can go to the moon, but what really matters to us is how we feel inside, day after day. The sense of inner satisfaction we want for ourselves is only made permanent through the development of consciousness.

Religion is the vehicle for the development of inner values for many of us. In my work as a doctor I've seen the way consciousness, when energized by religious feeling, can create recoveries that seem miraculous. The effects of consciousness on health inspire me; they also give an indication of how strong consciousness is when it works for life extension.

CONSCIOUSNESS AND OUR SENSE OF OURSELVES

When we think of consciousness in our lives, we tend to think just of the mundane level of consciousness—"maintaining an even strain," as they say in the military. The fact is, though, that our real inner selves are much better than the even strain we're trying to keep. A really developed consciousness is more stable, more relaxed, and more alert than this; but since an even strain all we know, we're reluctant to give it up. We're afraid to give up the sense of well-being and satisfaction we have now, even though it's flawed, for a changed perspective on consciousness that we're afraid may not be as good.

Every aspect of the Body Type Health Program is designed to replace a type of awareness that is dependent on compulsive, repetitive bad habits (bad nutrition, over- or underexercise, stress, chronic fatigue, etc.) with a sense of well-being that is more stable and permanent. It does this through the use of techniques to improve the functioning, synergy, entrainment, and integration of mind, brain, and body. Without this stable sense of inner well-being, longevity and perfect health are out of the question. With it, they open up possibilities in an entirely new way.

CONSCIOUSNESS, LONGEVITY, AND THE JOY OF LIFE

We are trying with all our strength, in our every action, to maintain a state of consciousness that feels comfortable, right, and truly like ourselves. But doing this through food, exercise, supplements, and so on is only partial and indirect. It's a little like trying to water a plant, but having most of the water fall on the leaves instead of the roots. What's needed *in addition to all our health-care measures* is a way of developing our consciousness directly, by work on consciousness itself.

Norman Cousins, in his book *Anatomy of an Illness**, described the way he was able to use his consciousness to overcome a disease medical science thinks of as incurable. He did it by assuming the responsibility for his own recovery, and by making laughter and joy an intimate part of his cure. His story is wonderful to read for the evidence it provides that awareness and attitude can cure disease.

This idea has become part of our general awareness— big hospitals now have programs in awareness for patients. Even though disease, when it hits one of us, is often so devastating that we have difficulty keeping a positive attitude with enough aplomb and detachment to make it work, we still feel that the idea is valid. But if the idea is correct, we need to be able to put it into practice. Creating a situation within ourselves in which we can rely upon our consciousness to make us well is the proper goal of this level of life extension.

How is this to be done? If you weren't born strong and funny, like Norman Cousins, or if you think you lack willpower or faith, what can you do to develop yourself more fully? Systematic development of consciousness, like life ex-

*W. W. Norton & Company, Inc., New York, 1979.

tension, is a series of decisions on an ongoing basis to make development of consciousness a priority in your life.

Meditation is the traditional way to full development of consciousness. You must be aware by now that I practice transcendental meditation for this purpose (I've mentioned it several times already). The research that has been done on TM is extremely encouraging. The available evidence suggests that the development of consciousness through TM provides genuine life extension, along with definite improvement in the quality of life. If you're interested in learning more about the research that has been done, you can contact a local transcendental meditation center or write to the Department of Neurophysiology, Maharishi International University, Fairfield, Iowa 52556.

The development of inner awareness is not incidental to life extension. It is its very essence, and you are not doing justice to your own potential unless you make it part of your own life-extension program.

CHANGE AND
GROWTH

These are the basic elements, then, of life extension. All the elements of the Body Type Health Program are directed toward the goal of taking care of your body. Development of consciousness becomes a priority. What can you expect to happen when you put these elements in place?

In the final chapter, I will give you a look into the future: how you can expect your body, your entire system, your health itself, to change and grow over the next several years. Whichever body type you are, it will change in the direction of balance, and the form of the changes is predictable within individual boundaries. I *can* tell you what to expect. In addition, there are changes, adjustments, which you must make in your program as the changes unfold in your system.

15

SIGNPOSTS TO CHANGE

Change: it's the most exciting, and at the same time, the scariest of life's realities—and the only real certainty we have. It's what the Body Type Health Program is about. It's not just about the novelty of the body-type concept, or the teas, or the soups, or the supplements. It's about real changes in the way you function and exist in the world. But what kind of changes will you experience? When will you experience them? Well—let's look at a case history of a typical patient.

Lisa B. is a P-type who has been on the Body Type Health Program for several years. She is a lovely woman I have known well for many years, both as a patient and as a friend; and when I saw her in my office recently, I reviewed her history in my mind.

In 1980, I'd started Lisa on the P-type Balancing Diet. She used it for weight control as well as balance—at that time she needed to lose about twenty-five pounds. She went through the Purification Diet in alternation with the Balancing Diet a total of three times before she reached her ideal weight of 135 pounds. She then went on to incorporate the principles of the P-type Health and Weight Maintenance Diet into her life. The effects were profound.

As she had gotten closer to her ideal weight, I recalled,

Lisa had done some serious thinking about her health. She started on the P-type Exercise Program—a real first for her, since she'd always hated even the idea of exercise. The effects of the exercising really turned her thinking around. (Like W.C. Fields, she had thought that if she went outside she'd be hit by a meteor.) She felt in touch with her body for the first time ever, and she liked it. For the first time, she even started to find sex interesting. Imagine.

So Lisa persevered with her Health and Weight Maintenance Program, even when her husband teased her for continuing to eat liver for breakfast. She did it because it *worked*—she felt stronger, more energetic, more sexual, more in touch with herself.

By the end of the first year on the program, Lisa became a really exemplary, balanced P-type. Then she got a new job. She'd been a computer programmer, but now she went into sales, where the potential for earning was much higher. There her three-piece suit, her running shoes, her energy and drive stood her in good stead; her income ratcheted upward, and her self-image went with it. She was reaping the rewards of change (the good kind).

She'd been doing well for the last year, and her office visits had been infrequent. On this particular day I happened to be quite busy and didn't focus on the way she looked until she was actually in my office for the consultation. Then what she said caught my attention immediately.

"Dr. Abravanel," she said, "I've been changing my diet gradually over the past year, and I think I've been doing the right thing. I feel great, but I wanted to get your opinion about it. What I think is that I've turned into an adrenal type, and the P-type diet isn't right for me anymore! So I've started following the A-type program rather than the P-type. It seems right to me, but what do you think?"

I looked at her closely. To the casual observer, there *was* something of the A-type about her. Her body was sturdier and stronger-looking. She'd put on muscle and had a more definite, feminine shape. The baby-fat cellulite around her knees was gone. Her breasts were more maternal. Her face had a better color and a more focused expression. There was an aura of warmth and power about her that hadn't been there before.

Nevertheless, despite all this, *Lisa was not an adrenal type*. She was unmistakably pituitary. Existing right along with the aura of A-type warmth and power was her unmistakable P-type coolness, her intellectual detachment, and that almost angelic, childlike quality that sets P-types apart from all the world. Clearly, Lisa was a P-type who had successfully balanced her system with the Body Type Program, and who was now in need of fine-tuning. She'd reached a *signpost to change*.

THE NEED FOR ADJUSTMENT

Like Lisa, *everybody who is on the Body Type Program for some time is going to have to adjust the program to his or her changing needs*. This is true whether you have been following the Body Type Diet for a year or two already, or whether you're just beginning on your Body Type Perfect Health Program.

Life is dynamic. Your body is dynamic. The body-type programs are dynamic too. They are intended to make changes in your entire system, and they do. They take you toward greater balance and integration, and away from imbalance, fixed tendencies, cravings, cellulite, and your typical body-type "windows of vulnerability." Of course, you know all this. I've been writing about the imbalances of each type and the techniques we use to offset them in every chapter of this book. But it's very important to emphasize that using these techniques results in predictable changes, and that *your* changes require, in turn, changes in the way you use the body-type techniques.

For each body type, the basic technique of change is to rest the overused functions and to nourish and support the functions that are less active. What this means, as you know, is that we use diet, exercise, supplements, stress-reduction techniques, acupressure, and the Long Weekend of Rejuvenation to reduce overstimulation of the dominant gland and to encourage stronger functioning in the less-active glands.

For each type, we use specific methodologies to bring up the *balancing glands*. This means

FOR PITUITARY TYPES: reducing stimulation of the pituitary, and supporting the adrenal and sex glands.

FOR THYROID TYPES: reducing stimulation of the thyroid, and supporting the adrenals primarily, the sex glands to a lesser extent.

FOR ADRENAL TYPES: reducing stimulation of the adrenals, and supporting the pituitary primarily, the thyroid to a lesser extent.

FOR GONADAL TYPES: reducing stimulation of the sex glands and supporting the pituitary and thyroid glands.

After you've been doing this for some time, you will find that *your balancing glands become much stronger and more active*. After about two to three years on the program, you will experience the following results:

Pituitary types become more adrenal and/or gonadal.

Thyroid types become more adrenal and/or gonadal.

Adrenal types become more pituitary and/or thyroidal.

Gonadal-type women become more pituitary and/or thyroidal.

It's important to note that these changes occur at different rates for different people. The time scale is an average, not an absolute. Some people have these effects sooner, some later. Some people change gradually, some quickly. Some change slowly at first, then more rapidly, or vice versa.

Even people of the same body type respond to the Body Type Health Program in a very personal way. If you've gone on the program with a friend or in a group, you may have noticed that some of you lose cellulite first, others notice increased mental clarity first, and so on. In the same way, after several months one T-type may become very "adrenalized" on the program, and another may become just slightly so. Some people approach balance slowly or gradually, and some overshoot and have to make corrections.

I, as a T-type, have become gradually more adrenalized over the past years. But just recently I took a camping trip with a lawyer friend who had been on the T-type program for a mere eight months. He had become so adrenal that for a moment on the trail I thought I had somehow forgotten his body type. A moment's reflection told me he was still the T-type I knew, but his physiology was very sensitive to the balancing effects of the Body Type Health Program.

ADJUSTMENTS: KEEPING THE SEESAW IN BALANCE

Once you have increased your balance through the program, you have created an entirely new situation. You have made the necessary corrections, but you don't want to *over-correct* and end up with imbalance again. So, to maintain your balance, you have to adjust your program to *reduce* stimulation of the glands that you needed at first to stimulate.

What you need is to take the same body-type techniques you used in balancing your system originally—but to turn them around, adjust them, so as to maintain the balance you have now acquired. Just as you once used food, exercise, and the other techniques of the Body Type Health Program to quiet your dominant gland and encourage your less-active ones, you must now use these same things to give a light amount of stimulation to your dominant gland. At the same time, you reduce (but do not entirely eliminate) stimulation of your balancing glands. Like a seesaw, you keep yourself in balance by adjusting the weight on each end.

In the years since I began using the Body Type balancing techniques with my patients, I have noticed that the majority of them have reached the point where they must make these adjustments. It's not uncommon, in fact, for patients to begin making the necessary adjustments in their program *on their own,* quite spontaneously, as Lisa B. did when she began adjusting her diet to the adrenal-type program. Other times, patients come to me with questions; they feel that it's time for them to make some changes, but they're wondering exactly what they should do, and when.

To help them respond to their changing needs, and to help you in the years to come, I use the concept of *signposts to change.* These are specific and impossible-to-miss events that alert you that you have reached a significant point in your progress. These signposts are like any other roadsigns: they reassure you that you are still on the way to your chosen destination, and they point the way if it's necessary to change your direction in order to stay on the road. The direction we've chosen, remember, is toward the best possible health; these signposts indicate that you're moving steadily toward that goal.

The signposts I'm going to discuss have actually been experienced by thousands of people who have followed the program. You will come to each of them in turn—but how soon you do so depends on a unique combination of personal factors. The most important ones are your degree of imbalance when you begin the program, how well you are able to follow the various techniques in your lifestyle, and the particular balance in the metabolism of your *less-active,* or nondominant, glands. This factor—the balance that you have in your secondary glands—is important in assessing the signposts to change, and so it has significance for you at this point.

THE SECONDARY GLAND

The basis of understanding your metabolism is knowing which of your glands is dominant in your system. But at this point in your progress you also need to be aware of which gland is *next strongest* after the dominant gland. This is your "secondary gland." The secondary gland is the one for which you got the next highest score, after your dominant gland, on the PMI. It is interesting to be aware of your secondary gland while you are going through the first year of the Body Type Health Program, but it becomes more relevant when you reach the first signposts to change.

The secondary gland is what accounts for the different ways people of the same body type can look. All thyroid types, for example, have the same basic body shape and the same metabolic style. But an individual T-type might have secondary adrenal glands, a secondary pituitary gland, or secondary gonads if a woman. Which of these glands is the secondary gland accounts for differences in T-type appearance and has an influence on the metabolism as well.

The secondary gland also gives you insight into how to adjust your diet, once you've reached the Health and Weight Maintenance stage, to your individual needs. Individual, notice—not just the needs of your body type. It didn't make sense to say that one diet will work for everyone, and it doesn't make sense either to say that one diet will work for every fourth person—in the end, for a lifetime, your diet must be personalized for you and only you. Awareness of your secondary gland is a factor that will help you do this.

HOW THE
SECONDARY GLAND
WORKS

I'll use some famous people to illustrate how the secondary gland contributes to the metabolism, but you can observe this for yourself if you wish. Just spend a few moments looking around you on a busy street corner or shopping mall, noticing the G-type women who go by. (I'm sure that by now you can identify G-type women at a glance.) If you look at five or six G-types, you'll notice that they aren't all shaped in quite the same way. The dominant gland has contributed the main features, but the secondary gland has made its contribution. There's a big difference between dominance and contribution.

Some G-types, for example, are very slender everywhere except the derriere. These women have a *secondary thyroid gland,* which accounts for their slenderness elsewhere. Brooke Shields has grown up to be a good example of this kind of G-type. When she was very young you might have thought that she would be a thyroid type, but when she grew out of childhood her G-type quality emerged.

Another possibility is the G-type who is built more solidly, with larger breasts and fuller arms. These women have *secondary adrenal glands* that give them their shape above the waist as well as below. Ann-Margret is a good example. Finally, there are G-type women who are more childlike in appearance, with calm, round faces and undeveloped bodies (except for their rear end). These women have a *secondary pituitary gland*. Charlene Tilton is a perfect example of a G-type with secondary P.

All these women I've mentioned have well-balanced metabolisms. All are beautiful. None is overweight. All have the glow of health. They have achieved balance: which is to say, they aren't "all gonadal," as unbalanced G-types are. At this stage the secondary gland can be seen clearly, and only at this stage is it relevant to the Body Type Health Program.

THE SECONDARY GLAND IN T-TYPES: SOME FAMOUS EXAMPLES

In the same way, you can discover variations in each of the body types that come from the secondary gland. In T-types, for example, there is quite a bit of variation within the basic T-type pattern. While a thyroid type is characteristically streamlined in the underlying bone structure, the degree of delicacy varies according to the secondary gland.

Those T-type women who have secondary sex glands get a certain increased roundness to the derriere from this secondary gland. Barbra Streisand is an example of a T-type woman with secondary G. In fact, her thyroid and her sex glands are very closely balanced, and the casual observer might well wonder whether she's a T-type with secondary G or a G-type with secondary T.

The fact that Ms. Streisand is a T-type comes out in several ways: her hands are delicately thyroidal, her face has the T-type shape and the T-type teeth, and she has larger breasts than you'd expect in a G-type with secondary T. Also, she acts like a thyroid type. Her intense creativity is very thyroidal, as are her occasional inconsistency and insecurity. Only a T-type would work four years to bring a movie project to life, then ask an interviewer anxiously if he thought *Yentl*'s subject matter "too ethnic."

Debra Winger is another example of a T-type with secondary G. Her liveliness and her chameleon acting ability are typical of a T-type, but you can see the qualities of her secondary sex glands from her sexiness in *Urban Cowboy* and her warmth in *Terms of Endearment*. Obviously, only women can have secondary G—since male G-types don't exist.

When a T-type has secondary adrenal glands, he or she has a strong but very finely-tuned body. Basketball players like Kareem Abdul-Jabbar and Magic Johnson are great examples of T-types who have developed their bodies to a peak of athletic ability and have taken full advantage of the qualities of the adrenal glands for a T-type body. In these men, solidity supports their height. Amy Irving is a good example of a T-type woman with secondary adrenals. The warm, solidly feminine atmosphere conveyed by this actress comes from strong adrenal glands playing a supporting role in a basically T-type body.

A T-type whose secondary gland is the pituitary is the most delicate of all the thyroid types. Here you may find extreme slenderness and a certain ethereal quality that comes from the pituitary gland. They usually have fine, angelic, but strong, hair. They don't look like P-types—their heads aren't too small for their bodies—but they have something of the same childlike appearance. Meryl Streep is an example of a T-type with secondary pituitary. The intellectual and thoroughly thought-out quality she brings to her roles shows the influence of her pituitary gland.

THE SECONDARY GLAND IN A-TYPES: A SURPRISING INSTANCE

Believe it or not, Princess Diana is a striking example of an adrenal type with secondary thyroid. At first glance she looks like a T-type: she is tall and, since she has turned from Lady Di into the Princess of Wales, very slim. But if you look back at pictures of her earlier days, you can see that she's an A-type. Square face, strong, adrenal legs, full bust, flat rear—a classic English schoolteacher. These are the signs that don't lie.

Princess Diana is reported to eat very lightly—she is mostly vegetarian, eats a lot of salads, and drinks no alcohol. Also, she eats quite a lot of sweets. If she were a T-type, she'd have all kinds of problems with this. As it is, she eats correctly for her body type and maintains excellent balance. On the other hand, Prince Charles is a T-type, and if he becomes a vegetarian as well, he has to be more careful than she does not to become *too* thyroidal. Queen Elizabeth, by the way, is a classic A-type, and she and Princess Diana may have more in common than appears at first sight. In fact, from her pictures the young Queen Elizabeth shows many features in common with Princess Di.

A-types with secondary pituitary glands look very different from A's with secondary T. This is a very common combination, incidentally. In these people the body type is unmistakably that of an A, but there is a more intellectual or spiritual feeling to go along with it. There is a feeling of "raised" energy, as if more of the body's energies were in the head than in the body, although the body does have the stocky adrenal look.

This body type is common in people in public life who combine action with qualities of thought and intellect—for example, President John F. Kennedy and Bobby Kennedy were adrenal types with strong secondary pituitaries. Ted Kennedy is an A-type as well, but his glandular system is not as well balanced, and his pituitary is not very active.

Linda Evans is an example of an A-type woman with secondary pituitary. Her adrenal body type appears in her shape—full bust, small rear, squarish face—and the more delicate influence added by her secondary pituitary shows in her finer skin and delicacy of appearance.

THE SECONDARY GLAND IN PITUITARY TYPES: AN INTERESTING CONTRAST

Pituitary types can have either secondary adrenals or a secondary thyroid. I have not found a P-type with secondary G in this country. However, I'm sure that somewhere in the infinite variety of the population explosion there is a P-type woman with secondary G! After all, there are a billion Chinese, most of them P-types.

In P-types with secondary T, the classically childlike P-type body is *very* slim and fine-boned. If a P-type has secondary adrenals, he or she gets the look of a sturdier sort of child: a "tomboy" look in women, the look of a sturdy young boy in men.

Fred Astaire and the late Truman Capote are examples that show the difference between secondary thyroid and secondary adrenals in a P-type man. Both these men have the basic shape of a P-type: big heads, large, clear eyes, fine skin, a general air of brightness, and relatively small and childlike bodies. But note the differences. Astaire's body is lithe, light, and limber; Capote's, by contrast, had a squarer and distinctly more adrenal shape. It's not just that he was heavier than Astaire, and not a dancer; it was the squareness of his face and hands and the more solid look of his body that revealed secondary gland.

Michael Jackson is, like Fred Astaire (one of his heroes), a P-type with secondary thyroid. He's a good example too of the way a P-type changes as he grows up. We've all seen him since he was a little cherub. Now that he's grown up, he's angelic.

Nancy Reagan is an example of a P-type woman with secondary thyroid. Like Fred Astaire, she has a radiantly childlike, interesting face, and a slim, fine-boned, and remarkably childlike body. Nancy Reagan's beauty, while very real, is elusive and has not been easy for many people to understand. She is described in the press as "dainty" or "elegant"—which are not the most modern of adjectives. It just shows what happens when T-type journalists try to describe the rare P-type!

THE SIGNIFICANCE OF YOUR SECONDARY GLAND

To get started on the Body Type Health Program, all you need to know is your body type—that is, your dominant gland. You don't need to worry about your secondary gland until you reach the third "signpost"—which I'll explain below. At this point, having balanced and adjusted your own program, it will be helpful to know your secondary gland. However, by the time you reach this point, you will have a very deep knowledge of your body and will have the ability to be sensitive to your secondary gland.

Actually, there is very little to *do* with the knowledge of your secondary gland—other than to be aware of it in the back of your mind. Know that your secondary gland will affect your fine-tuning of diet, exercise, and the other techniques. If your secondary gland turns out to be one that balances your dominant gland, then it will be easier for you to stay in balance. On the other hand, if your secondary gland doesn't balance your dominant gland, you will have to watch yourself more closely to stay in good adjustment.

To make this general idea more concrete in your mind, refer to these lists.

BALANCE WILL BE EASIER TO KEEP IF YOU ARE A:

Pituitary type with secondary adrenals
Thyroid type with secondary adrenals

Thyroid type with secondary gonads
Adrenal type with secondary pituitary
Adrenal type with secondary thyroid
Gonadal type with secondary pituitary
Gonadal type with secondary thyroid

BALANCE WILL REQUIRE MORE ATTENTION IF YOU ARE A:

Pituitary type with secondary thyroid
Thyroid type with secondary pituitary
Adrenal type with secondary gonads
Gonadal type with secondary adrenals

Whatever your particular combination of secondary glands may be, you will come to these signposts in turn, and you should be aware of them. Some people will reach them sooner, some later, but all will get there. For each signpost, there is an adjustment in the program that you will learn to make.

YOUR BEGINNING BALANCE AND THE FIRST SIGNPOST TO CHANGE: NO CRAVINGS

From the first days of your Body Type Program, when you first start adjusting your diet to your particular needs, you start to bring your system back from imbalance to balance. As you add the other elements—exercise, supplements, acupressure, stress reduction, the Long Weekend—your balance increases. The entire program is designed to work as rapidly as possible, but in an integrated and careful way, because this is the only way to make changes stick.

Again, like a seesaw, your body suffers if it changes too quickly. Whenever you try to do too many things too rapidly, it "hits bottom" (remember that sickening thud you used to get on the playground seesaw when you were a kid?) and then bounces back in the other direction. If you fast to lose weight, you may drop pounds rapidly, but find yourself over-eating in the days and weeks after the fast. If you overexercise, you become stiff, strained, and fatigued, and stop exercising sometimes forever! But if you make your changes in a measured way, your body can absorb the changes; the seesaw-swings become smaller, and eventually you are at that enjoyable point where neither side is likely to go up or down very far.

When you begin the body-type program, you will notice this kind of gradual shift taking place. But you may have been very, moderately, or scarcely out of balance, when you started. And of course the program can only begin working on you from where you are. Remember, people are different, and your friend is not the measure of *you*. Depending on how far out of balance you were, you will come to your first signpost within a few days to several weeks.

This first signpost is a reduction in the intensity of your cravings. It constitutes a definite sign that your dominant gland has started to recover from overstimulation, and that your system is beginning to develop alternate pathways to get the feeling of relaxed alertness that it formerly craved from your downfall foods.

Most people, as I say, reach this signpost within the first two to three weeks. But for your cravings to disappear completely, several months on the program are usually needed. A craving is gone, or cured, when you are not tempted at all by the craving food. I, as a T-type, can now look at cookies without longing. I can even eat one, without feeling I have to eat six more. To be honest, I never thought this would happen, but it did.

Curing cravings is accomplished with diet, exercise, and nutritional supplements; assuming you follow the guidelines in all three of these areas, you will get your cravings under your control completely. The same goes for other body-type compulsions, like the compulsion P-types sometimes have to run obsessively, or the A-type compulsion to pump iron. If you're a P-type and can run a reasonable amount and stop, or if you're an A-type and can lift weights just once a week, you're doing well. The intensity of these cravings, as well as cravings for food, is a good sign of the degree of your imbalance, so a big change in cravings means you have shortened the seesaw swings a lot.

THE NEXT SIGNPOST: YOUR IDEAL WEIGHT

The next signpost to change comes when you reach your ideal weight. Overweight, as you know, is a sign of imbalance, and controlling your cravings is a sign that your balance is reaching the point where you can reach *and keep* the weight you want. Once your cravings are controlled, how long it takes you to reach your ideal weight depends (no surprise here) on how much you needed to lose (or gain). To get an idea of how long it will take you, use this formula: if you follow the Balancing and Purification Diets in sequence, you will lose about two and a half percent of your body weight per week.

If you are one of those individuals who began the program at or about your best weight, there is still a significant signpost for you when your ideal weight becomes stable and comfortable. Many people who believe they don't have a weight problem are actually maintaining their weight only through rigid self-control, constant dieting, and attention. Fighting to maintain your weight is also a weight problem. You are only really at your best weight when you are totally craving-free, can eat what you want, and don't have to watch every bite you put in your mouth. Such vigilance isn't life, after all—and it hardly can be called *ideal*!

When you reach the signpost of your ideal weight, you naturally have to make an adjustment in your program. What you do at this point is change to the Health and Weight Maintenance Program for your body type—the adjustment is built into the nutritional program.

As you know, the Health and Weight Maintenance Program is not a diet—it's a set of guidelines for you to keep in mind and use for yourself. The Plenty Foods, Moderation Foods, and Rarely Foods are listed, but quantities aren't spelled out for you, nor do I give an exact definition of what "plenty," "moderation," or "rarely" actually mean. How are you to determine what "plenty" or "rarely" means for you? What information are you going on? You determine it through the intuition of your own needs, intuition that is actually developed by following the Body Type Program. Even so, the Health and Weight Maintenance Program does give you some guidance, because even at this stage your weight is not absolutely stable. It's *very* stable, but can still swing. The same goes for your energy.

Built into the Maintenance Program is a mini-adjustment that allows you to reduce your swings even further. You learn from the Maintenance stage how to make adjustments on your own. You don't necessarily think about it—but when you use a Rarely Food, you are doing it because you sense some kind of need in your system. When you reduce the Plenty Foods, or increase Moderation or Rarely Foods, you are responding to that intuition which is the sum total of your body's feelings. The better your balance, the more accurate your feelings will be. By this time, you are free of cravings, which allows you to reach a finer sense of yourself from the inside. This freedom of intuition is the exact opposite of the slavery to cravings.

This was what Lisa B. was doing, it turned out. Dairy products are a P-type Rarely Food. Lisa had been increasing her use of light dairy (yogurt, occasionally cottage cheese, once in a while an extra-cheese pizza) because she sensed intuitively, through awareness of her own body, that her adrenals were becoming more active and needed to be balanced by pituitary stimulation. I never had to tell her this—she just knew, because she knew herself. In her case, she wasn't responding to a desire to pig out on what previously were her downfall foods—she was just responding to a natural desire, a spontaneous movement to keep things in balance. Had she pigged out, she would have lost her balance, started having cravings, and started to gain back her weight. In fact, even wanting to pig out would have shown that her balance wasn't truly stabilized. But this hadn't happened—a sure sign that she was at the second signpost.

People of all body types who have reached this stage of balance usually continue for a year or so at this very comfortable stage. The comments I hear during this stage are all about how well they feel, how much more energy they have on their body-type program, and so on. This is the experience you, too, will have on your own body-type program. (You may think now, "Oh, I'll never stay on any program for over a year." But that's because you've never felt as good as you'll be feeling on the program.) And there will come a point—as with Lisa—when you'll feel that your system has swung as far as it should go in the direction you've been taking it—and then you'll know you have reached the next signpost to change.

THE ADJUSTABLE SYSTEM: SIGNPOST NUMBER THREE

The next signpost is the one that comes to most people after about a year—although it can be as much as two years if you were very out of balance to begin with. Two years is pretty unusual—a year is about average. Now, don't despair and start howling, "Do I have to wait that long?" The fact is that your body is conservative, even if you're liberal. It took a long time and great diligence to get into the state you were in when you started. Anyway, you'll be feeling fantastic all this time—it's just that your body still will be quietly making fine adjustments.

The third signpost is reached when you become aware that you have enlivened your balancing glands enough so that you have given yourself some of the characteristics of the "opposite" body type. The best way for me to tell you how you'll know when you've reached this signpost is—you'll just know. Your body intuition and your daily experience will make it obvious. You will become aware (which means that your body will tell you) that your metabolism has undergone some real changes, and they have become permanent. P-types and T-types will realize that they have become "adrenalized"; A-types and G-type women will notice that they have become more "thyroidal" or more "pituitarized." (These words are strange ones, but they do describe the reality!) Certain basic characteristics of the balancing body type are now a permanent part of *you.*

When you do get to this point and are clearly aware of it, then you are at a signpost to change that is really a signpost to freedom. It means that you now have the freedom to adjust your system *in any direction you want it to go.* You can use the principles of the body-type program to tilt your seesaw just a little bit in any direction—enough to get the kind of extra energy you need for whatever you want to do. I hope you realize what this means. It means that your body will be close to perfect balance and very flexible. No job will be impossible, no sport will be impossible, no *idea* will be too hard to accept, no relationship will seem too difficult.

For example. You're a T-type who has been on the program for about a year. You have nourished your adrenals very well, and they're working—you're steadier in your energy, less easily fatigued, less up-and-down in every way. But you're still a T-type, and your creative genius is still formed around your original body type. So what do you do if you have a sudden, intense call on your T-type creativity—such as a demand from your boss to produce a terrific, snappy report, yesterday? You stimulate your thyroid. You give yourself some thyroid-stimulating food and adjust your diet and your exercise just enough to create the kind of energy you need for the task at hand.

It's a tremendous relief to reach this signpost—as I can confirm, having become a balanced T-type on my own program! Occasionally someone will see me having a cup of coffee or eating a Danish or some such and reads me chapter and verse from the *Body Type Diet*. Yes, these would be mistakes for an unbalanced T-type, but I'm not one anymore. I lost my "jelly roll," and my body has learned to keep its balance. After following the T-type Health Program for ten years now, I know what I'm doing.

Suppose, on the other hand, that you're a gonadal type like my coauthor, who has lightened up by "pituitarizing" and "thyroidizing" her system for all these years. She still may use adrenal-stimulating or gonadal-stimulating foods if she has a physical challenge coming up, or if she just wants that G-type energy for a special party. But when she has creative work to do, she sticks with thyroid or pituitary stimulants; she might even go on the G-type Balancing Diet (full of thyroid-stimulating foods) for several weeks to get the effects she wants.

THE STABILITY AND FLEXIBILITY OF BALANCE

The balanced system, in other words, is now *fully adjustable*. You're in charge—and can do whatever you want with it. Of course, it takes a real understanding of the *principles* of the Body Type Health Program. You have to know what you're doing—but once you get to this signpost to change, it's actually easy to observe your body's reactions and gauge what you do accordingly. You can see the seesaw clearly and alter its balance however you wish. Your increased sensitivity to your body's responses and inner workings are another big plus of improved metabolic balance. It is now much easier to know thyself than before.

Your metabolism is now in such good balance that it's stabler *and* more flexible than it was when it was out of balance. It is more stable in that you don't disrupt it with small deviations from your diet, or by missing your regular exercise, or by unexpected stress or fatigue. Like a top that's spinning fast, it comes back to center when given a knock. A slow top falls over. As Lisa told me, "I find I can eat all kinds of food now that I couldn't handle before. Ice cream, for instance—it used to be if I ate it, I'd have a craving for it the next day. Now, I can eat pretty much whatever I want, and the next day it's no problem to stick to my basic food guidelines." This is the answer to the frightened question people always ask when looking over the Body Type Health Program for the first time: "Do I have to stay on this all my life?"

Along with this stability you're also more flexible—you can adjust your basic energy this way and that by your own, conscious decisions. The combination of stability and flexibility is a very favorable sign, not just a signpost to change but a sign of excellent health.

PERFECT HEALTH: THE LAST SIGNPOST

Now you know all you need to know about your dominant and secondary glands, so let's project into the future for a moment. It's important to have a clear idea where you're going, even though the destination may seem remote. The future I want to talk about is perhaps two or three years from now, "now" being the time you start on the program. Whenever you start, you need to be aware of the final goal, which is to make your health the best it possibly can be.

When you get your system in total balance, however long that takes, your health will be the best it can be with your particular physiology. Your body's self-repairing mechanisms will be so much more effective, and they are extremely powerful, but the passage of time isn't stopping either; there will be some deterioration, some aging, some possibility of disease. None of us, as the saying goes, is getting any younger.

What you will have now is very close to perfect health. It's the best health you can have, taking only the body into consideration. But the ideal of health goes beyond what can be achieved by attention to your body alone. A perfectly balanced system is a prerequisite. It's the foundation, but it's not the whole story. To create the full reality, you need to continue to take care of your body *and your consciousness*.

In the Introduction of this book, I projected a vision of ideal health. But what is actually the ideal? It's not just being free of disease. It's not just being resilient enough to stay up late and party and not feel hung over the next day, or to work hard and not burn out. These things are fine, and it's nice to have them—with the Body Type Health Program, you will have them. But ideal health is more than this. It's not even what today is called "positive wellness," which carries with it the idea of constant improvement. Again, you will have this with the Body Type Health Program, but again, the ideal of health includes even more.

In truth, I believe that perfect health is about the expansion of consciousness. I think we all instinctively feel that ideal health must include the quality of inner life, which means perfect inner balance—emotional, mental, spiritual—along with outer, bodily equilibrium.

I have had the privilege of observing up close this kind of inner and outer balance in a few individuals, and from a distance in a few more. Maharishi Mahesh Yogi, founder of the Transcendental Meditation movement, possesses an inner and outer equilibrium and radiance that is truly amazing. So does the Dalai Lama of Tibet. Pope John Paul II seems to me to have it also. This state of health has a recognizable glow, a radiant power, that once seen is unmistakable. In such people their radiant physical health seems to act like a perfectly constructed edifice that is designed to support, nourish, and reflect the life within.

THE META-BODY TYPE

Interestingly, all the people I'm aware of who have reached this level of health appear to have gone *beyond* their original body type. They have a discernible underlying metabolic body type, but their physiology appears to have a more general and more organized structure about it. There are a number of biochemical studies that suggest that the hypothalamus, neuro-glandular control center located in the brain, may be their "dominant gland." However, rather than refer to a "hypothalamic type," I have chosen to refer to these people as having developed a "meta-body" type. I want to set these highly developed individuals definitely apart from the four body types.

The meta-body type is not a fifth body type; it is a *development* from *any* of the four body types. Pope John Paul II and Maharishi Mahesh Yogi both appear originally to have had A-type metabolic styles, but they are not A-types, nor have they turned into one of the other types. They have gone beyond the A-type metabolism to a new and more organized state. The pope appears to have become a meta-body type after the attempt on his life. He went from being a healthy, glowing A-type to an even more glowing and more spiritual meta-adrenal type. What made the difference? I would say that the evolution of his consciousness, as demonstrated in the act of forgiving his would-be assassin, is somehow responsible.

The Dalai Lama appears to me to be a former T-type, but, like the Maharishi and Pope John II, he has evolved beyond any limitations of body type to the meta-body type. Popular representations of religious figures also suggest the meta-body type. Buddha is usually represented as a meta-pituitary type, Jesus as a meta-thyroid type. I can only make these observations from looking at representations of them—what these great historic individuals actually were, of course, I am in no position to say.

There is, however, a logic about the idea that our health will continue to evolve, even from the excellent physical balance created with the Body Type Health Program, and that the further evolution of health is inextricably bound up with the development of consciousness. Research on the development of consciousness suggests strongly that the best definition of the goal toward which health might evolve is a "physiological state that can support fully developed consciousness." Another way of saying it is that perfect health is simply a body pure enough to sustain a pure soul.

Meta-body types—people who have reached this goal—are rare, but they exist. And as I said in the Introduction, even if there were only one living example in the world, it would still be worth trying for in our own lives. The Body Type Health Program is designed to lay the groundwork: to develop such a refined state of balance and integration that further development is made easy and natural. The Body Type Health Program will help you think about your health in an efficient and scientific manner, but attention to your consciousness and your spirit will still be absolutely necessary for this development to continue.

Until there are more people who have reached this goal, there is little more that can be said to describe it. There is no current theory, except those offered by religion, to account for the level of neural and physical integration the meta-body types exhibit. It appears that aging in the meta-body type, also, is on its own terms. They're not getting older, they're getting *much* better—effortlessly. Whole new theories of aging, and of health itself, will have to be developed for individuals with this status.

And lest this seem like a daunting goal, remember that consciousness has its own momentum. There is in all of us something that wants to live, grow, and evolve—and this is consciousness in its purest state. This factor deserves all our attention; it is what makes individual life work, family life work, the whole of society work. It is the most precious value in human life, and it is my hope that the Body Type Health Program, by creating the most perfect physical health, will enable all of us to reach our highest goals.

APPENDIX
NOTES FOR SCIENTISTS

The *Body Type* theory is a general theory that attempts to give practical organization to the facts about the way people differ. It therefore accepts that people do differ. Resting upon established research in biochemistry and physiology by respected workers in the various fields, the Body Type theory provides a general structure for understanding why and how people are different and a clinical framework for making use of that knowledge for the benefit of patients.

In medicine we accept individual differences, but we usually do so in a way that tends to close off review as to their causes. There is a tacit assumption that human physiology is essentially the same in everyone; that each of its features falls on the bell-shaped Gaussian distribution curve; and that all variations, since they fall somewhere on the curve, have somehow been accounted for. But the curve itself is a description, and a prediction of differences; appreciation of their statistical reality is not the same as accounting for why they occur.

By its general nature, the body-type theory takes chances. General theories are inherently more falsifiable than specific hypotheses, which is to say that the bigger your generalization, the more chances you have to be wrong. The upside is that if you are right in postulating a general theory,

347

you have said a lot. The downside is taking the risk of making a big mistake, which is one of those little gambles we have to take if our lives are to remain interesting.

The Body Type theory essentially says that:

1. People are basically different. Packed into the fact that we are all human lies the fact that different chemistries motivate us, and that there are basic differences in the organization of how we function.

2. A key feature of the difference in organization is that each person is somehow governed, or dominated, by one of the four major glands—pituitary, thyroid, adrenals (or in men, adrenals/testes), ovaries—and that this dominance or governance determines the body type.

3. This governing gland tends to impose certain typical physical, personal, and behavioral characteristics, and these features reflect how that gland functions.

4. All people tend to use certain known effects of stimulation of these glandular functions to achieve, or activate, a comfortable state of awareness that has the combined features of tranquillity and arousal. This stimulation is pursued independently of whether the stimulus has any good or bad effects on the body. In general, because the stimulation is constant and unrelenting, the effects tend to be bad, or deleterious to the body. Yet the psychological need for a state of induced tranquil arousal overrides the importance of the effects on the somatic physiology in most, if not all, cases.

5. Almost all of the bad effects on the body created by compulsive attempts to sustain tranquil arousal can be reversed and reduced by proper changes in diet, exercise, nutritional supplementation, and other lifestyle adjustments; these changes correct the errant physiology. This can be done without giving up the tranquilly aroused state.

6. In the end, by making these adjustments, the physiology is more balanced, the body less tyrannized, and the actual tranquillity and arousal achieved are deeper and more varied than in the compulsive state of glandular overstimulation.

From the foregoing delineation, the reader can see that the Body Type theory is indeed a general one. It includes physiology and consciousness. It is not a theory like the one that says a certain strain of lab rat will do something a certain percentage of the time under controlled circumstances. Such studies test small, specific hypotheses. The Body Type theory is a way of organizing many such studies on rats, on people, to provide an overview or context, to explain trends. We are not just plugging in the numbers and running the statistics. We are viewing many aspects of physiology and behavior, attempting to tie them together to try to see *why* people look and behave the way they do, and, finally, to determine what we can do to help them.

However, to be fair, I must say with all this, I believe there are still areas to be explored. I have now seen tens of thousands of patients in the Los Angeles area. I have seen many hundreds of others all over the country—not just talk show hosts, but talk show guests. Their bodies, as it were, leave the door ajar to more general considerations. There is the *rare* person who confuses me, who makes me think that the drivers or governors of the physiology that generate the undeniable but fairly plastic differences among people do in fact lie deeper than the major glands. It is still my most definite impression that the glands and the types are critical and major links in the causal chain that creates body types. But, as in *The Wizard of Oz,* maybe there is a Frank Morgan behind the fluttering curtain making that big head speak. I don't plan to stop looking for one just because I have finished writing this book.

Intelligent skeptics will naturally wonder about extrapolations of the theory to predictions of, and accountings for, body shape and fat (cellulite) distribution. The whole notion that food affects glandular function and, with it, body shape, fat distribution, personality, and so forth is interesting. Such a view is not without suggestive and indicative evidence. Certainly, for example, all fat cells are not the same, either in size or in hormone responsiveness. Some are larger, some smaller. This suggests at least some basis for glandular differences affecting fat metabolism. Hormone receptors in fat vary absolutely and with changing milieu. Fat cell responsiveness to individual hormones varies by cell location, by current and prior hormone and biochemical influences, by genetic influences.

Additionally, the relationship of hormones to personality is well known to all of us in extreme cases (hyper- and hypothyroidism, Cushing's disease), and in more subtle cases, as indicated by menstrual, adrenal diurnal, pituitary diurnal, and thyroid effects. The wealth of new evidence of hormonal effects on brain function indicates the subtlety of responsiveness of this organ to endocrine influences.

One basic tenet of the body-type concept is that human physiology is susceptible to biochemical driving by loading certain reactions using high doses of substrate (chemical drivers). This is standard organic and inorganic chemistry. The new idea is that people can do it with diet—they eat what drives their glands, use ordinary foods to stimulate their dominant gland or any other gland, and rely on the results of that stimulation for alteration of consciousness, thereby effectively using foods as drugs. We all manipulate our conscious states chemically, usually using foods, often adding drugs (such as caffeine and alcohol) into the nutritive milieu. The body-type theory simply systematizes the way we unconsciously do this and reveals its consequences and its chemistry.

The following is a general outline of how each body type uses food to alter awareness.

THE PITUITARY TYPE

Every body type has its own biochemical "style" for achieving a relaxed state of arousal. So it is with the Pituitary Type, which uses characteristic foodstuffs and activities to control and modify the physiology of consciousness directly, through the local release of peripheral and brain hormones.

Vasopressin release is a key feature of P-type arousal, but it does not take place in isolation. As in all body types, the effects provoke constellations of influences that taken together create the kind of awareness with which a person of that type is most familiar and comfortable. As you will see in reviewing the other types, some of these mechanisms cross over from one type to another and share common features. All people have all the features; emphases differ. The universality of glandular biochemistry is in fact what makes treatment and change possible.

Vasopressin release can be triggered by many factors. The important ones for the P-type are high glutamate diet, high fructose diet, and long-duration exercise. Other effects will work, but these are the ones P-types choose. The effect on awareness of vasopressin is general arousal and memory consolidation with the affective addition of reduced depression.

Concurrent with this is prolactin stimulation and prolactinlike brain activation effects through ingestion of milk products. The effect of prolactin is abstract, integrated arousal. This combination of effects gives rise to the typical P-type kind of ivory-tower intelligence. In addition, the above effects cause the CNS (central nervous system) arousal effects of ACTH (adrenocorticotropic hormone) release from the pituitary gland, CRF (corticotropin release factor) release from the hypothalamus, and beta-endorphin release from numerous brain structures. The net effect is a sort of detached cerebration, reduced responsiveness to somatic (body) input, and a generalized mind-body dissociation with emphasis on the mind. These last effects are the result of increased alertness due to secondary steroid and ACTH in the brain, calmness and reduced aggression due to beta-endorphin and ACTH, and generalized hippocampal (limbic system) influences on memory and memory affect.

Another factor that favors the typical P-type detached calm is the effect of sugars and starches in releasing serotonin, with its tranquilizing, somatic, and sexual de-emphasizing effects.

De-emphasis of the anterior pituitary, coupled with the CNS effects noted above, which tend to reduce attention to the body, give rise to the characteristic undefined, childlike appearance of the P-type. Also, lack of an emphasized somatic major gland (thyroid, adrenal, or ovaries) results in a fat distribution that also lacks specificity. Conversely, dietary and exercise influences of the P-type Health Program reverse these tendencies (see below, A-type and G-type).

THE THYROID TYPE

We must now explain how the T-type acquires its characteristic oscillation of hyperactivity alternating with exhaustion, in the face of what we know about how the thyroid functions—i.e., that its actual hormonal output is actually quite stable. The T-type is interesting in that the effect of diet on actual thyroid output is very gradual. It is a long-term effect caused by increased T_4 levels at the pituitary. The effects of the so-called thyroid stimulants are actually in the periphery.

The effects of T-type dietary habits in inducing a transient hyperthyroidlike state in the body are actually based on the effect of the stimulating foods to affect the ratio of T_4 to T_3 in blood and tissues. Circulating thyroid hormone is mostly present in the bound, relatively inactive form T_4. Virtually all T_3, the active form, arises in the periphery (the bloodstream and tissues) from the peroxidative splitting of T_4 to T_3, which is facilitated by what in this book I have called the "thyroid stimulants"—sugar and caffeine. In actual fact, it is this chemical reaction that is stimulated—i.e., driven.

The outcome is essentially identical to what would happen if one added thyroid hormone to a person's diet—an increase in the metabolic effects of thyroid hormone. These effects include increased energy production, tachycardia, increased synaptic rate in the brain, increased alertness, faster reflexes. These same carbohydrates also release serotonin to produce a modicum of tranquillity. The degree of activity, the degree of sexual interest in T-types, along with many other factors, also reflect the balance of these effects. Serotonin effects are rather more stimulus-dependent than thyroid effects.

The increased arousal caused by the various effects of thyroid hormone on brain metabolism, on arousal-inducing effects of ascending somatic pathways, and on neuromuscular integration, combined with the tranquilizing effects of the serotonin and the diffuseness of the thyroid effect, create the characteristic T-type calm alertness.

Deterioration in this state of affairs takes place for two reasons. First, the caffeine and sugar increase the dissociation of T_4-protein, and this increase in free T_4 (unbound from protein) has the gradual effect of suppressing pituitary stimulation of the thyroid. This is the source of the oft-seen gradual suppression of thyroid activity in T-types who often present themselves to the physician as reversibly hypothyroid. Second, the effects of sugar and caffeine on the brain are biphasic—that is, stimulants at low doses and depressants at high doses. They eventually reduce the sensitivity of the brain to the stimulating effects of T_3, resulting in compulsive overuse of these foods in an attempt to gain stimulation. The serotonin effect of carbohydrates is not so reduced, and tranquillity or dullness eventually overrides arousal. This is the obese, exhausted T-type.

The effect of exercise on T-types, especially the best type of strenuous exercise, is to increase the ratio of T_3 to RT_3, the active to the inactive form, resulting in more efficient energy utilization and mental stimulation.

The effects of overuse of caffeine and sugar also tend to increase cholesterol levels directly by sucrose and indirectly by lower T_3, and reduce the lipolytic responsiveness of fat cells to catecholamine-T_3 complex. The result is reduced fat utilization, and when weight is lost, it is protein rather than fat that is utilized for energy. On the wrong reducing diet a T-type may lose weight but is weak and flabby.

THE ADRENAL TYPE

The A-type gains his dramatic sense of invincible power and wide-angle alertness by the confluence of a number of pathways. Characteristic of the A-type experience at its most typical is this sort of indomitable willfulness and strength.

The hormonal/neural pathways that give rise to this experience are numerous.

A-types consume salt to stimulate vasopressin release—note the difference from P-types. This release directly affects mental alertness and triggers in turn the release of ACTH, which has a direct tranquilizing effect on the mind. In addition this effect is reinforced by the ACTH-mediated release of cortisol by the adrenals, resulting in increased blood pressure and blood sugar, thereby increasing substrate availability to the brain. Cortisol also acts directly on the brain to increase general arousal and aggressive behavior. This is the effect in A-types of a sense of invincibility and power and is heightened in this type by the release of large quantities of aldosterone (another adrenal hormone) in the presence of sodium, resulting in beta-endorphin release into the brain from the neuro-intermediate lobe of the pituitary. Here, then, we have the typical A-type tranquil arousal, less tranquil, more globally aroused.

When an A-type ingests alcohol, the effects are characteristically biphasic. Low quantities of alcohol result in the typical anti-ADH* effect, which triggers the renin/angiotensin mechanism and aldosterone release, with the same effect noted above. In addition, the resulting hypovolemia (low blood volume) caused by secondary diuresis and the direct pituitary effect causes the ACTH-cortisol chain reaction, with the tranquilizing and general arousal effects also noted above. The exact balance of the effects is the result of quantity of intake, and individual factors interplaying with the direct CNS effects of alcohol. Agitation and/or depression are of course well-known effects of alcohol intake.

The effect of a cholesterol-loaded meal, especially in the presence of digested food, results in a de-esterification of cholesterol esters, with the resulting increase in cholesterol available as substrate for the creation of adrenal hormones. This is one of those clear cases in which substrate loading leads to hormonal loading, with resultant increase in hormone effect.

The total effect of these dietary habits is the loading of

*ADH. antidiuretic hormone.

reactions that increase general arousal, memory consolidation, tranquillity, insensitivity to pain, and aggression.

Much of the beneficial effects of aerobic exercise in A-types stems from the reversal of these effects, reducing cholesterol, insulin, triglycerides, and cortisol, with secondary reductions in arousal, blood sugar, blood pressure, and the general reduction by numerous pathways of the aggressive/arousal pattern of the A-type.

THE GONADAL TYPE

The *sine qua non* of the G-type physiology is the intense stimulation of the ovaries and pelvic organs, and the resultant characteristic body shape and energy.

The stimulation of general arousal in G-types is activated by two main pathways—ovarian stimulation by congestion, caused by greasy and spicy foods, and limbic-hippocampal stimulation caused by olfactory influences of spicy foods. These are generally supplemented with the A-type sodium consumption effects, but these adrenal effects are very highly modified in the G-type physiology; they increase arousal, but have little effect on aggression (see A-type discussion). The combination of these causes a generalized arousal characterized by a sort of maternal or "nesting" behavior. This is what gives rise to the magnetic character of the G-type and is reinforced by the hormonal effects of apocrine gland aromatics (i.e., G-types are attracted by smell).

Alcohol in the G-type tends to cause pelvic and lower intestinal congestion by vascular dilatation in a vascular bed already sensitized by other habits. Also, similarly to the A-type, alcohol results in aldosterone release (resulting in the release of beta endorphins) and cortisol release (resulting in increased arousal).

In addition to the pelvic congestive effects of a fatty, spicy meal, cholesterol ingestion also results in making more substrate available to produce more hormone in the already activated and stimulated ovaries. These effects are also bi-phasic, with low doses resulting in stimulation and high doses resulting in secondary suppression. The effect is the "nesting" effects noted above, followed by their suppression. It is at this point that the G-type gain weight, caused by ineffectual overstimulation, becomes most marked.

Some helpful references for further reading on this subject are noted below.

BIBLIOGRAPHY

Bacchus, Habeeb. *Essentials of Metabolic Diseases and Endocrinology.* Baltimore: University Park Press, 1976.

Balthazart, J., E. Prove, and R. Gilles, eds. *Hormones and Behavior in Higher Vertebrates.* New York: Springer-Verlag.

Baertschi, A. J., and J. J. Dreifuss, eds. *Neuroendocrinology of Vasopressin, Corticoliberin, and Opiomelanocortins.* London: Academic Press, 1982.

Bray, George A., ed. *Obesity in Perspective.* Washington, D.C.: U.S. Government Printing Office, 1975.

Brodish, A., and E. S. Redgate, eds. *Brain-Pituitary-Adrenal Interrelationships.* Basel: Karger, 1973.

De Nicola, A., J. Blaquier, and R. J. Soto, eds. *Physiopathology of Hypophyseal Disturbances and Diseases in Reproduction.* New York: Alan R. Liss, 1981.

Everitt, Arthur V., and J. A. Burgess, eds. *Hypothalamus, Pituitary and Aging.* Springfield, Illinois: Thomas, 1976.

Ishi, S., T. Hirano, and M. Wada, eds. *Hormones, Adaptation and Evolution.* Tokyo: Japan Scientific Societies Press, 1980.

Jones, Mortyn T., et al., eds. *Interaction Within the Brain-*

Pituitary-Adrenocortical System. London: Academic Press, 1979.

Korenman, Stanley G., ed. *Endocrine Aspects of Aging*. New York: Elsevier Science Publishing Co., 1982.

Moses, A. M., and L. Share, eds. *Neurohypophysis*. Basel: Karger, 1977.

Motta, M., M. Zanisi, and F. Piva, eds. *Pituitary Hormones and Related Peptides*. London: Academic Press, 1982.

Munro, J. F. *The Treatment of Obesity*. Baltimore: University Park Press, 1979.

Peptides of the Pars Intermedia. Ciba Foundation Symposium 81. Pitman Medical Press, 1981.

Svare, B., ed. *Hormones and Aggressive Behavior*. New York: Plenum Press, 1983.

Weingartner, H., et al. "Effects of Vasopressin on Human Memory Functions." *Science* 221, II (1981): 601–603.

Williams, E. D., ed. *Current Endocrine Concepts*. New York: Praeger, 1982.

Yagi, Kinjii. *Neuroendocrine Control*. New York: Wiley, 1973.

INDEX

ABOUT THE AUTHORS

ELLIOT D. ABRAVANEL, M.D., graduated from the University of Cincinnati Medical School. He now divides his time between his clinics in the Los Angeles area, writing and lecturing. ELIZABETH A. KING is the wife of Dr. Abravanel. She is a frequent contributor to the major American magazines. Their first book together, *Dr. Abravanel's Body Type Diet and Lifetime Nutrition Plan,* was a national bestseller.

This second book, now appearing for the first time in a paperback edition, was also a bestseller in hard cover.

BANTAM'S
PILL BOOK LIBRARY

━━━━━━ ℞ ━━━━━━